AFRICAN STUDIES SERIES
General Editor: J. R. GOODY

AFRICAN RAILWAYMEN

BOOKS IN THIS SERIES

AFRICAN RAILWAYMEN

SOLIDARITY AND OPPOSITION IN AN EAST AFRICAN LABOUR FORCE

R. D. GRILLO

Lecturer in the School of African and Asian Studies
Sussex University

CAMBRIDGE

AT THE UNIVERSITY PRESS, 1973

Published by the Syndics of the Cambridge University Press
Bentley House, 200 Euston Road, London NW1 2DB
American Branch: 32 East 57th Street, New York, N.Y.10022

Library of Congress Catalogue Card Number: 73–79302

ISBN: 0 521 20276 0

Printed in Great Britain
by The Eastern Press Limited
London and Reading

CONTENTS

v

FIGURES

TABLES

Tables

viii

ACKNOWLEDGEMENTS

During fieldwork I was attached as an 'Associate' to the East African Institute of Social Research (EAISR) at Makerere University College, Kampala. I would like to record my thanks to the various chairmen of the institute for the facilities they offered. Anyone connected with the EAISR will appreciate the many debts one owes to colleagues and friends, not least to the members of the clerical staff. I should particularly like to mention Professor Raymond Apthorpe, then Professor of Sociology at Makerere, and Dr Josef Gugler who supervised my work in the field. In the UK, work for the dissertation on which this monograph is based was supervised at various times by Professor Lucy Mair, Dr Audrey Richards and Dr Cyril Sofer, each of whom provided much helpful advice. As an undergraduate and a postgraduate at Cambridge I received every encouragement, practical and intellectual, from Professor Meyer Fortes and Dr Edmund Leach, both of King's College. More recently I have benefited from the stimulus of Professor F. G. Bailey and Dr Harvey Sarles when our tenures at the University of Sussex coincided. May I make special mention of the very many debts I owe to an old friend and colleague, Dr David Parkin, now also of the University of Sussex.

The research for my dissertation was financed by grants from the then Department of Education and Science, and by generous awards from the Smuts Memorial Fund and the Fellows of King's College, Cambridge. Without their support this study could not have been made.

Debts to informants in the field can never fully be repaid. Without the co-operation of the EARH, fieldwork would have been impossible. I am very grateful to Mr L. L. Brown and Mr C. Tamale (then AGMs of the Uganda Region) for allowing me to work at Kampala, and to Mr Z. H. Kaheru (then Chief Assistant to the GM at Nairobi) who accorded me every facility when collecting material at Headquarters. To the railway employees themselves I owe an obvious debt. To single out a few is invidious, but I would particularly like to thank the following past and present members of the EARH staff: E. E. Akena, J. Aswani, J. Isiche, S. Mwinamo, J. Ochola, J. Odonde, G. Okoth, M. Okum, J. Okwiri, M. Opiyo, and A. Rwakubale. Let me also thank the Hon. H. M. Luande, MP, President of the RAU(U), and many other union officers in both Kampala and Nairobi, especially C. Lutta. I wish also to thank J. Siso, D. Okumu and A. Adhanja of the 'Nylon Bar' and all their families for their generous hospitality at

Acknowledgements

all times. The final draft of this manuscript was typed by the Secretarial staff of the School of African and Asian Studies, University of Sussex, and I would like to thank Miss Yvette Ashby, Administrative Secretary, for according me this facility.

Finally I must pay tribute to my wife without whose tolerance and understanding neither this book nor the dissertation on which it is based would ever have been written.

R. D. G.

Sussex
August 1971

ABBREVIATIONS

AGM	Assistant General Manager
AME	Assistant Mechanical Engineer
ATS	Assistant Traffic Superintendent
CxR	Carriage and Waggon Examiner
DE	District Engineer (official or department)
DME	District Mechanical Engineer (official or department)
DTS	District Traffic Superintendent (official or department)
EACSO	East African Common Service Organisation
EAISR	East African Institute of Social Research
EARH	East African Railways and Harbours
FUTU	Federation of Uganda Trades Unions
GM	General Manager
HI	Health Inspector(ate)
ICFTU	International Confederation of Free Trades Unions
IRO	Industrial Relations Officer
IW	Inspector(ate) of Works
PWI	Permanent Way Inspector(ate)
RAU(U)	Railway African Union (Uganda)
RSF	Running Shift Foreman
RTS	Railway Training School
TTE	Travelling Ticket Examiner
UTUC	Uganda Trades Union Congress

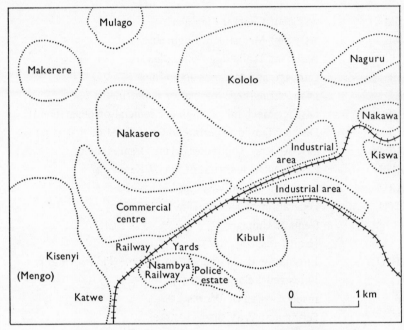

Fig. 1. Kampala City: main urban area and suburbs

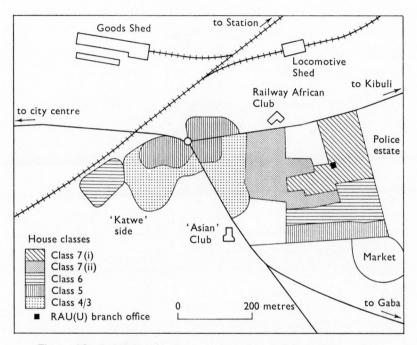

Fig. 2. The EARH Housing Estate at Nsambya and immediate environs

INTRODUCTION

This monograph deals with a number of problems in the field of urban and industrial anthropology in East Africa. It concerns the members of a largely migrant but nonetheless 'committed' labour force employed as railwaymen in Kampala, Uganda, and shows how workers in this industry form a distinct community, even a subculture, in the urban area. The form of this community is provided by the industrial process which generates a framework by reference to which certain relationships of solidarity and opposition are articulated. Of particular significance in this respect is the differentiation of the labour force in terms of occupation, 'grade', income and position in the industrial hierarchy, factors which give rise to inequalities of status and power and lead to alignments based on relative position in what are conceived of as systems of stratification and class. To this extent the study documents a particular example of the general trend toward status differentiation in urban Africa which has been noted in many recent publications. It will be seen, however, that such alignments are in this instance tempered by other factors. For although railwaymen are committed to industrial employment and have in many ways absorbed the values of industrial society they remain migrants. They do not form an urban proletariat which has severed all connection with its rural origins. This fact in itself raises a number of questions much debated among social scientists and others concerning the conditions necessary for urban and industrial growth in the so-called underdeveloped countries, but has a major consequence for the more limited purposes of the present study. Almost all railwaymen continue to maintain networks of social ties outside the community, principally with those from their rural homes. Such ties which are broadly those of kinship and ethnicity both link the individual with others in the urban and rural areas and generate within the community alignments of solidarity and opposition which frequently run counter to those derived from the industrial framework. Thus any individual railwayman may order his social world from two contrasting view-points and may have at least two sets of norms and values by reference to which he may conduct his relationships with others. How and why he operates in such a system form the principal problems of this monograph.

THE CHOICE OF COMMUNITY AND RESTRICTIONS ON THE SCOPE OF THE STUDY

The fieldwork for this study was carried out in East Africa in 1964/5, for the most part in Kampala, the capital and principal city of Uganda. The people with whom it is chiefly concerned are the African employees of the EARH, stationed at the Railways' Kampala Depot and living on the railway-owned Nsambya Housing Estate which lies on the southern edge of the city. The EARH, or simply the Railways, is the largest employer in the heavy industrial sector in the three East African territories – Kenya, Uganda and Tanzania. This in itself was one of its principal attractions for an anthropologist since until then, in contrast with, for example, the Copper Belt, there had been no major study of the labour force of a large-scale industrial enterprise in East Africa. Other factors indicated that fieldwork in this industry would be both practicable and interesting, including the diverse occupational structure of the labour force – the EARH employs a wide range of skilled labour – the presence of large and active trades unions and the existence of special housing estates for the use of railway employees. It was anticipated that the congregation of workers in such estates would not only facilitate fieldwork but would also provide some basis for comparison with those industries such as the copper mines in Zambia where employees are both workmates and neighbours. Finally, there already existed a short survey of railway employees in Nairobi carried out in 1946 (Northcott 1949) and although its purpose was not primarily anthropological it contained many interesting social observations which might be compared with findings in Kampala. The Kampala Depot itself was chosen as the point of departure for fieldwork partly because the labour force was of a convenient size and partly because previous publications and work then in progress in other areas of the city meant that a considerable amount of information on the urban context was readily available.

The choice of an urban and industrial community reflected both my own personal interests and the increasing involvement in such studies among British anthropologists, notably, of course, those working in Central Africa. The selection of the EARH was made essentially on pragmatic grounds and did not indicate a romantic attachment to railways *per se*.

There are a number of restrictions on the scope of the study which may impose limitations on the value of its findings. Although the EARH employs workers of all races I concentrated on the African element in the labour force to the virtual exclusion of the European and Asian members. This was partly dictated by the focus of my own interests and partly by the exigencies of the situation, for it was found that outside work each race mostly went its own way and consequently gathering material on each group would have involved an unacceptable diversification of time and resources. Important, too, was the fact that the climate of the times made it extremely unlikely that a single anthropologist could successfully maintain rapport with all three groups simultaneously. The fieldworker may be felt by his informants to have acquired commitments and loyalties, and anything which throws doubt on these may disrupt relationships which in the nature of things may have taken months to establish. Nevertheless, I recognise that the failure to treat Europeans and Asians except in so far as they impinged on the African employees represents a major limitation.

A second restriction comes from the fact that fieldwork was carried out principally at one depot only, Kampala. The EARH maintains several hundred stations, jetties and so on of varying size and importance all over

East Africa. Although my original intention had been to sample several of these, time and the funds available made this impossible. Even a less ambitious plan to study three depots each of a different size had to be abandoned when it became necessary to spend much longer than anticipated at Kampala in order to complete a thorough study. Nevertheless, I was able to spend some time at a much smaller station, Kasese, in western Uganda, and at a much larger, Nairobi, and am therefore in some position to be able to judge how far the findings of the Kampala study apply in general terms to railwaymen elsewhere in East Africa. This position is bolstered by the fact that among railway personnel there was at the time a high inter-depot transfer rate which meant that at Kampala one could meet railwaymen who had served in almost every part of East Africa. Conversely, many informants first met at Kampala were in their turn transferred elsewhere and when contact was maintained it was possible to gain some insight into how conditions varied from place to place.

There are other restrictions, too. The major part of fieldwork at Kampala was undertaken at the Nsambya Housing Estate. Since some employees live off the estate and these may represent a distinct section of the labour force the relative neglect of that section may indicate another gap in the field-work and another possible source of bias in its findings. More important in this respect was the considerable ethnic diversity of the labour force and hence in the cultural origins and background of its members. Restrictions of time and to some extent loyalties made it impossible to investigate every ethnic group as thoroughly as could be desired. Since two groups – the Luo and the Luhya, both from western Kenya – were numerically of great significance and of especial importance in the trade union movement I found myself concentrating on them to the partial neglect of others. I will try to assess where this has biased the findings. Finally, my information on relationships within the work process is not as detailed as one could have wished since the EARH management felt unable to allow me to observe systematically workers at the depot. It was, however, possible from time to time to undertake sufficient fieldwork of such a kind at least to allow for the substantiation of statements made by informants about relationships in the work context.

So, then, the study primarily concerns a particular segment of the railway labour force or alternatively the residents of one housing estate in the city of Kampala. This section of the population, African railwaymen and their families living at Nsambya, numbered about 2,800 persons. Nevertheless, contacts and information were drawn from a wider range of sources than this implies. On the one hand the relatively high turnover in the estate population brought about by transfers, visits to Kampala by other railwaymen in the course of their duties and my own trips to Kasese and Nairobi considerably extended the range of informants in the labour force. Secondly, I came to know Kampala itself tolerably well and was able to maintain contacts with residents other than railwaymen, particularly among those living in the neighbourhoods around Nsambya, and these extended my knowledge of the urban context. Finally, through the

3

hospitality of several informants I made several extended visits to the rural areas, particularly to the Western and Nyanza Provinces of Kenya and to parts of Tanzania. Consequently, despite the restrictions, I feel reasonably confident about judging the extent to which the findings at Nsambya apply to railwaymen throughout East Africa, to the residents of other parts of Kampala and to certain ethnic groups from particular areas of rural East Africa.

METHODS

A variety of methods of data collection were employed. The bulk of information was obtained in the time-honoured way by intensive observation. During a period of eighteen months, from March 1964 to September 1965, I was in almost daily contact with railwaymen in Kampala and elsewhere. Unfortunately it proved impossible, owing to a shortage of housing, to obtain accommodation on the estate and so I was forced to live on the Makerere campus about a mile away. Eventually many friends were able to offer accommodation locally as the need arose. Besides gathering information casually in the seemingly endless hours of social drinking which proved to be the principal leisure activity of the majority of railwaymen, I kept in daily contact with a relatively small number of informants whose lives I studied in detail. These, some of whom I sought and some of whom sought me, represented a rough cross-section of the various elements in the population and it was thus possible to keep in touch with events in various parts of the community. Although the frequency of inter-depot transfer had some advantages it also posed a problem in that sometimes months of effort spent in establishing rapport would seemingly be lost when the subject was suddenly moved, perhaps to Mombasa. The population was thus considerably more fluid than that which an anthropologist studying a rural or some urban communities is likely to encounter. The fluidity meant a continual influx of new residents to whom one's existence had to be justified afresh. Partly because of this, formal interviews were rarely found to be acceptable as a method of gathering information, at least until a close understanding had been developed. Even the sight of a notebook seemed to be counter-productive. Thus like Whyte (1943) I found it necessary to memorise the events of a day until an opportunity occurred to record them in a diary. For this reason many statements by informants quoted in this monograph are unavoidably couched in *oratio obliqua* which, wherever possible, retains the vocabulary and phrasing of the original.

As to language, both English and Swahili, which I studied in London before entering the field, were important means of communication between residents on the estate. In order, however, to enter more fully into relationships with informants it would have been desirable to learn a dozen or more local languages and dialects. This being impossible, I had to pick up what I could of the languages of the two most important ethnic groups, Luo and Luhya, together with some Luganda which is used by many as a common language.

4

Besides these intensive methods it was found both possible and desirable to conduct a survey of a randomly-selected sample of household heads, the details of which are given in Appendix I. This survey, undertaken after a full year's fieldwork, provided invaluable information which often corroborated and sometimes extended hypotheses derived from intensive work as well as occasionally confounding them. There was also available a considerable body of published and unpublished statistical data relating to the EARH and its predecessors which was particularly valuable for obtaining a historical perspective on the development of the labour force. Finally, documents, public and private – newspapers, magazines, pamphlets, leaflets, memoranda, letters – were also a useful source of material. It was particularly gratifying to obtain through the good offices of numerous officials considerable quantities of documents relating to the affairs and policies of the principal trades unions, though some of this data must await analysis in a subsequent publication.

ORIENTATIONS

A brief summary of the principal issues has already been presented and here I will do little more than explain how the discussion in each chapter relates to the central themes and develop one or two points concerning the theoretical orientations of the monograph. It will be found that while most chapters contain some theoretical discussion, the wider implications of the findings for urban and industrial studies in Africa are for the most part confined to the Conclusion.

Chapters 1 and 2 establish the general background and the specific context of the study. Chapter 1 examines the social and economic framework of Kenya and Uganda in the early 1960s with particular reference to the development of the labour force and the urban population. A contrast is drawn between two types of migration, one of which may be said to have characterised the urban African workforce until the late fifties, the other of which is of more recent appearance. It is argued that increasing labour force stability and growing commitment to an urban and industrial way of life has not been accompanied by 'proletarianisation'. This theme is taken up and documented for the railway case in Chapter 3.

Chapter 2 deals specifically with the EARH and clears away a number of technical issues necessary for understanding the subsequent discussion. The proposition that railwaymen have absorbed the norms and values of industrial society and that participation in the industry generates lines of differentiation within the labour force is examined in Chapters 4, 5 and 6. It is hoped that the discussion goes some way to substantiating a hypothesis put forward by Mitchell, who makes the following comment on what he terms 'structural relationships'.

These are relationships, within an urban social system, which have enduring patterns of interaction and which are structured, i.e. the norms are defined in terms of the role expectations of others. Perhaps the most important of these in terms of the amount of time which urban Africans spend in them are work relationships. These are probably the most tightly structured of all urban relationships in the sense that the statuses and roles among workers are rigidly defined in terms of the productive activity in which they are engaged. Yet, in general, the interaction of African townsmen in industrial and commercial environments has been little studied.

(Mitchell 1966: 51)

Although the present monograph hopes to contribute to this aspect of African urban anthropology it must be stressed yet again that this is not primarily a study of people *at work*, but of the extent to which participation in the 'productive activity' of the industry structures relationships both in and outside work. As has been suggested, of particular importance in this connection are the inequalities imposed by differences of occupation and so forth from which is derived consciousness of status and class allegiance. This theme is examined in Chapters 5 and 6 where a further point is made, namely that within the community great emphasis is placed on achievement measured in terms of advancement within the industrial hierarchy. Railwaymen are conscious not only of differences of status but also of the possibilities of achieving higher status through competition with others. The intensity of competition is reflected in the responses to success and failure documented in Chapter 6. The competitive spirit engendered within the industry is reflected in urban life in general as may be seen in Chapter 7 which recounts the history of struggles for power within the RAU(U).

It is through an examination of status differences and the competition for status that two major themes are brought together. For it is at this point that two sets of norms and values – those generated by the industrial framework and those derived from the need to retain ongoing links with rural homes and hence within the ethnic group of origin – are potentially in greatest danger of conflicting. This theme is mentioned briefly in Chapter 3 and taken up more extensively in Chapters 5, 6 and 7.

The argument throughout accepts and confirms the now widely-held proposition that relationships between individuals in both the rural and urban areas are interconnected into a single system, or to use another term, 'field'. Since this concept is used with a different emphasis by various writers some clarification is necessary. Mitchell, for example, notes that:

A social field may be thought of as a series of interconnecting relationships all of which in some way influence one another. As Barnes (1954) used the idea, each field is a segment of the social system which may be isolated in terms of the interdependency of the relationships and of the activities of the people involved in it. Overlapping fields together, therefore, comprise the total social system.

(Mitchell 1966: 57)

The term 'field' as used in this quotation apparently has the same meaning as the term 'set' as used by Epstein, who suggests that an African town may be seen as: 'A field of social relations which is made up of sets of social relations of different kinds, each of which covers a distinct sphere of social interaction, and forms a sub-system' (Epstein 1958: 232). In order to avoid possible terminological confusion the concept of a 'field' is used here in Epstein's sense. Thus the rural and urban areas of East Africa constitute a single social field and the norms of the industrial and ethnic sets of relationships, using those terms as a kind of shorthand, form subsystems of this field. Any individual is likely to have a wide range of contacts within his personal network drawn from both sets of relationships and from others, and we will see in Chapter 7 how competitors for leadership in an urban association may use this fact, perhaps to their advantage. Within the railway community, however, individuals are frequently linked by multiplex ties, joined in relationships ordered by reference to both the industrial and the ethnic frameworks. It will be seen that there is a normatively acceptable solution to the problems posed by this situation which emerges through a consideration of individuals' attempts to reconcile the conflict of norms and allegiances with which they are faced.

Finally, a number of minor points concerning the presentation of data may be noted. When the present tense is used in ethnographic description the time referred to is the period of fieldwork, i.e. 1964/5. Throughout the text African countries are usually referred to by the names by which they are known at present even where these are anachronistic. Throughout the monograph use is made of a number of technical terms and abbreviations which form an integral part of a railwayman's vocabulary: all abbreviations used are listed on p. xi. Numerous individuals are referred to by name in the text, and I have taken the liberty in all but a few cases of using pseudonyms. Lastly, the currency referred to throughout is the East African £ which at the time of the study was on par with sterling. Subsequently each of the three territories issued their own currency. After the devaluation of 1967 the Ugandan and Kenyan pounds had an official value of £1.16½ sterling.

CHAPTER 1

THE SOCIAL AND
ECONOMIC FRAMEWORK

East Africa – Kenya, Uganda and Tanzania – is what used to be called an 'underdeveloped' area. The fashion in labels has changed, but the facts remain. They are vast countries, sparsely inhabited overall, but with dense concentrations in fertile areas. The majority of the population gain a livelihood as peasant farmers whose standard of living measured in conventional economic terms is low. *Per capita* income in 1969 was in Kenya £47 per annum, in Uganda £33. Disease, illiteracy, hunger, are the features commonly associated with such economies. In the last decade the area has experienced rapid political and social change associated with the end of colonial rule and the attainment of independence. In broad terms this is the context in which this study is set. This chapter will document such features of the social and economic backgrounds of Uganda and Kenya as are necessary for an understanding of what follows. The discussion covers ground familiar to those acquainted with the African literature on urbanisation and migration. The first sections deal with the place of wage employment in the two economies and the structure of what is still largely a migratory labour force. The Uganda material updates existing studies by social scientists working in that country in the fifties (e.g. Elkan 1960, Powesland 1957, Richards (ed.) 1954) and in some respects confirms their findings. Some important changes will, however, be noted, especially the tendency towards greater 'stability' on the part of African workers. This leads to a discussion of the causes of migration of either a short-term or long-term type, and to a provisional assessment of some of the arguments used to account for the presence or absence of 'commitment' to industrial employment in this area.

THE LABOUR FORCE IN THE ECONOMY [1]

According to the 1969 censuses the population of Kenya was approximately 11 million, that of Uganda 9½ million. Comparison with earlier returns (see Table 1) shows that the population is increasing at an estimated 3½% to 4% per annum. Those in wage employment are but a fraction of the total (see Table 2). In Kenya and Uganda combined about 17% only of African males of working age [2] were engaged in wage labour in 1969. Many of these are unskilled agricultural labourers, and only a fifth work in industry. A study concerned with railwaymen, heavy industrial workers many of whom have skilled or white collar jobs, deals with a minority of

TABLE I. *The population of Uganda and Kenya at census dates ('ooo person)*

Race	Uganda			Kenya		
	1948	1959	1969[a]	1948	1962	1969
African	4,900	6,425	9,456	5,251	8,366	10,674
Others	42	88	92	155	270	269
Total	4,942	6,513	9,548	5,406	8,636	10,943

[a] Uganda 1969 figures are provisional.

employees in a labour force which itself constitutes a minority of those engaged in productive activities.

The principal features of the labour force in the early sixties may be noted briefly. Wages are, of course, abysmally low in world terms. In 1963 the average African income from employment was under £100 per annum. It is significant, however, that in the period 1954–69 African wages were increasing at an annual rate of over 12%. African average wages may be compared with those for Asians (c. £600 per annum) and Europeans (c. £1,500) in the same year, 1963. The second feature which is to be emphasised is the distribution of employment. In Uganda in 1963 nearly 53% of all workers were located in the adjacent Districts of Mengo and Busoga, in and around the towns of Kampala and Jinja and along the 50-mile road which joins them. In this area, Uganda's 'golden triangle', 75% of workers in manufacturing industries were concentrated. More recent figures suggest that there have been some attempts to spread the distribution more evenly, though in 1969 this area still held 49% of the country's labour force. The only other major concentration is at Kasese in the west, the copper-mining centre and railhead. In Kenya the principal centres of employment are to be found roughly on the line Mombasa–Nairobi–Kisumu. Nairobi itself and the surrounding Central Province contained over 40% of the national workforce in 1962.[3]

Table 2 shows that in the early sixties there was a fall in the absolute numbers of those employed in both Kenya and Uganda.[4] Subsequently there was an upward trend, largely due to government intervention, but at the time the present study was made there were fewer Africans in employment than for many years, and since the population had been growing steadily this meant a reduction in the proportion of the population at work. Indeed, despite the expansion of the workforce in the late sixties, there were still relatively fewer Africans employed in 1969 than there had been in 1954. We will return shortly to estimate the consequences of this development.

Although average wages may seem low, in contrast with what is generally available from other sources – trade and agriculture – they provide a relatively high cash income. Estimates of income outside the employment sector are difficult to obtain and highly speculative but in Table 2 an attempt is made to provide such figures for various years between 1954–69.[5] It can be seen that in 1963, for example, an adult male in employment could

TABLE 2. *Trends in employment and earnings, Kenya and Uganda, 1954–69*

	1954	1963	1969
Uganda			
Total employed all races '000	236	222	295
Africans in employment '000	225	208	281
Estimated African population '000	5,682	7,499	9,456
% African population employed	4.0	2.8	3.0
Mean African income from employment £.p.a.	£40	£99	£158
Mean African income other sources £.p.a.	£44	£37	£38
Kenya			
Total employed all races '000	543	533	627
Africans in employment '000	491	479	582
Estimated African population '000	6,610	8,658	10,674
% African population employed	7.4	5.5	5.9
Mean African income from employment £.p.a.	£45	£95	£174
Mean African income other sources £.p.a.	£8	£10	n.a.

For sources and commments, see notes 1 and 5 to Chapter 1 (p. 193).

expect to earn 2½ times as much as his counterpart in agriculture or trade and that the gap between the two has continued to widen. The figures in Table 2 are of necessity crude approximations. That they correctly represent the direction of developments may be seen in the fact that while between 1963–9 in Uganda the amount paid out in wages to African workers rose from £m.21 to £m.45, the value of the principal cash crops, cotton and coffee, increased by only a little, from £m.30 to £m.36.[6]

Another feature of the rural economy which has a bearing on later discussion is the variation in average income derived from farming between provinces and districts. Once again figures are largely speculative, but taking into account the population of each province, and the reported acreages of cotton and coffee, it may be estimated that in 1963 the average income per adult male varied as follows: Buganda Province £78 per annum, Eastern £39, Western £14, Northern £20. Variations at the district level are equally marked.[7] Comparable figures for Kenya are not available, but it may be noted that in Nyanza Province, an area from which come large numbers of those who work in the EARH and with whom therefore we will be especially concerned, the annual monetary product – per adult male – was estimated in 1962 at £20.[8]

Migrant labour

Since the earliest days of colonial development a large section of the East African labour force has consisted of migrants, men who have left their homes to travel, often great distances, to find employment. Table 3 shows that in Uganda in 1963 56,600 workers, 27% of the labour force, were actually born outside the country. To this number must be added a further 60,700 Uganda-born workers employed outside their district of birth.

TABLE 3. *Uganda African employees, place of birth, 1963 and 1969*

District/Country of origin	1963		1969	
	Number [a]	%	Number [a]	%
Mengo	24,000	11.5	35,500	12.6
Masaka	6,400	3.1	12,100	4.3
Mubende	2,300	1.1	5,500	2.0
Total Buganda Province	32,700	15.7	53,100	18.9
Busoga	11,200	5.4	19,200	6.8
Bugisu	5,900	2.8	10,600	3.8
Bukedi	8,200	3.9	14,000	5.0
Teso	9,700	4.6	12,900	4.6
Total Eastern Province	35,000	16.7	56,700	20.2
Acholi	10,000	4.8	13,900	4.9
Lango	5,800	2.8	9,500	3.4
Karamoja	2,100	1.0	3,000	1.1
West Nile	12,700	6.1	} 18,800	6.7
Madi	2,100	1.0		
Total Northern Province	32,700	15.7	45,200	16.1
Bunyoro	8,300	4.0	11,700	4.2
Toro	13,500	6.5	14,400	5.3
Ankole	12,400	6.0	17,800	6.3
Kigezi	17,200	8.3	25,700	9.2
Total Western Province	51,400	24.8	69,600	25.0
Total Uganda born	151,800	72.9	224,600	80.2
Congo	4,800	2.3	5,300	1.9
Rwanda and Burundi	24,900	11.9	28,200	10.1
Kenya	16,600	8.0	14,400	5.2
Tanzania	2,200	1.1	1,600	0.6
Sudan	6,700	3.2	5,400	1.9
Other	1,400	0.7	700	0.2
Grand total	208,400	100.1	280,500	100.1

[a] Individual district totals are rounded up or down to the nearest hundred.

SOURCE: Figures derived from Uganda Government, *Enumeration of Employees*, June 1963, Tables 6 and 7, and from *Enumeration of Employees*, June 1969, Appendix VI and VII.

Migrants in both categories make up 57% of all employees. These figures underestimate the full extent of migration in this area. There are the farm labourers who escape enumeration, the thousands who have moved from one rural area to another to rent or buy land, the many petty traders in the towns and, of course, the wives and children of all these. According to the 1959 census, the latest available at present, over 50% of the African population of Kampala consisted of migrants and their families – i.e. non-Ganda. In Mengo and Busoga, including Kampala and Jinja, migrants actually constitute 70% of the labour force. Among non-Ugandans working in the area the greatest number are from Rwanda and Burundi who mostly find employment in plantation agriculture in Mengo and Busoga. The other large group is the Kenyans who tend to work in light industry in Kampala and Jinja, though in 1963, at any rate, many were employed in the public services. Each district of Uganda sends at least some representatives into the area, though the absolute numbers from each district vary considerably. Among Ugandans in the labour force as a whole in 1963 those born in West Nile, Acholi and Kigezi Districts were particularly strongly represented, each district contributing over 10% of the migrants, while at the other end of the scale areas such as Mengo, Masaka, Mubende, Busoga, Bugisu, Lango and Karamoja each provided less than 5%. These variations remain even when factors such as population, size and distance from employing centres are held constant. They are, however, strongly associated with the regional variations in rural cash incomes, mentioned earlier. This will have a bearing on later discussion.

Between 1963 and 1969 there were some changes in the composition of the labour force, notably the decline of the non-Ugandan element, in particular the Kenyans, partly as a result of government policy. Similarly there appears to have been increasing employment among Africans from areas such as Lango District. The extent and significance of these changes cannot be discussed here.

The 'classical' pattern of migration

The fact of extensive migration in Uganda was noted in the fifties, and the data presented here simply update published material. The causes of migration in all parts of Africa have also received considerable attention (e.g. Gugler 1968, 1969, Gulliver 1960, Hutton 1970, Mitchell 1959, among many others). The argument most generally accepted runs as follows. Whatever motives an individual has for migrating, the rate of migration from any area is generated by a nexus of social and economic factors, with emphasis on the economic. This argument may be used to explain the variation in migration rates from different areas noted above. It has been suggested, and much evidence offered in support, that there is an association between a high rate of migration and an absence of alternative opportunities for earning a cash income, e.g. in agriculture. This is certainly the case for Uganda. Areas such as Kigezi, Acholi and West Nile Districts have in general low average agricultural incomes and high rates of migration when compared with other Uganda districts. The reverse applies to areas such as Bugisu. Other studies (e.g. Southall 1954) have shown that there may be variation between different parts of a district which may be explained in similar terms. While this type of economic argument may be generally accepted, it is well to take note of some areas, e.g. Karamoja, which have low migration rates and poor opportunities for earning cash in agriculture or trade. A rider needs to be added to the effect that when within two areas there is an equal demand for cash, then differential rates of migration may be explained by reference to the presence or absence of alternative income sources. The problem, which cannot be explored here, then becomes one of explaining why areas like Karamoja have low cash needs.

Not surprisingly, then, most migrants come from areas poorly endowed with alternative income sources, and they come to work to earn a living rather, than as sometimes suggested, to view the 'bright lights'. From the many migrant studies undertaken in East Africa in both rural and urban areas it is possible to draw up a set of characteristics, an 'ideal type', of what, for reasons which will become clear, I will call the 'classical' pattern of labour migration. The principal features appear to be as follows. The migrant leaves his rural home to visit the urban and other centres of employment for a period of perhaps two years. He is usually a young man and either a bachelor or a married man who has left his wife and children back home. He may enter the labour market only once in his life-time or may make several excursions, interspersing each work-spell with periods spent, as they say in Kampala, 'sitting at home'. His motives for entering employment, when cast in economic terms, often refer to a limited goal – money for taxes, bridewealth, a bike. Because of this he is often called a 'target worker', a concept whose origin is obscure but which crept into administrative and academic jargon some time in the thirties, and then dominated thinking on African labour. The short periods spent at work mean that in industry there is a high turnover among employees and in the towns an extremely fluid and unstable population. Demographically the areas of immigration are 'abnormal' in that they contain a high proportion of young men, but few women, children and old people. Because of this it is frequently argued that this pattern of migration is costly (for the employer), inefficient, unreliable and socially undesirable (e.g. ILO 1958: 145). The social and economic consequences for the rural areas are also deprecated – split families, the absence of men for farm work and so on – though others have suggested that the rural economy does not suffer as much as is often supposed (Berg 1961, 1965).

In many respects, then, this type of migration is felt to constitute a problem the dimensions of which, for the industrialist, may be documented by reference to some figures from Uganda industry in the fifties. For example, the Uganda Labour Department annual report for 1955 provided estimates of the mean monthly turnover rates in a number of enterprises, which averaged out at no less than 15%. In a Kampala factory studied by Elkan in 1954 the rate was 8%, lower than average but still very high by European and American standards. In that factory 71% of the workers had served for less than three years (Elkan 1956: 6, 10). For anthropologists, economists and others the explanation of this pattern and a resolution of the associated problems seemed a critical issue.

Just as the standard explanation for the causes of migration focuses on economic factors, so do those offered for the causes of short-term migration. With respect to Uganda a major contribution was made by Elkan, who in his study *Migrants and proletarians* surveys a range of possible explanations including the unattractiveness of urban conditions, the lack of housing suitable for family units, the insufficiency of urban wages to support families and the importance of land in social and economic life, a factor on which he himself lays considerable emphasis:

So long as a man cannot obtain compensation for vacating his land, and on the other hand cannot normally maintain his right to it unless he or his family are in actual occupation, he has no inducement to vacate it and he is therefore bound to regard employment as in some sense temporary. (1960: 136)

Elkan adds later:

Once an entire family leave their holding in the countryside it ceases to be theirs and it ceases to afford them further income and security. The success of stabilization policies in the Congo may therefore be attributable as much to this compulsory severance from the land as to the positive inducement of employers. (ibid.: 137)

We will return to this argument again.

A changing pattern?

Although the classical pattern of migration may have characterised the East African labour force perhaps until the late fifties, there is evidence, scattered and fragmentary though it be, that the pattern has been changing. For example, the average turnover rates recorded by the Uganda Labour Department reports had fallen in 1957 to 10.2% and by 1960 to 6.5%; later figures are not available. Further evidence of this trend may be seen in the fact that in Elkan's tobacco factory the turnover rate in 1960 was as low as 0.7%. A follow-up study by Baryaruha showed that by 1965 the median length of service among the factory's employees was 9.5 years, compared with 1.7 years in 1954 (see Table 4). Further work by Baryaruha

TABLE 4. *Length of service of African employees in two industries*

	Railways		Tobacco factory	
Years of service	Nairobi 1946	Kampala 1965	Kampala 1954	Kampala 1965
0–4	56%	10%	83%	8%
5 plus	44%	90%	17%	92%
Median length	4.0	12.0	1.7	9.5

SOURCES: Railways Nairobi: Northcott 1949; railways Kampala, my own data; tobacco factory: Elkan 1956, Baryaruha 1967.

on other firms, my own data for EARH employees, and a United Nations enquiry establish a widespread trend towards increasing stability.[9] Further indications of this trend may be seen in the changing demographic structure of East Africa's towns.

URBAN GROWTH AND CHANGE IN KENYA AND UGANDA

Like many underdeveloped countries Uganda and Kenya have a low level of urbanisation, defining the urbanised population in the straightforward sense of those resident in town at any time. In the censuses of 1959 and

1962 about 5% of the African population in the two countries lived in urban centres of over 5,000 inhabitants. Comparisons from census to census for the purposes of estimating urban growth are tricky because of the rapidity with which boundaries change. Provisional returns for 1969 give Greater Kampala a population of 330,700, as against 157,825 in a comparable area in 1959. This represents an intercensal growth rate of 7.6% per annum. Nairobi is now said to have a population of over 500,000 compared with 314,760 in the Extra Provincial District in 1962. Tables 5 and 6

TABLE 5. *Demographic structure of Kampala, 1948 and 1959*

	Adults				Children			
	Male		Female		Male		Female	
	No. '000	%	No. '000	%	No. '000	%	No. '000	%
1948	23.2	49.0	12.5	26.4	6.6	13.9	5.2	10.9
1959	42.6	46.2	22.5	24.4	13.6	14.8	13.4	14.6

SOURCES: Uganda Census 1948: 5–6, Uganda Census 1959b: 35–7.

TABLE 6. *Demographic structure of Nairobi, 1948 and 1962*

	Adults				Children			
	Male		Female		Male		Female	
	No. '000	%	No. '000	%	No. '000	%	No. '000	%
1948	45.6	70.7	9.3	14.4	5.6	8.7	4.0	6.2
1962	75.9	48.6	30.4	19.5	25.9	16.6	24.0	15.3

SOURCES: Kenya Census 1948: 6–7, Kenya Census 1962: 36.

compare the demographic structure of the African populations of the two cities at two censuses.[10] Besides the growth in numbers the principal feature of the changing structure in both cases is the increase in the numbers of women and children compared with adult males, and the declining preponderance of the latter. This trend has continued, as far as can be seen from the figures so far published, into the late sixties. For example, the male:female ratio in the African population of Nairobi at successive censuses was, 1948: 3.85, 1962: 1.89, 1969: 1.58. Whereas in Kampala in 1948 among migrants males outnumbered females by 3:1, by 1959 this figure was down to almost 2:1.

The census material suggests that the urban African population is becoming increasingly 'normal' in a demographic sense, a conclusion which may be substantiated by reference to the numerous studies undertaken in Kampala since the pioneering work of Southall and Gutkind in the early fifties.[11] Some indications of the kinds of change occurring may be seen in a comparison of the findings of Southall and Gutkind's survey of Mulago and Kisenyi with those of the 'Kampala Survey 1965' which covered

TABLE 7. *A comparison of two surveys of Kampala*

	Kisenyi–Mulago 1953/4	Kibuli–Kiswa–Nsambya 1965
Population enumerated	3,493	2,285
Adult males per cent	47.9	38.0
Adult females per cent	33.3	26.8
Children per cent	18.9	35.2
Number of households	1,146	866
Persons per household	2.47	2.65
1 person households per cent	40.0	35.0
2 person households per cent	37.0	24.0
3 or more person households per cent	23.0	42.0
Rooms per household	1.45	1.16
Persons per room	1.70	3.29
Employed/self-employed per cent [a]	57.0	38.3
Non-employed per cent [a]	43.0	61.7

[a] Based on Mulago and Kibuli data only.

SOURCES: Kisenyi and Mulago figures derived from Southall and Gutkind, Tables I–XV; Kibuli etc., figures derived from 'Kampala Survey 1965'.

Kibuli, Kiswa and Nsambya (see Appendix I). Data from the two surveys are presented in Table 7. Since they covered different suburbs of the city the comparison has to be undertaken with caution; nonetheless each may be taken as representing 'typical' areas of the city at different points in time. The findings are consistent with those of the censuses. Females and children are much more prevalent, household size has risen, there are fewer single-person households, population density as measured in persons per room has increased and the proportion of the population engaged in earning a living has declined, i.e. there are a greater number of dependants per worker.

These changes in the urban structure may be set alongside those that are occurring in industry. They indicate a new pattern of migration characterised by increasing commitment to employment and a greater tendency to bring families into the town. Further evidence for this, and discussion of associated factors, is provided in Chapter 3, which deals with the Railway labour force at Kampala. This trend towards urbanisation and stability is to be found in many parts of Africa, especially Kenya (Amsden 1971, ch. 2, and future publications by Parkin) and on the Copper Belt.

An explanation of the change

How can we account for this trend? First, it is significant that during the fifties and sixties there was a change in the state of the labour supply in the two countries. Whereas government reports of the early fifties reflect the complaints of recruiting officers about the difficulty of filling vacancies for even unskilled jobs, by the end of the decade the problem became not the shortage but the surplus of labour, and during the sixties there was generally recognised to be widespread unemployment among all but those with the highest level of skills and training.[12] Since, as we saw earlier, the labour force actually contracted during the fifties, while the population continued to expand, this change is not unexpected. Evidence, however, suggests that the proportion of the population wanting work also increased. This again is not unexpected, for during this period, which coincided with falls in world prices for primary products, wages increased much more rapidly than earnings from agriculture. If, as may be accepted, the demand for employment on the part of the African peasant farmer is related to the availability of acceptable returns from agriculture, then a decline in the latter would produce a greater propensity to seek work in the wage sector. A parallel trend which seems to have increased the supply of work seekers was the vast expansion in the output of primary and intermediary schools.

While it cannot be entirely discounted that, as has sometimes been argued (Amsden 1971, Weeks 1971), wage increases themselves created stability and led to unemployment, it is more likely that stability itself reflected a more fundamental change in the society. Indeed there is some evidence to suggest that wage increases, or at least demands for wage increases on the part of the emergent trade union movement, were generated by an existing trend towards stability (Grillo, forthcoming 1974). It is not immediately obvious that the situation outlined in the preceding paragraph would affect the behaviour of the classical migrant. The target worker with his once-for-all need for cash would not necessarily lengthen his stay in employment, though economic opinion on this is divided (cf. Berg 1961). Indeed, unless as Gulliver (1955: 21) suggested, the target was a period of time rather than a fixed sum, rising wages might induce him to shorten his term of employment. Job shortages would only be relevant in so far as he would be unable to find employment exactly when he wanted it. A combination of high unemployment and high, if not increasing, labour turnover would not be impossible. Increasing stability in fact suggests a change in the attitudes and needs of those entering the labour market, and here unemployment is relevant.

The migrant with intermittent but recurring cash needs is likely to find that his chances of returning to a job are slim if he quits the labour force when his present needs are fulfilled. If a future need is recognised, there would seem to be an inducement to stay on. As a corollary, increasing stability could be taken as *prima facie* evidence of a change in cash needs. By the sixties the cash economy had advanced almost throughout East Africa to the point where the fulfilment of many needs and desires, both economic and social, required a continuing income. Given that this could generally be guaranteed only in a job rather than in trade or agriculture it seems inevitable that employment should stabilise. To this, perhaps because of this, should be added the fact that for many people a job itself seemed desirable for the prestige attaching to possession of employment.

Many of the points raised here will be documented in Chapter 3, for railwaymen are, as I said, very much the products of these trends. A problem which will concern us then is that of relationship to the land.

It will be remembered that Elkan has argued that a cause of short-term migration is to be found in the continuing need to retain a hold on land. This theory suggests that increasing industrial and urban commitment is likely to be accompanied by a severance of rural ties. Whether this, too, forms part of the modern type of migration is a subject likewise reserved for Chapter 3.

To sum up, then. The workers considered in this monograph are part of a small industrial labour force which, compared to the majority of peasant farmers, is relatively well off in terms of cash income. Railwaymen also form part of a small but rapidly growing urban population. There is evidence that over the past fifteen years there has been a change towards a new type of migration, associated with increased labour force stability and normalisation of the demographic structure of the towns. This trend may be explained by reference to the changing economic needs of the population coupled with the slow growth of rural incomes and the resulting demand for jobs. The picture presented here as well as providing background for the current study also indicates some of the problems which confronted the newly independent governments which came to power in East Africa in the early sixties.

THE POLITICAL CONTEXT

Uganda and Kenya were granted independence in 1962 and 1963 respectively. Overnight the African inhabitants of the two countries ceased to be the subjects of a distant alien power and became citizens of sovereign states. It is easy to overdramatise the significance of this step, for many changes had already occurred. Nevertheless, the actual achievement of independence was seen by many to mark a dramatic turning point in their lives. No longer third-class subjects but first-class citizens, for their benefit was the economic strategy of government to be directed, their interests were to be given priority in the new order.

For railwaymen, at least for some railwaymen, the most tangible benefit of independence derived from the policy followed throughout East Africa of lessening the new nations' dependence on expatriate workers. As rapidly as possible Africans were to be placed in positions of power and authority in all areas of society. Although this policy of ' Africanisation ' had in fact started to take effect before independence it was not until political control had actually been achieved that really large numbers of Africans were able to advance into jobs previously restricted to Europeans and Asians. The policy affected all departments of government and all industries in the public sector, not least the Railways. Private industry followed, but more slowly. During the period when this study was undertaken Africanisation was a major source of change in the community, giving as it did rapid advancement to thousands of employees. It may be said to be one of the principal factors behind the growth of an urban middle class in both Kampala and Nairobi. The consequences of this change, both for the community as a whole and for particular groups of individuals, will be considered extensively in later chapters of the monograph.

CHAPTER 2

THE RAILWAY COMMUNITY
IN EAST AFRICA AND AT KAMPALA

In East Africa the average urban employee is likely to be better off in terms of cash income than his compatriot gaining a living through peasant farming. The urban labour force as a whole, therefore, represents something of an elite minority. As we shall see later, railwaymen are generally better paid than other workers: a fact which places them in an advantageous position in the urban situation. On these and other grounds railwaymen constitute a special segment of the industrial labour force. A further contrast which may be drawn between railwaymen and other workers derives from the organisation of employment in the EARH, for railwaymen may be said to form a distinct industrial community in East Africa.

Whether one is willing to apply the term 'community' to the labour force of the EARH depends in the end on which of several dozen definitions one finds acceptable (cf. Hillery 1955). Although territorial aggregation is not a necessary component of an agreeable definition – some communities transcend physical boundaries – railwaymen in fact constitute a series of local communities, for, as we shall see, it is EARH policy to maintain closed housing estates for its workers wherever they are stationed. There are, however, more salient reasons for supporting an application of the term to the people who are the subject of this monograph. All railwaymen, wherever they are stationed, share a common interest and experience derived from the industrial milieu in which they operate. This provides a set of values, expectations, even a language, which is unique to workers in the industry. Any railwayman may leave one depot and enter another, no matter where in East Africa, and immediately enter into relationships with fellow workers in a way which would be impossible for an outsider. Railwaymen thus come close to having a 'culture' as that term is used in American anthropology (cf. Goodenough 1961). A small example will suffice. Among railwaymen there exists a specialised set of words and phrases which derive from the work context. 'Letter One', 'CxR', 'Number 1 Up', are all terms incomprehensible to others which any railwayman would know. Sometimes this jargon is used metaphorically outside work, as when a drunken man walking unsteadily is referred to as having an 'off-gauge load'. This communality is reinforced by the close-knit network of ties which link railwaymen both at and outside work. These derive from the system of housing, the frequency of inter-depot transfers, the training system, and from certain aspects of the work process. None of this need imply harmony or homogeneity. The industrial framework at

19

the same time unites and divides, as we shall see in later chapters. The purpose of this chapter is to establish the basic features of this industrial framework. Its sociological significance will become manifest as the study proceeds.

THE EARH IN THE EAST AFRICAN ECONOMY [1]

The EARH was created in 1949 when its predecessors – the Kenya Uganda Railways and Harbours and the Tanganyika Railways and Ports Services – were amalgamated within the framework of the East African High Commission. By that time the services were over fifty years old, for rail construction had begun at Mombasa in 1896 and by the turn of the century stretched far into the interior, reaching Kisumu on Lake Victoria in 1901. The original plan to take the line on to Kampala was not completed until 1931, although a number of unconnected lines operated in Uganda as early as 1912.[2] In 1961 the EARH was placed within EACSO, an embryo federal body to which the GM was made responsible through a ministerial committee whose members were supplied by the governments of the three East African territories. The EARH, therefore, is a supra-national public corporation.

The EARH has a monopoly of all public passenger and goods rail transport and runs extensive marine and road services. Its operations extend to most parts of East Africa and take in the main centres of urban and rural population. As the main transport agency the EARH has a key role in the movement of exports and imports and its principal contribution to the economy comes from its ability to move, at the appropriate season, vast quantities of primary products – cotton, sisal, copper, coffee – from up-country to the coast. In 1964 85% of its earnings came from goods traffic, passenger services being relatively insignificant. The EARH is big business. In 1964 with working earnings of £30 million there was a surplus of nearly £5 million of the working account. In that year it operated on 9,543 route miles, serving 334 stations, piers and jetties. By employing over 40,000 workers of all races, nearly 4% of the entire East African labour force, it made a further substantial contribution to the economy. A breakdown of the labour force, by race, over the period 1949–65 is given in Table 8. The total employed fluctuated considerably during this period and fell away

TABLE 8. *EARH staff by race, 1949–65*

Race	1949	1955	1961	1964	1965
African	41,789	56,295	43,952	41,619	39,171
Asian	4,274	5,580	4,230	2,259	2,029
European	1,002	1,643	1,509	709	702
Total	47,065	63,518	49,691	44,587	41,902

SOURCES: EARH Annual Reports, 1949–64. 1965 figure supplied by the Administration.

TABLE 9. *EARH staff by occupation, 1961 and 1964*

Occupation	1961	% African	1964	% African
Senior officers	318	5	267	20
Clerical and station staff	4,994	59	5,647	83
Surveyors and draughtsmen	195	27	228	59
Inspectors, overseers, passed gangers	474	47	763	80
Foremen	723	33	749	60
Workshop chargehands and artisans	3,872	69	4,725	83
Ticket examiners	81	15	62	74
Guards	464	85	516	98
Locomotive drivers	929	63	876	85
Locomotive firemen	696	100	751	100
Crane and motor drivers	1,039	98	1,000	100
Welfare staff, non-clerical	39	72	57	100
Welfare staff, subordinate	186	100	58	100
Apprentices	349	88	406	98
Artisans, subordinate	4,472	91	4,438	99
Tugmasters, mates, engineers	227	68	367	89
Labourers, porters, etc.	30,013	100	22,548	100
Cooks, stewards, vanmen and others	620	58	1,129	88
Total	49,691	89	44,587	93

SOURCE: EARH Annual Reports 1961 and 1964.

during the early sixties, in line with the East African labour force as a whole. That the labour force differs from others in East Africa by employing large numbers of skilled and white-collar workers may be seen in Table 9. The significance of this occupational structure and in particular of the changes that occurred between 1961 and 1964 which Table 9 also indicates will be considered subsequently.

Organisation: departments, districts and depots

The EARH is organised into a number of *departments*, each of which has a head or chief officer whose headquarters staff is usually located at Nairobi. In control of the entire enterprise is the GM. The functions of his and the seven other departments are outlined in Appendix II. Each department is made up of a number of subdivisions known as *sections*. In Appendix II the responsibilities of only the major sections is described, i.e. those sections invariably found in each district in which the department is represented. At departmental headquarters there are many more small sections engaged in highly specialised tasks. Sections are further divided into what I call *subsections*, an obvious term but one which is not employed in the EARH.

The territory in which the EARH operates is divided into a number of *districts* of which in Kenya there are five, while Uganda forms a single district. In each there are a number of *depots* – rail and road stations, ports, piers, jetties – of which one is designated the district headquarters, e.g.

Mombasa, Nairobi, Nakuru, Eldoret, Kisumu and Kampala. Each department with personnel in a district has a departmental head, e.g. DME, who reports to the departmental head at Nairobi. Within the district the local head of the Commercial and Operating Department (the DTS) usually has overall control. However, in the early sixties, for purposes of liaison with the three East African governments the territories of Kenya, Uganda and Tanzania were designated *regions* in which overall control was allocated to an official described at varying times as the Regional Representative or the AGM. Uganda had the unique distinction of constituting a single region and district. The departmental structure of the EARH in a district will be illustrated later in this chapter through the example of the organisation in Uganda. Table 10 shows the distribution of staff by department in 1964.

TABLE 10. *EARH staff by department: whole network 1964, Uganda District 1965*

Department	Number	%	Uganda District	%
GM's	476	1.1	30	0.6
Engineering	18,252	41.0	2,662	56.2
Commercial and Operating	10,798	24.2	1,378	29.1
Mechanical Engineering	12,320	27.4	666	14.1
Accounts	464	1.0	–	–
Stores	681	1.5	–	–
Ports	1,596	3.6	–	–
Total	44,587	100.0	4,736	100.0

SOURCES: EARH Annual Report 1964 and EARH Administration, Kampala.

The grading and salary systems

Another principle of organisation whose significance will be discussed extensively in this monograph is the grading system. Each employee is allocated to one of a number of hierarchically ordered categories which determine his rank in Railway terms and basic salary. The main features of this system are shown in Table 11, and further details may be found in Appendix III. There are four main categories known as *Groups* each divided into *grades*. Each grade has a salary starting point and a number of incremental points. There is a fifth major category of employees who are technically outside the system, viz. 'day wage' or 'casual' labour. All other workers are on contract and are paid monthly. The internal structure of each Group differs, sometimes considerably. Superscale, the highest, has six grades, only two of which have incremental points. Group A has three *segments* and a cadet grade for trainees who will eventually fill posts at the Group A level. Group B is the most complicated, being divided in the first instance into four *divisions*, the lowest grade of each representing the entry points for trainees at different levels. Group C, the lowest, is also the simplest, containing only three grades.

TABLE 11. *The grading system of the EARH as at 1964/5*

(1) Group	(2) Grade	(3) Salary Minimum	(4) £ p.a. Maximum	(5) House class	(6) Leave days	(7) Ticket class
Superscale	1	–	3,600	1	30	First
	2	–	3,100			
	3	2,550	2,700			
	4	–	2,370			
	5	–	2,160			
	6	1,650	1,950			
Group A	Segment I	1,335	1,524	2		
	Segment II	1,101	1,272			
	Segment III	900	1,044			
	Cadet	762	826			
Group B Executive	A	–	1,500			
	B	–	1,350			
	C	–	1,200			
Division I	I	1,065	1,110	3		
	II	975	1,020			
	III	786	903			
	IV	618	726	4	27	Second
	V	510	582			
Division II	VI [a] ⎱ VII [a] ⎰	402	474	5	24	
	VIII	294	366			
Division III	IX [a] ⎱ X [a] ⎰	222	270	6	21	
	XI	150	186			
Group C	NC 1	132	156			Third
	NC 2	96	120	7		
	NC 3	78	84			

[a] Grades VI and VII and IX and X were amalgamated as a result of the Harres recommendations. See Appendix III, p. 191.
SOURCE: EARH Administration.

This basic system is modified in a number of special cases, there being special scales for secretarial staff, for footplate staff, i.e. engine drivers and firemen, and running staff, i.e. guards and TTEs. Details will be found in Appendix III. Finally the basic salaries for Group C given in Table 11 are raised by a cost-of-living allowance for employees stationed in the main East African cities. At Kampala, for example, a Group NC 3 worker receives £105 per annum instead of £84.

All contract staff are entitled to a number of perquisites. Each is allowed two free return travel passes for himself and his family each year, the class of ticket to which he is entitled depending on his grade (see Table 11, column 7). He is also allowed an annual leave, the amount of which also depends on grade (Table 11, column 6). Finally he is given a rent-free house, the kind or – to use the technical term – *class* of which likewise varies by grade (Table 11, column 5 and below). If he is not able to be housed by

TABLE 12. *EARH staff by race and grade, 1965*

	European	Asian	African	Total	Per cent African 30 April 1965	1 Oct. 1962
Superscale	113	1	22	136	16.2	0.8
Group A	90	10	20	120	16.7	4.0
Cadets	2	1	24	27	89.0	76.8
Group B Executive	52	1	–	53	–	–
B Division I	388	741	941	2,070	45.5	13.4
B Division II	3	1,028	2,952	3,983	74.2	39.1
B Division III	–	48	7,321	7,369	99.5	99.0
B Secretarial	53	126	56	235	23.8	2.7
Group C	–	–	24,066	24,066	100.0	100.0
Casual workers	1	73	3,769	3,843	98.1	n.a.
Total	702	2,029	39,171	41,902	93.4	91.0

SOURCE: EARH Administration.

the EARH he receives a house allowance equivalent to 15% of his basic salary or 25s. per month, whichever is greater. A comparison of the emoluments of EARH workers with those in other industries shows that railwaymen are relatively well paid. Since this study deals principally with EARH staff at Kampala a comparison with wages in that city is obviously most appropriate. The Nsambya Railway sample which did not include Group A or Superscale staff obtained information on both basic and take-home pay which is recorded in Table 13. The average (mean) basic wage was found to be 377.8s. per month, the average take-home pay, including overtime, 436.6s. In order to arrive at a comparable figure for total emoluments we need to include an amount for housing. Since this may be taken as equivalent to 15% of the basic wage we arrive at a total monthly average of approximately 493s. This may be compared with an average emolument (including wages, rations and housing), of 315s. in Kampala in 1965.[3]

The EARH offers its workers a number of other fringe benefits, including

TABLE 13. *Wage distribution of African railwaymen at Nsambya, April 1965*

Shillings per month	Basic pay Number	%	Take-home pay Number	%
175–99	20	33.9	12	20.4
200–99	11	18.7	14	23.7
300–99	9	15.2	10	17.0
400–99	9	15.2	8	13.6
500–99	7	11.9	10	17.0
600 plus	3	5.1	5	8.4
All	59	100.0	59	100.1

a Pension Fund. This provides on retirement at age 55 a monthly pension equal to half the basic salary of the grade on which the worker retires. This scheme was introduced in 1954 when it replaced the Provident Fund, a form of saving in which the employee contracted to have part of his salary each month put aside, to which the EARH added an equal amount. Some employees who joined before 1954 are still in this scheme, though all those who entered subsequently are in the Pension Fund. A number of welfare services are also provided of which the most important are the Railway Clubs. These are open to all railwaymen on payment of a small monthly fee and activities include film shows, meetings, lectures, dances, women's classes and sports. A bar is usually attached which is a convenient meeting place. At Nsambya and on other estates the welfare services include a nursery and a small primary school. The EARH publishes a monthly magazine, *Spear*, and a fortnightly newspaper, *Sikio*, which means ' ear ' in Swahili. This is distributed free to all employees.

Posts and the establishment

Each railwayman is appointed to a *post* designated by a title or occupation, a grade, the department or section in which the post is established, and the depot or district where it is located, e.g. RSF Grade VII, Loco Shed, Kampala; Clerk, Grade IX, Goods Shed, Mombasa. In sociological jargon each post is an ' office ' which has a ' specified sphere of competence ', i.e. ' obligations to perform functions which have been marked off as part of a systematic division of labour ' (Weber, 1947: 330ff.). The sphere of competence is defined by reference to the organisational unit in which the post is established and by the Staff Regulations (see below) which specify the tasks the occupant is to carry out.

At any point in time the number of persons each department may employ in total, at each depot, and in each grade, is in theory limited by what is termed the *departmental establishment*. Through time the number of posts that make up the establishment may change and at any one time the departmental strength may be above or more usually below its official establishment. In this study the term ' post ' is used in a wider sense than that railwaymen themselves usually employ. Ordinarily a station porter would not be referred to as occupying a post. Yet technically his position is exactly comparable to that of someone in a more exalted position, e.g. the GM. Both hold positions in the railway establishment to which they are appointed after going through a specific mode of recruitment. Both occupy those positions until transferred to another or leave the EARH. Neither ' owns ' the post or any of its appurtenances.

Each post is graded and the occupant usually receives the salary and other perquisites attaching to the grade, though he may sometimes be required to ' act unpaid '. Some posts carry a range of grades and a post may be regraded at any time. The factors which affect the grading of a post must be taken as given in this study, since the principles which underlie them derive ultimately from the values of the British social system.

Among these principles one may cite the amount of power and responsibility attaching to a position, the kind of work done, the amount of training or level of skill deemed to be necessary, and the importance of the depot in which the post is established. All unskilled and most semi-skilled jobs are graded in Group C. Almost all clerical jobs are in Group B. Skilled jobs are found in Group C and the lower levels of Group B. Supervisorial posts are generally graded in the middle and upper ranges of Group B, while administrative work usually receives a Group A or Superscale grade.

Any railwayman is eligible for promotion from a lower grade to a higher, though the chances of promotion for Group C staff are fewer than for those in higher grades. In the early 1960s, the period of rapid Africanisation, opportunities for promotion for those in Group B were immense. During 1962–4 an average of nearly 5,700 posts in Group B and above changed hands annually, compared with an average establishment of *c.* 13,600.[4] That is to say, some 42% of all staff at this level were promoted each year. Since promotion is often accompanied by transfer, most of those involved have to move to another depot. This frequently means that the depot where a worker is currently stationed is unlikely to be that at which he first served in the EARH. In the Nsambya sample only 22% of respondents had served continuously at Kampala since first joining the Railways. The average period spent at any depot was three years, but varied with occupation. Whereas unskilled workers served an average of six years per depot, the figure for clerks was less than one-and-a-half years. The mechanics of promotion and its sociological significance are considered in Chapter 6.

Recruitment and training

How and where a railwayman joins the EARH depends partly on the level at which he wishes to join. Group C workers are taken on by the section of a department at a particular depot as vacancies occur, and candidates are interviewed by the section head or a designated member of staff and perhaps tested. Those who wish to join at one of the higher levels apply in writing to a district departmental head or direct to Nairobi. They are interviewed and if selected sent to one of the two RTSs, where they are assigned to one of the training divisions and to a department. The division to which they are assigned depends largely on their academic qualifications. In the past those with eight years' schooling could expect to enter Division III, those with twelve years' Division II. During the sixties, however, the expansion of the educational system and the shortage of jobs meant that even those with eight years' education were having to take unskilled work in Group C. The extent to which the EARH was at that time in a buyer's market may be judged from the fact that in 1967 there were over 50,000 applications for 180 places in the RTS at Nairobi.[5] The general educational standard of Railway workers is relatively high as may be seen from the figures in Table 14 taken from the Nsambya sample.

At the school recruits are assigned to a class which stays together throughout their course which may last from one to three years. The

TABLE 14. *Educational standards of railwaymen at Nsambya*

Years at school	Standard	Group C %	Group B %	All %
0	–	48	7	27.1
1–6	Primary	28	27	27.1
7–8	Intermediary	17	20	18.7
9–12	Secondary	7	47	27.1
Total		100	101	100.0
Numbers in sample		29	30	59

school also offers courses for established railwaymen, some of which form part of the regular career pattern, others of which may be taken by workers hoping to transfer to a different job. There are also 'refresher' courses. During his working life a railwayman, especially if he is in Group B or above, may make several extended visits to the school. This is one of the mechanisms through which he extends his network of contacts among fellow railwaymen.

Discipline and industrial relations

The conduct of railwaymen at work is governed by the *Staff Regulations* which lay down in considerable detail how jobs should be performed. It is the duty of every railwayman to follow these regulations and should they be infringed an offence is committed. These are defined in the following terms by Staff Regulation G.2:

(a) An employee may be dealt with under these Regulations and charged with committing an offence if he: neglects, disregards or without sufficient reasons fails to comply with an order, regulation, standing order or departmental instruction; or incapacitates himself for the performance of any of his duties by indulgence in any stimulant; or improperly discloses any information respecting the affairs of the Administration to any unauthorised person; or is convicted by a court of an offence; or otherwise misconducts himself within the meaning of paragraph (b).

(b) For the purpose of this regulation, 'misconduct' means dishonesty, serious neglect of duty, disobedience to the order of a superior, any act of insubordination, being under the influence of liquor whilst on duty, and such other behaviour as the GM may certify to be misconduct.

Offences are dealt with as follows. Any section head or other officer wishing to press a charge sends the offender a 'Letter for explanation': for a serious offence a 'Letter Two', for a minor offence a 'Letter One'. If the defendant fails to provide a satisfactory explanation he may be punished – reprimanded, suspended, discharged – according to the gravity of the offence and his record.

Industrial relations are guided by the Industrial Relations Machinery

Agreement of 1962 between management and unions. This established a hierarchy of joint consultative committees at depot, territorial and inter-territorial levels. Further details are given in Chapter 7.

In the Uganda District there are sixty-five EARH depots of which twenty-one employ more than ten members of staff. Table 10 (p. 22) shows total EARH strength in the district to be under 5,000 and of these about 1,600 are stationed in and around Kampala. Four departments only have an establishment in the district and only at Kampala are each represented. The strength of each department and section at the depot in June 1965 is given in Table 15. A sketch of the organisational structure at the depot, including the key units and the chain of authority, is shown in Figure 3. Figures 4 and 5 present similar information in greater detail for the DME's and DTS's departments respectively. It is hoped that these figures will help to guide the reader through some of the material to be presented later.

Table 16 presents a breakdown of the Kampala EARH labour force by department, race and Group. The ratio of Group C to higher grades of staff varies considerably between departments since some, e.g. DEs, employ a high proportion of unskilled labour. The proportion of non-African staff in Group B and above also varies, largely because of the way in which Africanisation has been carried out. Both DE and DME employ technical

TABLE 15. *Departmental and sectional strengths at Kampala, mid-1965*

Department	Section	Africans	Non-Africans	Total
GM	Office	5	1	6
	IRO/PO	2	–	2
	Welfare	22	–	22
	Total	29	1	30
DE	Office	41	6	47
	PWI	305	7	312
	IW	279	13	292
	HI	81	2	83
	Total	706	28	734
DTS	Office	42	13	55
	Station	115	–	115
	Goods	327	8	335
	Yard	93	–	93
	Total	577	21	598
DME	Office	11	3	14
	CxR	49	5	54
	Loco Shed	204	13	217
	Electric	13	2	15
	Total	277	23	300
Grand total		1,589	73	1,662

SOURCE: EARH Administration, Kampala.

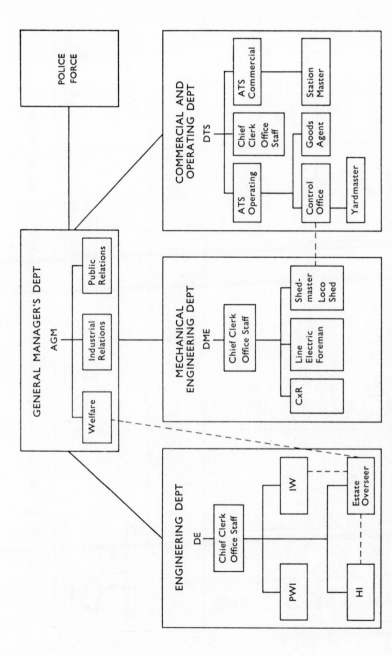

Fig. 3. EARH Kampala Depot: departmental organisational structure

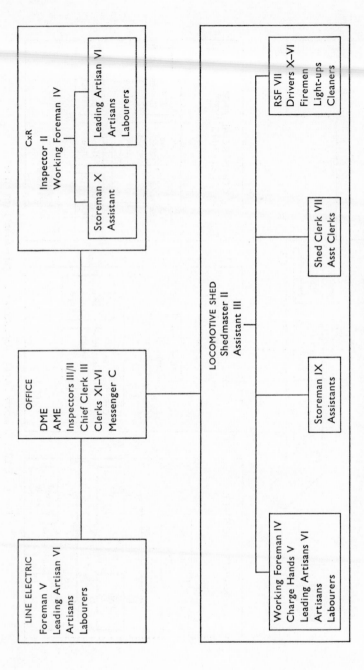

Fig. 4. EARH Kampala Depot: Mechanical Engineering Department (roman numerals refer to grades)

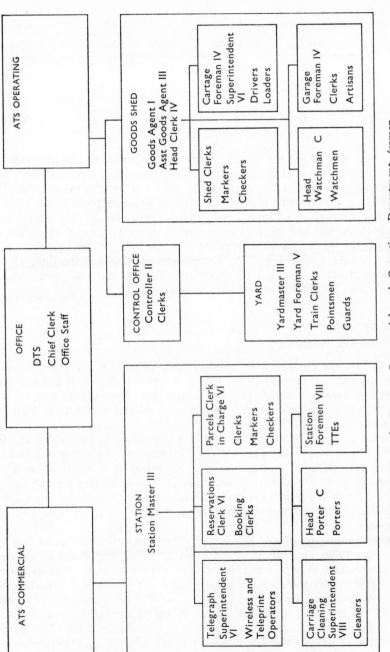

Fig. 5. EARH Kampala Depot: Commercial and Operating Department (roman numerals refer to grades)

TABLE 16. *EARH staff at Kampala by Group, race and department, mid-1965*

Department	Superscale/A		Group B		Group C
	African	Non-African	African	Non-African	African
GM	2	–	9	1	18
DE	–	3	88	25	618
DTS	3	3	209	18	365
DME	1	1	127	22	149
Total	6	7	433	66	1,150

staff with highly specific qualifications and experience, and although it proved possible to Africanise administrative posts with some rapidity, the replacement of expatriates in technical posts had to wait on the completion of long-term training programmes. Out of 25 senior posts at the depot – departmental heads, assistant heads, chief clerks and section heads – ten had been Africanised by mid-1965, almost all since nearly 1964. These included the AGM, the IRO, Welfare and Publicity Officers, an ATS, the Station Master, Goods Agent and Yardmaster, an AME and the CxR. These represented major changes in depot organisation and had great social significance as we shall see.

EARH HOUSING

The Estate at Nsambya

The EARH has continued its predecessor's policy of being responsible for employees' accommodation. Historically this policy derives from the pioneering nature of early railway construction. The railhead opened up new territory creating towns where none existed and houses were built as the need arose.

The EARH thus finds itself the heir to a large stock of housing in all the centres where it operates. This has the advantage of facilitating movement of personnel since no matter where an employee is transferred, or how frequently, he should in theory have no difficulty in finding a home. Since in many places the housing is located near the depot employees are spared the inconvenience of long journeys to work and emergency staff can be summoned rapidly.

EARH housing is divided into seven classes and allocated according to grade (see Table 11, column 5). In most areas housing is collected into estates and there may be more than one estate per depot. At Nairobi there are several estates some distance apart, each comprising a single class of house. At Kampala the bulk of housing is at Nsambya, though this estate contains no units in classes 1 and 2. On Nsambya the houses in each class tend to be placed together, as may be seen in Figure 2 on p. xiii. Altogether the EARH owns some 850 housing units in the city providing accommodation for rather more than half its workers. The rest may be divided into four categories: wages staff, who are not eligible for houses; PWI and IW staff quartered out in several small estates along the line of rail around the city; senior officers eligible for class 1 and 2 houses of which the EARH owned few – they for the most part rented bungalows in the residential suburb of Kololo; and the rest who had to find their own rooms while waiting for units to become available at Nsambya. A number of people actually preferred to find their own accommodation, in particular those from Ankole District who lived in an ethnic cluster on nearby Kibuli Hill.

Table 17 gives details of the houses in each class. Class 7 (i) units are known as 'Landies', a term which has come to be applied to the whole

TABLE 17. *EARH house classes in Kampala*

Class	Rooms	Amenities on premises	Comments
7 (i)	I	None	The 'Landies'
7 (ii)	I	Kitchen	
6 (i)	2	Kitchen, shower	Semi-detached
6 (ii)	2	Kitchen, shower, veranda	'Asian' style
6 (iii)	2	Kitchen, shower, toilet	Maisonettes
5 (i)	3	Kitchen, shower, storeroom	Semi-detached
5 (ii)	3	Kitchen, shower, storeroom, veranda, toilet and court-yard	'Asian' style
4	3	As 5 (ii) but no veranda, larger rooms	Semi-detached
3	4	As 4 but larger	
2/1	No particular specifications. Usually large bungalows in own grounds		

estate. Each consists of a single ten-by-ten room with a window at the rear and at the front a small veranda formed by the overhang of the roof. They are made of prefabricated concrete, roofed with iron, and arranged in barrack-like lines of ten or twenty units in a row. Five units share a kitchen shelter and forty units a latrine block. Most of the Landies were built when the estate was first established in the thirties and were originally intended as bachelor quarters though many now house whole families. Usually the single room is divided by a curtain thus providing a 'bedroom'. Class 7 (ii) quarters are more spacious – the kitchen serves virtually as a second room – and are arranged in blocks of four. In the higher class quarters both the kitchen and the storeroom often serve as extra bedrooms.

Table 18 shows the numbers of houses in each class at Nsambya.[6] Note that all Asian employees are housed in class 5 (ii) or above. These properties are all located on the western or 'Katwe' side of the estate and there was thus until recently a *de facto* policy of racial zoning. By 1965, however, there were more Africans than Asians in this area, and indeed one young railwayman who had actually been born and brought up at Nsambya once remarked that for him the most significant sign of the advent of independence was the fact of Africans living in 'Asian houses'. Although the two groups now live side by side there is little social contact between them, none of the visiting, gossiping, drinking that characterises relationships between Africans (or Asians) themselves. Interaction is so infrequent that its occurrence constitutes a special occasion and one such is noted later in the volume. Both races have to interact at work, but in very formal situations. Outside work the two groups form separate communities, geographically intertwined, socially isolated. The forty-one policemen recorded in Table 18 are members of the Uganda force seconded for Railway duty. They too, for different reasons, form a relatively separate element.

TABLE 18. *EARH housing at Nsambya, house usage, April 1965*

Class	Occupied by Railwaymen		By police	Otherwise	Total
	Africans	Asians	Africans	engaged	
7	381	–	20	24	425
6	81	–	19	4	104
5 (i)	73	–	2	–	75
5 (ii)	43	33	–	–	76
4/3	35	9	–	–	44
Total	613	42	41	28	724

SOURCE: EARH Administration, Kampala.

The estate is close by the depot as may be seen from Figures 1 and 2 (pp. xii and xiii); indeed, since it is situated on the lower slopes of Nsambya Hill the houses to the south actually look down on the Loco Shed and the Marshalling Yards. The estate itself is split into two – Nsambya and the 'Katwe' side – by the Gaba Road. The part at Nsambya proper is divided by a metalled road off which run a number of alleyways surfaced with murram. Patches of grass serve as children's play areas or provide convenient spots for laying out washing and holding meetings. A few trees give some shade. In places, mainly around the higher-class houses, there is enough soil space for small gardens where some people grow a little maize, cassava or plantain. A few chickens are kept and an occasional duck or turkey.

There are a number of buildings on or associated with the estate. There are three shops – a charcoal seller's, a tailor's and a general store – the veranda in front of which is used as a place to sit and talk. It was an ideal spot from which to operate in the early stages of fieldwork. There is also the Estate Overseer's Office, Welfare Office, Nursery and Primary School and a small hut used as the branch office of the Railway African Union. Across the Kibuli Road, closer to the depot, is the Railway African Club with bar and dance hall, while near the Asian houses on the Katwe side is the building known formerly as the 'Asian Club', but now called the 'Railway Gymkhana Club'. A sign of change may be seen in the state of the cricket ground. The whole estate occupies an area of approximately 58 acres, and the total population may be estimated at 3,324 persons, a density of 57 per acre, 36,000 per square mile.

Nsambya in Kampala

Greater Kampala may be described as consisting of a number of suburbs which are in certain respects socially and economically independent.[7] Within each suburb there are a number of local neighbourhoods. The EARH estate at Nsambya – ' Nsambya Relwe (or Lerwe) ' as it is sometimes called – is one such neighbourhood in the suburb which may be termed ' Nsambya-Kibuli '. This area lies along the southern boundary of what was then Kampala City. To the west are Katwe and Kisenyi, to the north the railway, to the north east the industrial estate. To the south and east the suburb merges gradually with the peri-urban, semi-rural fringes of the metropolitan area. It is essentially a residential suburb feeding commuters into the commerce and industry of the city. It has its own markets and shopping centres and contains a number of small-scale manufacturing enterprises. There are local churches, a mosque, a hospital, schools, dance halls and bars used primarily by local residents. The population is overwhelmingly African.

Next door to Nsambya Railway are the police and special force barracks and the area known sometimes as ' Nsambya *matoke* ' (*matoke* being the Ganda word for plantain). These four neighbourhoods share a small market with, among other facilities, three highly popular bars much frequented by railwaymen and others. Immediately to the east is Kibuli Hill which is residentially a strong contrast to the highly organised and planned Railway and police estates. At Kibuli there is no apparent order, the few large and well-constructed buildings being heavily outnumbered by the hundreds of small mud-built huts, often hidden behind clumps of plantain.

Railwaymen and the other inhabitants of the area have little need to venture into other suburbs. They do so, of course, for the reasons one might expect: to attend major sports events at the big city stadiums, to go to the cinema, to buy clothes and other goods which perhaps cannot be acquired locally, to go to ' high-class ' bars and night clubs in the centre, and to visit friends and relatives. Such journeys are, however, infrequent and for the most part at work and at leisure daily life in the urban area is circumscribed by the depot and the housing estate.

CHAPTER 3

TOWARDS AN AFRICAN PROLETARIAT?

Although the primary purpose of this monograph is to explore how the industrial framework outlined in Chapter 2 moulds relationships between railwaymen in the urban context, other issues have to be accorded priority. The first relates to a point made in Chapter 1. A common preoccupation of African urban studies has been the ' problem' of stability. That and the associated question of ' urbanisation' are the principal subjects of the present chapter. Briefly, although railwaymen are far from being ' target workers', and are on the contrary strongly committed to an urban and industrial world, they continue to maintain active contacts with their rural areas of origin through networks of ' extra-town ties', as Mayer (1962: 576) calls them. How and why such networks are maintained and with what consequences for the structure of urban relations will be explored here. The findings of this chapter provide an interesting contrast with those of earlier researchers in Uganda, particularly Elkan, but largely confirm, and I hope amplify, the conclusions of Parkin's Kampala study (1969a, etc.) and of his subsequent work in Nairobi (forthcoming). They also bear out the implications of recent research on the Copper Belt (especially Harries-Jones 1969, 1970). On the other hand they provide opportunities for comparison and contrast with a recent Ghanaian study (Peil 1972). Peil's research, which was published when this monograph was virtually complete, included intensive surveys of Ghanaian factory workers in which information similar to that discussed in this chapter was sought. The results, for example in respect of employment histories and future ambitions, indicate something of the different social and economic frameworks operating in East (and Central) compared with West Africa.

THE ORIGINS OF THE LABOUR FORCE

Most railwaymen are migrants in that they are working away from their place of birth. This may be seen in Table 19 which shows the district (in Uganda) or country of origin of Kampala railwaymen in 1965. In the EARH labour force we find workers from seven different countries, with the majority from Uganda and Kenya. Every Uganda district has at least a few representatives, though none provides a major contingent, in contrast with the labour force of Kampala as a whole, where nearly 30% come from the surrounding Mengo District. People from this area (Ganda) are poorly represented on the Railways. Although the published statistics tell us nothing beyond the country of origin of the non-Ugandans, some supplementary

TABLE 19. *Percentage distribution by place of birth of African railwaymen at Kampala, mid-1965*

District or country	EARH Kampala labour force	Kampala City labour force
Mengo	8.6	29.9
Masaka	1.2	3.6
Mubende	1.9	1.5
Buganda Province	11.7	35.0
Busoga	4.7	2.4
Bugisu	1.3	1.8
Bukedi	7.6	2.4
Teso	1.2	2.7
Eastern Province	14.8	9.3
Acholi	3.2	3.9
Lango	0.8	2.7
Karamoja	0.3	0.3
West Nile	3.7	3.6
Madi	1.5	0.6
Northern Province	9.5	11.1
Bunyoro	4.7	3.0
Toro	0.8	5.1
Ankole	5.5	5.4
Kigezi	1.4	7.8
Western Province	12.4	21.3
Total born in Uganda	48.4	76.3
Kenya	41.2	15.6
Tanzania	2.7	1.8
Sudan	5.5	0.6
Congo	0.5	0.9
Rwanda and Burundi	1.8	3.0
All countries	100.0	100.0
Numbers	1,284	33,400

SOURCES: Kampala City figures, *Enumeration of Employees 1965*; EARH figures, Kampala Administration. These figures exclude 305 workers in the PWI whose place of birth was not recorded in the returns.

information is available from the Nsambya sample. Of the Sudanese, most are Acholi by tribe from the area between Juba and the Uganda border, many having in recent years made their homes in northern Uganda. In many respects they and the Uganda Acholi can be considered as a single group. Most of the Kenyans come from the west of that country. In the sample 60% were Luo from Nyanza Province, 36% Luhya from Western Province. Ethnically the Kenya Luhya are closely related to the peoples from Uganda's Bukedi District – the Samia and Gwe – who frequently identify themselves with the Luhya. Using the evidence from both the Nsambya sample and the published enumeration statistics the ethnic composition of the labour force seems to be roughly as follows: Luo 25%, Luhya–Samia 23%, Ganda 12%, Acholi 8%, the rest, including perhaps as many as two dozen different ethnic groups, 32%. Using the distinction developed by Parkin, roughly a fifth of all African employees are 'Hosts', i.e. from societies with among other features traditional kingdoms and shallow lineage systems, while the rest are 'Migrants' from traditionally acephalous societies with strong lineage systems (Parkin 1969a: ch. 5). The significance or otherwise of these differences in cultural background will be considered subsequently. Most of the workers come from the relatively poorer areas of East Africa. Only 16% have their homes in the more affluent districts such as Mengo, Masaka, Busoga and Bugisu. In this respect the Railway labour force is much the same as those of many other enterprises in the Kampala area.

THE EVIDENCE FOR STABILITY

It was pointed out in Chapter 1 that it used frequently to be assumed that the 'typical' African worker had the following characteristics: he was a young man, usually a bachelor, who left his home for short periods, perhaps for a year or two, to enter the labour market for a brief spell in employment. Evidence from the Nsambya sample shows how far most railwaymen diverge from this pattern. Each respondent was asked to give his total length of service with the EARH, the year in which he joined, and whether at any time he had 'broken service', i.e. had left the EARH and rejoined later. The average (mean) length of service was found to be 12.96 years. Just under 20% had served for twenty years or more. About a fifth had joined the EARH before 1945, while only 10% had joined the Railways in the five years preceding the survey. Only 5% had ever broken service. The significance of these figures only becomes apparent by comparison with those available for employees in other East African industries, e.g. in the work of Elkan and others which was cited and discussed in Chapter 1. Nowhere in East Africa has there been reported a labour force whose members have such a high average length of service, though the figure is comparable to those found on the Copper Belt.[1] When the sample was broken down by ethnic group and area of origin no significant difference emerged, though there were differences between occupational groups. The mean length of service for unskilled workers was 13.8 years, for semi-skilled 10.8, skilled 15.6, white collar 8.5 and supervisorial 22.6. The relatively low figure for white-collar workers – the clerks – is related to the fact that they are younger than average, having been recruited largely during the period of Africanisation of the lower–middle grades in Group B which took place in the late fifties. Semi-skilled workers, too, are generally younger since many are in jobs which are apprenticeships leading to careers in skilled occupations. Note that among unskilled workers, often thought to be among the more unstable elements in the labour force, length of service is slightly above average.

Another index which may be used to measure stability is the turnover rate. Unfortunately the EARH does not at present keep such figures. The Uganda Labour Department Annual Reports for 1958 and 1959 gave rates of 3.81 and 2.38 respectively for turnover among EARH employees. My experience would suggest that the current figure is lower. Voluntary separation appears to be confined to those reaching the retirement age and to a few workers – mainly with high academic or technical qualifications which are in short supply – who are able to find better prospects elsewhere. Among day-wage labourers, of course, the rate is much higher since they are taken on for short periods only, at the height of the cotton season for example, but their separation can scarcely be said to be voluntary. The falling turnover rate among railway employees during the fifties and sixties is in line with what appears to have been happening in other Uganda industries, as we saw in Chapter 1. It is probable, however, that the EARH labour force has in this respect been in the vanguard.

The contrast between railwaymen and the traditional migrants is further strengthened when previous work experience is considered. Of respondents, 66% claimed never to have worked for any previous employer, and a further substantial number had previously worked in one job only for a short time, less than a year, before settling down with the EARH. Only 15% had, in more typical short-term migrant fashion, moved from job to job before committing themselves to the railways. Thus 85% of the sample had spent all or nearly all their working lives with a single employer. What constitutes a working life? On average people first entered employment at the age of twenty-three, a figure which is much the same for both younger and older workers, and again on average some fifteen years had elapsed between first entering employment and the time of the survey. Of those years, thirteen – 85% of the time – had been spent with the EARH. Although predictions as to future performance based on stated intentions are inherently dangerous it may be noted that few people in the sample or in my experience envisaged leaving the Railways until reaching the retirement age of fifty-five, and many expressed a hope that they would be able to continue beyond that point. Indeed, in the sample a small number (5%) were found to be above retiring age.

Consistent with the high average length of service is the age distribution recorded in Table 20. The (ungrouped) mean age was found to be 36.9 years, that calculated using the groups in Table 20, 38.3. Of the sample, 44% gave their ages as forty or more. The calculation of the average age and an assessment of its reliability raises a methodological problem.

TABLE 20. *Age distribution of household heads at Nsambya*

Age in years	Number	%
20–4	7	11.5
25–9	10	16.4
30–4	9	14.8
35–9	8	13.1
40–9	19	31.2
Over 50	8	13.1
Total	61	100.1

Respondents were asked to state their age and, when known, their year of birth. The stated age was checked against the internal evidence from other answers in the survey and found to be highly reliable, at least for those under 35. Older people tended to underestimate their real age, many declaring themselves to be ' forty ' when other evidence showed this to be impossible. This finding is consistent with that of the Uganda Census, which discovered that ages ending in nought and five were very popular.[2] In all probability, then, the means are on the low side, though for technical reasons those calculated from the grouped data are likely to be more accurate.[3] This is simply to reinforce the point that by African urban standards railwaymen are quite old, a fact which should be borne in mind when we discuss marital status and family size. Since most Africans in this area tend to marry by age twenty-five we can expect few bachelors among railwaymen.

According to criteria considered so far – length of service, turnover rate, job loyalty, age – we can conclude that the railway labour force is relatively mature and stable, committed to employment in a way which is often considered rare in underdeveloped countries. This impression is reinforced by other data.

The demographic structure of the estate population

In the Nsambya survey a considerable amount of information was collected on the size and composition of railwaymen's households. The ' household ' was simply defined as all those sleeping in the house unit assigned to a particular worker, and each was asked to list all those who stayed under his roof on the night preceding the survey. The results, by class of house, are tabulated in Table 21. A total of 281 men, women and children were enumerated for sixty-one houses, giving a mean of 4.61 persons per household, median 4.44. Over 20% of the households contained more than seven persons. The average for Nsambya may be compared with that for the three areas of Kibuli, Kiswa and Nsambya combined – 2.65; see Table 7.

TABLE 21. *Household size by house class at Nsambya*

Household size	7 (i)	7 (ii)	6	5	4/3	House class All
1	8	1	–	2	–	11
2	3	2	2	–	–	7
3	4	4	–	1 ·	–	9
4	2	1	2	3	–	8
5	2	4	1	1	–	8
6	1	1	–	1	2	5
7 or more	1	4	1	5	2	13
Total	21	17	6	13	4	61
Median size	2.8	5.1	4.5	5.5	8.0	4.44

Only in the class 7 (i) houses at Nsambya do we find a figure as low as that. At Kiswa and Kibuli most accommodation consists of single-room units, in size not unlike class 7 (i) railway housing. It would seem that, all else being equal, urban household size varies with number of rooms available. In class 7 (ii) units, which because of the separate kitchen may be categorised as a two-room dwelling, the average size household is nearly twice that in 7 (i) units. A similar pattern was found at Kiswa and Kibuli when the relatively few households living in two rooms were compared with those in single-room accommodation.

The age and sex structure of the population was as follows. Adult males (age sixteen and over) make up 31.2%, adult females 17.8%, male children 27.0% and female children 24.0%. Two contrasts may be made with other areas of the city. Whereas at Kiswa and Kibuli, for example, only one-third are under 16 – the arbitrary dividing line between adults and children generally employed in East Africa – at Nsambya over half come into this category. The adult:child ratio on the estate is close to what may be considered 'normal' for an African population.[4] The ratio does, however, vary between house classes. In class 7 (i) children form only 35% of the total, a figure much closer to the Kampala average (see Table 7). Secondly, the number of adult females per household is higher than in the rest of Kampala, eighty-two per hundred households at Nsambya compared with sixty-eight per hundred at Kibuli and Kiswa. Again, class 7 (i) is in contrast where the figure is only forty-eight per hundred. It is unfortunately impossible to provide a more detailed breakdown of the age distribution of the total population, for while the information obtained on the ages of household heads turned out to be reasonably accurate or at least readily checkable, the same could not be said for the ages supplied for the women and children. A comparison with the structure of the estate some seventeen years earlier illustrates some of the changes that have occurred. Munger (1951: 24, Table 4) presents figures derived from the 1948 Uganda Census and not published elsewhere showing details of the demographic structure of various Kampala neighbourhoods including the 'Railway Lines', i.e. Nsambya. At that time the total population of the estate was 877, less than a third of the present total. Males constituted 65% and children 37.5%. Interestingly the Railway population in 1948 was more 'normal' than that in other areas of the city where, for example, children constituted only 21% of the total. The preponderance of non-Ugandans on the estate which we noted earlier also existed in 1948 when they formed some 54% of the population, about the same as they do today.

If we consider the composition of households and the relationship of occupants to household head we find that 85% of the population consists of railwaymen and their immediate families, i.e. wives and children. A further 11% consists of siblings and more distant relatives. Wives and children alone make up 63% of the total, but once again a difference appears in class 7 (i) where they form 43% as against 68% in other classes. The data may be analysed rather differently, and perhaps more clearly, by dividing all the households into five basic types:

Type one: household head, no wife or children present.
Type two: household head without wife, but with children present.
Type three: household head with wife, no children.
Type four: household head with wife and children.
Type five: household head, wives and children, i.e. polygynous households.
The numbers of households in each type are listed in Table 22, where they are further divided according to whether the household contains any 'guests', i.e. other than members of the respondent's immediate family. The table also shows the proportion of household types in each house class. The majority of households are type four, but nuclear and extended families – types three, four and five combined – account for nearly two-thirds of the total. As may be seen in Table 22, the higher the house class, the greater the proportion of these types of household.

TABLE 22. *Types of household structure at Nsambya*

Type	Without guests	With guests	No.	%	% by class of house		
					7 (i)	7 (ii)/6	5/4/3
One	11	7	18	29.5	57	17	12
Two	2	1	3	4.9	5	4	6
Three	4	1	5	8.2	10	13	–
Four	16	16	32	52.6	29	61	71
Five	2	1	3	4.9	–	4	12
Totals	35	26	61	100.1	100	100	100
%	57.4	42.6		100.0			

Of all households in the sample, 42.6% had a friend or relative staying with them at the time of the survey. Some of these are unemployed visitors from the rural areas looking for jobs, others have jobs and are looking for accommodation. Another category consists of young people, mostly boys, 'schooling' in Kampala or perhaps looking for a school. Yet others are young female relatives brought from home to assist the wife with the children. A small group consists of children of neighbours, workmates and other urban friends. In many ethnic groups, particularly Luo and Luhya, it is customary for a boy past the age of puberty to sleep in his own hut, i.e. he should not share the same roof as his father. In order to conform to this practice the boys are often farmed out around several households. Although accurate figures are difficult to obtain it seems that the average length of stay on the estate of guests of all categories is relatively short, between three to six months. There is a high turnover in this section of the population and in the course of a year a household may have several different guests passing through, and most households have at least one. The proportion of the total population who may be said to be unemployed and actively seeking work is about 5%, though this figure may be increased if we include the somewhat nebulous category of school-seekers, who as likely as not will take a job should that materialise before a school.

In sum, then, a large proportion of households consist of families, usually with a number of temporary guests. Adult males living alone without family or friends make up only 18% of all households and the majority of these are in class 7 (i) units. However, just as a static count of guests present in a house gives an incomplete picture of that social phenomenon, a simple enumeration of households with wives present tells us little of the dynamics of family relationships. For the actual number of wives and children maintained on the estate should be compared, at least, with the total numbers available. Accordingly each respondent was asked how many wives they had married at any time, either by customary or church law, and how many of those marriages still survived. Excluding 'temporary' wives, a total of seventy-four marriages were recorded of which three were no longer in existence, two having ended in divorce and a third through the death of the spouse. On an impressionistic basis the figure for the number of completed marriages seems low and may in fact be an underestimate. There always seemed to be a certain reticence (even among close informants) about discussing marriages which had ended. Table 23 com-

TABLE 23. *Marital status of household heads*

Number of wives				Number of wives living at Nsambya	
	0	1	2	Total	%
0	6	–	–	6	10.1
1	11	27	–	38	64.5
2	2	9	2	13	22.0
3 or 4	–	1	1	2	3.4
Total	19	37	3	59	100.0
%	32.1	62.9	5.0	100.0	

pares the numbers of wives to whom the respondent is married with the number actually present in Kampala at the time of the survey. Only 10% of household heads were actually unmarried while 25% were polygynists. This may be compared with Parkin's finding that at Nakawa and Naguru 21% of household heads were bachelors (Parkin 1969a: 100). While in the sample as a whole two-thirds of respondents have at least one wife living with them, among married men 75% keep a wife or wives in town, and among polygynists 87%. The latter for the most part keep one wife in town and another in the rural areas, circulating them, as we shall see later. It may be noted here, for subsequent discussion, that the majority of marriages are intra-ethnic.

Information was also obtained on the number of children born to each wife, and the number still living. For present purposes the first category may be ignored. In all, 224 children were enumerated, in forty-five out of fifty-nine families. Of this total 144, or 64%, were stated to be living at Nsambya, though not all were sleeping in the respondent's house. Recalling the point made earlier about farming out young boys, it may be noted that some 7%

of children on the estate were sleeping away from their father's house. So then, 76% of all railwaymen had children present on the estate, while 85% of all fathers kept at least one child in town, and 45% maintained all their children at Nsambya. Table 24 compares these findings, and those for mar-

TABLE 24. *Households with wives and children present, by class of house*

Class	No.	% married	% with wives at Nsambya		% with children at Nsambya	
			of all	of married	of all	of fathers
7 (i)	20	80	45	56	40	73
7 (ii) 6	22	91	77	85	68	83
5/4/3	17	100	82	82	88	100
All	59	90	68	75	76	85

riages, by house class. As might be expected those railwaymen in the higher house classes are more likely to be married, to bring their wives to town, to have children, and to maintain some or all their children on the estate. In short, they are more likely to live in accordance with what may be accepted as a normal style of family life.

So then, the level of stability and commitment to urban industry which we find among railwaymen as workers is reflected in the extent to which there is a tendency where possible to bring wives and children to live on the estate. According to two of the indicators of urban commitment used in other studies – proportion of time spent in town since adulthood, and the presence of a wife in the urban area (Mitchell 1956a, Mitchell and Shaul 1965) – African railwaymen would seem to exhibit a relatively high degree of urbanisation, at least in a demographic sense (Mitchell 1956a: 694–5). However, as perhaps has been already indicated in our discussion of wives and children, the fact of presence in town does not necessarily indicate the severance of a connection with the rural areas. Railwaymen and their families may in some respects be highly urbanised, but they are by no means ' de-ruralised '.

RELATIONSHIPS WITH HOME AREAS : VISITS

In observing linguistic usage among informants it was clear that a number of recurring phrases, e.g. in Swahili *kwetu*, which are usually translated as ' home' never referred to the urban place of residence, but invariably to somewhere outside the town in the rural areas. The sample survey lent statistical support to this conclusion, for when asked to cite their ' home ' all respondents gave a location or subcounty outside Kampala. For 87% this was the place in which they and their fathers had been born. All of the remainder cited a rural home to which they or their family had at some time moved. None gave Kampala, in contrast to the respondents on the Kiswa Housing Estate, among whom some 9% said their home was in the urban area. One indication of the significance of home may be seen in the fact that 71% of the sample had built themselves a house there. Those who had not already done so were younger than average, about thirty, and perhaps many would build eventually.

The building of a house, whose symbolic and practical significance we will consider later, is not the only act which links railwaymen with their distant rural homes. For example, all employees are entitled to an annual leave, which they may take at one go, or accumulate over a number of years, or use piecemeal, taking a few days at a time if this is consistent with the staffing situation. In the seventeen months preceding the survey 68% had gone on leave, the modal period spent away being thirty days, i.e. a full working month. Fifteen per cent had not been away for more than two-and-a-half years. When asked where their last leave had been spent 85% gave their rural home. The vast majority of railwaymen, therefore, go home at least once every two years, at least as frequently, that is, as the traditional short-term migrant. Railwaymen, however, invariably return to their jobs. They take vacations almost in the orthodox European or American sense.

Among the household heads, then, there is a continual movement between the town and the countryside, and the same applies to their families, though the movement pattern of wives and children is rather different. Earlier we saw that 25% of married men did not have their wives in town at the time of the survey. Those who *never* have their wives with them are many fewer, only 5%. The synchronic picture of household composition presented earlier needs a more dynamic perspective.

Using information derived from answers to several questions in the survey married householders may be divided into three categories according to whether the residence pattern of their wives is 'rural', 'urban' or 'migrant' oriented. This typology which measures only residence and movement is based on the following criteria. Informants were asked whether their wives were 'usually resident' (as defined by the subject) in Kampala or the rural areas, and about the frequency of their wives' visits to the home or the town. Rurally oriented wives are defined as those normally resident outside Kampala who occasionally visit the town, i.e. once a year or less, urban oriented as those normally resident in Kampala who occasionally visit the rural areas. Migrants are a residual category including those frequently moving from one place to the other. The results shown in Table 25 indicate that about half the families are urban oriented in the

TABLE 25. *Movement patterns of householders' wives at Nsambya*

Orientation	Monogamous households		Polygynous households		All	
	Number	%	Number	%	Number	%
Rural	9	23.6	4	26.6	13	24.5
Migrant	4	10.5	9	60.0	13	24.5
Urban	25	65.8	2	13.3	27	51.0
Totals	38	99.9	15	99.9	53	100.0

sense defined. It is clear that it is useful to distinguish between monogamous and polygynous households, for there is a difference between the two. The majority of polygynists are classified as migrant because they seem to maintain two households, one in the town, the other in the country, with one wife permanently resident at each end, or more usually each taking turns in one place or the other.

This typology is relatively crude, implying, for example, a series of discrete categories when in fact there is a continuum with at one end those whose wives never come to town, and at the other those who never visit the rural areas. The numbers at each end of the spectrum are very small, in both cases about 5%. There is almost always some degree of movement. The fact that the residence and movement patterns of wives and, as we shall see, of children can be relatively independent of those of the husband has implications for the measurement of degrees of urbanisation or urban commitment. Such indices should perhaps treat the two variables as separate factors.

The factors associated with the three movement patterns may be indicated briefly, though the sample was too small and the potential variables too many for any firm conclusions to be drawn. Ethnic differences are not significant, neither is distance from Kampala. Among those whose homes are within ninety miles of the city 47% were urban oriented, compared with 53% for those at a greater distance. Railwaymen whose wives are rural or migrant oriented appear to be rather older than average, more frequently in unskilled and semi-skilled occupations, with below average income, living in class 7 (i) housing. None of these factors on their own accounts for the difference. It may be, for example, that orientation to the rural area is a product in part at least of the family developmental cycle and the stage the worker has reached in his career, as has been suggested by Mitchell (1969). As his family grows up he may be more willing to allow his wife to spend time away in the rural area. Similarly as he grows closer to the age of retirement his thoughts turn more to the area in which he will eventually live. Some indication of this may be seen in the fact that rural and migrant families tend to have a more active interest in land. It would, however, need a much larger sample to sort out the principal factors involved.[5]

The movement pattern of children is closer to the wives' than the fathers'. Very young children, as might be expected, accompany their mothers, older children, however, move rather more independently. They may perhaps be at school in the rural area and come to Kampala during the holidays or *vice versa*. As we saw earlier a small number of men look after their children in town while their wife stays at home. An example of this is a Luhya informant. His wife is usually resident in Kenya where she looks after their house and small farm, coming to Kampala perhaps once a year. Of four children, the three boys, aged seven to twelve, stay with the father, attending the Railway Primary School, while the daughter, aged ten, stays with the mother, helping her in the house.

This movement of railwaymen and their families between the rural homes and the towns is reinforced by the frequent visits of friends and relatives from back home who stay as guests in the urban households. All this establishes and maintains a constant ebb and flow of information, gossip and material goods. News of the weather, the crops, who is dead, who married, who has succeeded, who failed, is passed from the countryside to the urban area. Similar news is returned along with information on jobs, the accommodation market, political events and so on. The rural areas and the towns are junctions in the informal communications network of East Africa. Any local rural community will have detailed news about the progress of its sons wherever they are in East Africa or even abroad. This flow of information carried by letter as well as word of mouth has an obvious social significance, as we shall see.

RELATIONSHIPS WITH HOME AREAS: LAND AND RURAL INVESTMENT

These extra-town networks of social ties are not only channels for the flow of information, they are also the links along which a wide variety of material goods are passed. To the rural areas go money, clothes, gifts of all kinds to relatives and friends. To the towns comes food, particularly eggs, poultry, maize and millet which, while not making a substantial addition to urban living standards, may help keep down expenses. The existence of this movement of farm produce raises the question of the extent to which railwaymen keep up an interest in land and farming. A variety of information on this point was obtained from the Nsambya survey. Each respondent was asked whether he owned or had right of access to land, and whether he used it for farming. The replies are divided into three categories (see Table 26).

TABLE 26. *Land-holding among railwaymen at Nsambya*

	Father living	Father deceased	Total	%
With land they cultivate	5	19	24	40.7
With land they do not cultivate	3	10	13	22.0
With no land	14	8	22	37.3
All	22	37	59	100.0
%	37.3	62.7	100.0	

Those with an active interest in land, and those with a dormant interest constitute nearly 63% of the sample. In analysing the data it became clear that those in the third category, with no apparent interest in land, were younger on average than the rest. More important, it was found that a high proportion of this group (64%) had fathers who were still alive, whereas in the other two categories the figure was a much lower 22%. The implication of this is that those in the landless category might at a later stage of their family's developmental cycle acquire access to and an interest in land. The truly landless, those with no land whose father is dead, form only 13.6% of the sample.

Although a large minority (40.7%) are active farmers few practise agriculture on any substantial scale. Their holdings are generally small, on
average five or six acres, though this may be typical of the areas from
which they come. Two-thirds claim to grow cash crops, but average earnings
are low compared with incomes derived from employment, in most cases
being less than 100s. per annum. Only three respondents earned as much as
£40 per annum, and in each case their annual take-home salary from the
EARH exceeded £300. The most prosperous farmer, with a farm income of
£160 per annum, was a clerk from Gisu who had actually been born at
Eldoret where his father had been working as an engine driver. Given that
few obtain a substantial income from farming, why are so many railwaymen active farmers or at least retain a passive interest in land? The
reasons are both economic and social. Although farming does not usually
contribute a direct amount to the family's cash income, the farm may
subsidise income in two ways: first, but of least importance, by providing
produce for the urban table; secondly, by providing accommodation and
food for families while they are away from the urban areas. Even with the
relatively high incomes that railwaymen can earn, it may be costly to maintain dependants in town the whole time. At Nsambya most food must be
paid for, at home it is free, or rather the major cost is in labour which is, of
course, provided by wives, children and perhaps other relatives. Against this
benefit must be set the cost of travel, though for railwaymen who can
obtain free travel passes for their families, this is less significant than it
might be for other workers.

Another reason for the retention of an interest in land, and for the building of a rural home, is the provision of a livelihood and security in time of
difficulty or in the future after retirement. It was often said by informants
that a man might need his land should he become unemployed – there is no
unemployment benefit or redundancy pay. A farm was also considered a
useful bolt-hole should political developments make the town dangerous, as
happened in Kenya during the Emergency, or should the industry go on
strike, as happened in 1959 and 1965. At a union meeting in late 1964 which
was discussing a possible stoppage of work in connection with a pay claim,
officials urged workers to send their families home so that they should not
suffer and, as it were, clear the estate for action.

It has been seen that some writers, notably Elkan, have argued along
similar lines to account for the persistence of the practice of short-term
migration, i.e. the need to retain rights in land for economic reasons has
been proposed as a causal factor in labour force instability. Since in the
railway case interest in land is retained although the workers are not short-
term migrants it would appear that there is not a direct relationship
between the two variables of the kind suggested. The evidence from the
sample shows that in fact the economic benefits of the land are not as great
as has perhaps been supposed by Elkan, and moreover there appears to be
a greater interest in land among those with higher urban incomes, that is
among those who have less need of additions to their salary – taking only

those whose fathers were dead, the median income of those with no land was found to be under 200s. per month, compared with 266s. in the case of the farmers. A similar point is made by Gugler who reported that in a Nigerian sample he found that civil servants with well-paid urban employment were at least as likely as other workers to retain a rural farm (Gugler 1965). Without wishing to underrate the economic significance of the retention of an interest in farming I would argue that the retention of rights in land cannot be understood apart from the total set of ties which link the urban worker to his rural home, and that these ties are as important socially as economically.

In some respects the most important economic aspect of rural-urban links lies in the way that the town subsidises the countryside, rather than the reverse. In so far as railwaymen invest urban-acquired savings and techniques in their rural farms the retention of an interest in land functions as one of the mechanisms by which those earning high urban incomes transfer wealth, knowledge and resources to the rural areas. In fact this happens only to a limited extent. There are, however, other mechanisms. For example, the man who builds himself a substantial rural house, with bricks, mortar and an iron roof, may well employ local craftsmen and materials. He certainly improves the stock of rural housing. The social and symbolic significance of the house is less important for the present argument than the fact that it involves cash expenditure some of which must percolate into the rural economy. Moreover, anything which detracts from the worker's urban spending power should be seen as a manifestation of his extra-town orientation. Other forms of wealth transfer also take place. Some put money into local businesses, anything from a small shop to a fleet of fishing boats. Such an investment may be seen as a form of hedging, to solve the problem of insecurity in employment or after retirement, though it also has a social significance in that it reflects on the standing of the investor in the local community. It is in order to have a lump sum available for investment of this kind that some railwaymen expressed a preference for the old Provident Fund as against the Pension scheme, though one also heard cautionary tales of those who had squandered their savings in bankrupt businesses. Investments with a more obvious social than ecomonic pay-off are also made, as when a man donates a roof for a church or equipment for a school, setting himself up as a local philanthropist.

RELATIONSHIPS WITH HOME AREAS : REMITTANCES

While those who invest large lump sums may be in a minority there is one form of transfer which almost all employ, and which is in many ways the most important expression of the significance of rural ties – the remittance. By a remittance is meant any transfer of cash or kind from someone based in the town to someone based in the rural areas. They may be transferred by post or letter (not favoured), by hand via a friend or relative returning home, or by donation to an urban visitor. By far the most popular method is simply to take the gifts on a visit to the home area and distribute them personally. From observation of such visits by urban workers it is clear that there is every expectation that gifts will be made, and indeed there is a moral obligation to provide them.

From information in the survey at Nsambya it was possible to calculate a rough figure for the amount of the average monthly remittance (see Table 27).[6] It will be seen that the average amount remitted tends to increase with

TABLE 27. *Cash remittances to the rural areas*

(1) Salary group	(2) Mean wage	(3)ᵃ Mean remittance	(4) % of wage remitted	(5) Household size
0–199	180.0	25.2	14.0	3.8
200–99	238.4	28.1	11.8	3.6
300–99	355.2	34.3	9.6	4.9
400–99	453.4	31.2	6.9	6.0
500 plus	879.8	61.2	7.0	6.5
All	377.8	34.1	9.1	4.6

ᵃ Figures in columns (1), (2) and (3) are all shillings per month.

salary, though taking up a lower proportion of income. This reflects to some extent the fact that those with higher incomes maintain larger urban households. During the period January to May 1965 only 22% of the sample failed to make a donation of some kind, and only 10% claimed never to have given anything. Typically each worker sends or takes a cash gift once every three months when the average amount is about 100s., one red note. The usual practice, then, is to hand over largish sums at fairly frequent intervals. A survey of African householders in Nairobi in 1963, whose incomes ranged from 335s. to 1,399s. per month. estimated a figure of 9.9% of income handed out as remittances.[7] This accords in general terms with my own findings of 9.1%.

To whom does the money go? Excluding those who had never sent anything it was found that replies to the question ' To whom did you make a remittance last time? ' gave the following results. Parents 52%, wives and children 28%, siblings 13%, affines and others 6%. Clearly almost all goes to close relatives and others in the rural area with whom the urban worker maintains on-going social relationships. Cash transfers of this kind do not, of course, tell the fully story of the total amount of income that finds its way from the town to the countryside. Leaving aside farm and house investment which were discussed earlier there are other major items such as school fees which are paid directly to the authorities rather than handed over via intermediaries, and personal bridewealth contributions which are frequently financed directly or indirectly out of urban savings, possibly through an intermediate purchase of cattle. None of these is included in remittances as defined here. Thus the figure of 9% of urban income given in remittances very much underestimates the total transfer of wealth from the urban to the rural areas.

FULFILMENT OF SOCIAL OBLIGATIONS

Although the economic links between town and country cannot be dismissed as insignificant more crucial to our understanding of what has been termed the ' rural–urban continuum ' in East Africa are the social ties which cash transfers, investment and so on express and nourish. Most railwaymen have a network of rural contacts which they keep warm through a wide range of social and economic transactions. For example, visits to the home are frequently occasioned by the duty to fulfil some customary duty. On one occasion I accompanied a young Luo who had been summoned back home by his father to be present at the completion of the gateway of a newly established compound. According to Luo tradition the eldest son should witness this ceremony. Among both Luo and Luhya a visit is often brought on by the death of a relative or friend. If possible a man should return for the funeral of a close relative or as soon as he can make a special call at the deceased's homestead to pay his respects. At the very least he must send condolences by letter or word of mouth together with a small donation to help cover the costs of burial and provide support for the survivors. When an adult male or female dies in town it is most unusual for him to be buried away from home. Children and even young wives dying on the estate were often buried in town, usually at the Nsambya cemetery, but never to my knowledge an adult male. It is usual to despatch the body home by car or lorry after it has lain some time at the deceased's urban residence where his town friends pay their respects and a collection is made. The collection is reckoned to provide for the cost of transport. This insistence on burial in the rural home is widespread throughout urban Africa. In Kampala informants often suggested that ethnic associations were originally founded for this purpose, perhaps like the burial societies in Rhodesia. Be that as it may, the return of the body to the deceased's home is clearly an expression of the attachment that people retain for their primary place of residence. The act may also fulfil the functions of establishing in the home area the fact of death – which may be important for purposes of inheritance – of providing a means of ensuring that traditional customary obligations to the dead are carried out, and acknowledging ritually the deceased's status in the rural social system.

Links with the rural areas are also expressed and maintained through marriage. Previous publications have shown that most of the tribes in the Kampala migrant labour force try to enforce a rule of ethnic endogamy (Parkin 1966b, 1969a : Ch. 5, Grillo forthcoming). The evidence for this from Nsambya may be summarised briefly. In the sample only 8% of recorded marriages were inter-ethnic and all of these were between members of the Interlacustrine Bantu cultural complex. Moreover, in the case of Luo and Luhya most marriages were between those from the same or neighbouring locations in the rural area.[8] In the Luo and Luhya locations there are clearcut traditional limits to the geographical area from which individuals select spouses, and by and large these continue to be effective in the towns, i.e. an urban resident draws his partner from the same range of eligible girls as he would if he were living in the countryside. In Kampala and Nairobi all Luo and Luhya are identified by their location of origin no matter how long they have been absent. Take, for example, the case of a Luo named David who had in fact been born at Nsambya – his father was a railwayman – and had lived there all his life, being now the proprietor of a popular bar. His father's original location was Rusinga Island which lies at the mouth of the Kavirondo Gulf, in South Nyanza. On one occasion David attempted to marry a girl whose brother worked in the Railways and who lived at Nsambya. Their family was from Gem in Central Nyanza. The girl's mother objected to the match on the grounds that 'Rusinga is too far', namely from Gem – not, be it noted, Kampala, where the couple would be most likely to reside for most of their lives. For both Luo and Luhya the ethnic map is based on rural geography.

For the members of both the Kenyan ethnic groups failure to take an ethnically acceptable wife has important repercussions, as I show in another publication (Grillo forthcoming). Making an approved match not only demonstrates the individual's attachment to his home people and their values and indicates the strength of his ties with the ethnic community, but depends on their prior existence. Courtship and marriage frequently require the help of a network of extra-town ties, relatives and friends in the rural areas who can effect introductions to eligible girls. To illustrate this we will consider in some detail the case of the Rusinga Luo David whose problems were mentioned briefly earlier. Although David was not a railwayman the case is included here because it is the best available to illustrate the issues we are discussing, and in fact involves several people at least indirectly connected with the Railways.

David was the son of Opio (see Figure 6) who originally came to Kampala thirty years previously. The chain of migration which Opio pioneered will be discussed later. Opio had after a life-time's service in the Goods Shed retired with his savings to an area of North Tanzania which had been recently colonised by Luo from South Nyanza and elsewhere. His son David had been well educated and had worked for some years as an office clerk before taking up the management of one of the bars at Nsambya market jointly with his cousin Marcus. David had an important position in the neighbourhood as we shall see (cf. Chapter 5, Figure 10, and Chapter 7 passim) but although already thirty years old had failed to acquire a wife. David was a man about town and had so far successfully resisted pressures from his father and others who thought that for a man of his age and in his position to remain a bachelor was very shameful. David had in fact made some attempts to get married, but as with the girl mentioned earlier, these generally failed. In June 1965, however, his family and close friends decided that he must make a serious effort and planned an expedition for him to go to South Nyanza. Marcus and myself were deputed to escort him.

The preparations for this trip took some weeks and included the purchase of new clothes for all and new suitcases, and the planning of strategy. Our principal objective was to contact as many eligible girls as possible through the mediation of numerous contacts in the area. These contacts were to be used as 'pathfinders', as the Luo call them, to ease the way with introductions and help in any negotiations that might be necessary. There was already one important lead, a girl named Ruth. She was the cousin of a South Nyanza man who worked as an engine driver at Nsambya. She was still at school but had visited Kampala frequently during the holidays and on one occasion had been introduced to David. A lengthy and somewhat inconclusive courtship had followed and it was now decided to visit her at school and elicit her intentions. Ruth in fact fulfilled many of the criteria that David thought necessary for a good wife. She had acquired a certain level of education, about Standard 8, but not too much, and was about to leave school. She was from a respected family and she herself had a good reputation as far as men were concerned. She was also attractive. Martin, a relative of David's who worked in the Railways, had commented that although Ruth was eligible in other ways she did not look very strong. David replied that he was not looking for a wife to 'dig a *shamba* (farm) or milk cows'. He was concerned more with the shapeliness of her neck than the sturdiness of her legs.

We eventually left for South Nyanza and established our base of operations in the small trading and administrative centre of Homa Bay. Immediately on our arrival Marcus sought out three Rusinga men who it was thought could help us. One of these, Eric, was David's mother's brother through his father's second wife, the others – William and Anthony – were from lineages on Rusinga Island whose links with David or Marcus were more indirect. Simon, after some thought, produced the name of one girl who was in fact the daughter of a chief. She went on the list but David was dubious as he thought she must be sought after by many other suitors. William suggested the daughter of a relative of his. This girl, Miriam, was in the first year of secondary school, but would soon have to leave because her parents were running out of money for school fees, a good point, this. Accordingly, that evening, armed with a letter from William and with Eric to act as spokesman, we borrowed a car and drove over to Miriam's school. Although we arrived at 6 p.m., a very late hour to be visiting a girl's school, Eric was able to gain our admittance through a political contact of his. Miriam was summoned and introduced. Everyone ventured a few remarks, hinting at the purpose of our visit, but the girl was obviously nervous and said so. We left her with William's letter and said we hoped to see her again, but it was generally felt that Eric had pushed matters too fast and had probably ruined our approach. It should be said that Eric was under some pressure from Marcus who was most anxious for David to get married quickly and particularly wanted him to return to Kampala with a wife in tow.

The next day brought contact with another Rusinga man, Harry, who had worked for some years in Kampala but who was now the district organiser for the area's major politician, a minister in Nairobi. Harry was related to several Luo working on the Railways in Kampala. He felt he could help us, and mentioned several girls, but recognised that our first priority must be to visit Ruth. He offered us his car and his driver and together with Eric we set off for Ruth's school. There the headmistress, a European, was persuaded to let David talk to her on the grounds that he was a 'close relative' and he and Ruth spent some time together in private. Subsequently several of us added a few words, but it was clear that she was still hesitant. However, she promised to make up her mind when she came to visit Kampala in August. We left the matter without pressing her.

The following day Harry told of several visits that he would arrange, but in the meantime recommended to our attention a young girl called Matilda who was both attractive and apparently available. A brief introductory discussion confirmed her eligibility, Marcus in particular being very enthusiastic. There were, however, some doubts as to her ancestry. Her father had originally come from Alego Location in Central Nyanza and it was necessary to find out more about her family background, especially to discover whether there was any history of witchcraft (*juok*) in her lineage. Eric said he knew someone who could make the enquiries. A further meeting was arranged for the next day, and Marcus, who by now was convinced we had found the right girl, entered into serious private discussions with her. David then spoke with her and it seemed that she was most eager to marry him. We all adjourned to a bar for drinks in a congratulatory mood. During the course of the evening one or two disquieting notes were struck. For example, at one point David and Harry were joking together in Luganda which both knew because of their residence in Kampala, and it seemed that Matilda understood what they said because she began laughing. This prompted one member of the party to ask her whether she had ever been to Kampala and she agreed she had. Marcus immediately wanted to know when and with whom. Matilda replied that in 1963 she had stayed at Kibuli with one Stephen, the husband of a sister-in-law, a man who was well known to both David and Marcus. Further questioning elicited that Matilda had known several people working on the Railways and had visited the Railway African Club. Furthermore, when we discussed her among ourselves, it transpired that she had told conflicting stories about her educational standard. All of this information begged several urgent questions.

Next day various reports came in. Harry's driver had been asked by the proprietor of the bar where we had been drinking 'Where did you find that girl?' According to the bar-owner she had been living at another trading centre with a man thought to be her husband. Someone else reported that there was a rumour that a brother-in-law of hers had died in a mysterious fire, something which indicated a family history of *juok*. Moreover, Eric said that as soon as he learned that the girl had stayed in Kampala with Stephen he was against her. On top of this both Marcus and David thought that they now remembered seeing Matilda in Kampala in dubious company. It was accordingly decided to withdraw from the engagement. The problem was to break off the relationship honourably, because promises had been made. Fortunately, for our party, shortly after this her husband arrived on the scene and, although a fierce quarrel followed, the necessary excuse had been found. This was not quite the end of the matter, for when her husband went back to his business, leaving Matilda in Homa Bay – he had apparently dismissed her – she immediately became the target for another kind of approach. Although she had ceased to be eligible as a wife she had in fact gained an attraction as a girl who knew town ways. In short, although she could no longer be married, she could be slept with, a fact that several of the party proceeded to prove.

During the whole of our visit to South Nyanza nine eligible girls were contacted and visited through the courtesy of intermediaries of various kinds. The visits took us to nearly every corner of South Nyanza. Several of the candidates looked promising, but in no case could a definite decision be reached and we had to return to Kampala empty-handed.

Information on the extent to which particular individuals in the rural areas help those on visits from the town naturally percolate back to the urban areas. In the case described above, for example, Harry's reputation in Kampala suffered over the Matilda episode. He should have, must have, known about her husband. Conversely, the manner in which an urban host receives his rural guests is known in the countryside. Any visitor expects to be entertained in a fashion appropriate to his status, to be given at least food, drink and a bed and, depending on his relationship with his host, to be found a female companion. A host who fails to give satisfaction suffers a loss of reputation in his rural homeland. In another publication (Grillo forthcoming) I discuss the case of a Railway 'officer', a Luhya, who was imprisoned for theft of Railway funds. His father, who came to town to see what could be done, was thoroughly dissatisfied with his treatment as a guest, and when he returned home immediately spread the word among his neighbours. His complaint, which also reflected his belief that his son's case had received insufficient attention from his friends in town, was not just idle grumbling, but a serious criticism.

CHAIN MIGRATION

The urban worker is expected to share the benefits of his employment with those from his home area, and the extent to which he does so reflects on his standing in both the urban and rural communities. We saw that each household at Nsambya is likely to receive several visitors in a year seeking accommodation and jobs. In a survey at the Kiswa Housing Estate it was found that 78% of household heads had stayed with relatives and others from their home area on first arriving in town. Among railwaymen the figure was lower, not least because the EARH provides its own housing. The townsman not only provides accommodation, he also helps the visitor to find a room of his own, a process which in such areas of Kampala as Kibuli or Kiswa leads to the formation of ethnic clusters in multi-occupied dwellings and local neighbourhoods. This does not happen at Nsambya where housing is allocated on a formal basis.

The process by which ethnic or regional groups cluster into residential areas or into certain kinds of employment has been noted in many studies of migration. Sociologists in Australia have named the process 'chain migration' (Price 1969: 210, MacDonalds 1964: 90). A not untypical migrant chain in Kampala may be seen in Figure 6. This concerns the small group of Rusinga Island Luo, the exploits of one of whom were discussed earlier. In the early thirties Opio and Onyango left the island with their wives to walk to Kampala where they had heard that another Rusinga man, Hamisi, the pioneer, was working in the Railways. They contacted him and he got them jobs in the then Kenya Uganda Railways and Harbours Service. He also found them accommodation at Nsambya market. They were joined by various relatives including Martin, Maria and Marcus, all of whom married Rusinga people who also came to Kampala. Marcus, Martin, John O. and Francis were all found Railway employment over the years. In 1965 all those mentioned in Figure 6 were still living at Kampala except Hamisi

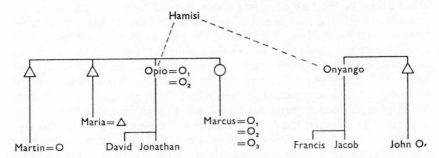

Fig. 6. A chain of migrants

(dead) and Opio who, as described earlier, had retired with his savings to the rural areas where he now managed a small fleet of fishing boats. Besides those listed in Figure 6 many other Rusinga people had passed through Kampala and attached themselves for shorter or longer periods to the core group, being found jobs and houses, though many of these had since moved on.

In order to elicit some quantitative evidence of the extent to which chains of migrants had established themselves in the Railway labour force each respondent was asked a number of questions concerning the current occupations of his close kin. He was also asked to name any 'relatives' employed in the EARH at Kampala. The replies must be treated with some caution since the questions were used in the first instance as an experiment to see whether a more detailed investigation was justified. Unfortunately this could not in the end be undertaken. The present evidence is incomplete for various reasons. Since the questions specified three broad categories of relative – patrikin, matrikin, and wife's relatives – information on several important groups, for example, sisters' husbands and children, was not obtained.

Moreover, the questions referred to current employment and therefore the results failed to pick up instances where fathers or elder brothers had formerly been employed with the EARH, although I knew this to be the case with several of the respondents. Finally, friends and neighbours from back home were also ignored, another significant omission. Thus the findings recorded in Table 28 probably severely underestimate the extent to which

TABLE 28. *Relatives in the EARH*

	% of respondents in each category with:		
	Relatives in Kampala depot	Other EARH depots	No relatives in EARH
All respondents	32.2	10.2	57.6
Kenyans	40.0	12.0	48.0
Ugandans	24.0	8.0	68.0
Group B	27.0	15.0	58.0
Group C	34.5	6.9	58.6

each railwayman is linked to others in the labour force by a network of ties of kinship and friendship based on the rural home. Nevertheless the figures for the sample as a whole show that over 42% of respondents had a relative, as defined, working in the EARH at Kampala or elsewhere. Interestingly, many more Kenyans than Ugandans had kinsmen in railway employment.

The clustering of those from the same rural area either in residence or employment arises largely through the operation of migrant chains of the kind described earlier. Those already working in a particular section or subsection know when vacancies occur and pass on the message. The recruiting officer is usually concerned only that a recruit is suitably qualified, though there is evidence that they favour people from areas or ethnic groups already well represented in the section. This situation brings to mind what has been reported for immigrant groups elsewhere, for example, in America. Warner and Low, writing on Yankee City, quote a foreman as saying:

> Among the men the national tie is strongest. . . If I want to take on a certain man whom I had working in the Department previously, all I have to do is ask one of the workers of the same nationality and he will bring him next morning. . . Also, if I want a new man of a particular national group, I merely ask one of that group to bring a man.
>
> (Warner and Low 1962: 40)

Among the migrants from a particular area there are often a few, like Opio, who are more willing or more successful than others in placing their relatives and friends in accommodation or employment. They therefore build up reputations as urban gatekeepers or perhaps patrons. Opio, who was famous in Kampala for the help he gave to fellow Luo, was able to establish himself as a key figure in one period of Luo associational politics.

Advancement through the manipulation of this kind of patronage is, of course, familiar elsewhere. It appears that potential migrants in the rural areas are fully aware of the strength of their home contacts in the town. Few leave without having someone to approach. It has also been reported that in Luo areas the direction of migration varies with the placing of local contacts. In one sublocation, for example, the members of one lineage invariably go to the post office in Nairobi for jobs, while those of another head for Mombasa docks.[9]

The consequences of all this are important, though perhaps peripheral to our immediate concern. Consider Table 29 which presents a break-down of the distribution by area of origin and departmental section of the African employees at the Kampala Depot. The significance of the table lies in the relative distribution of those from different areas in the various organisational units. Before this is discussed, however, a prior point needs to be established.

In Table 19 may be found side by side the composition of the EARH labour force and that of Kampala City as a whole. It has already been noted that in the EARH, compared with Kampala City, Kenyans are over-represented, while Ganda are conspicuously absent. A more accurate comparison may be made using a measure known as the Index of Relative Concentration,[10] which locates precisely those groups which are under- and over-represented. The theoretical justification for this measure has been put forward by an American sociologist who argues that if the labour force in a given area consists of a certain distribution of particular sets of people then we may treat the distribution as 'normal' for the area (Nosow 1962). If the distribution varies between sub-areas or industries then we are entitled to ask why. The Index of Relative Concentration compares the distribution in a sub-area with that which is 'normal'. An Index value over 100 indicates representation greater than might be expected. Calculation of Index values for each district and country of origin represented in the EARH labour force, compared with that of Kampala City, gives the following results—200 or more: Bukedi, Madi, Kenya, Sudan; 125–99: Busoga, Bunyoro, Tanzania; 75–124: Mubende, Acholi, Karamoja, W. Nile, Ankole; 25–74: Mengo, Masaka, Bugisu, Teso, Lango, Congo, Rwanda-Burundi; less than 24: Toro, Kigezi. This pattern appears to be consistent from year to year, and similar variations occur in other industries in the Kampala–Mengo area (see Grillo and Parkin, forthcoming: Introduction). Just as there is variation between industries so there occurs variation within an industry, which is what Table 29 illustrates. For example, in Kampala City as a whole Kenyans make up 15.6% of the labour force, within the EARH 41.2%, and within the Loco Shed 68.6%. The Index value for Kenyans in the Mechanical Engineering Department, compared with the city labour force is 452. Similarly, although there are not significantly more Ankole in the depot labour force than one might expect, most of these are concentrated in two sections, HI and the Station, where they form 39.5% and 16.5% respectively. If the relative distribution over several years is

TABLE 29. *African railwaymen at Kampala by area of origin and departmental section, mid-1965*

% distribution in each department and section

Area of origin (1)	Depot Total No. (2)	Depot Total % (3)	GM's All sections (4)	DTS's All (5)	DTS's Office (6)	DTS's Station (7)	DTS's Goods (8)	DTS's Yard (9)	DME's All (10)	DME's Office (11)	DME's Loco (12)	DME's CxR (13)	DE's All (14)	DE's Office (15)	DE's IW (16)	DE's HI (17)
Mengo	111	8.6	20.6	6.8	11.9	8.7	5.8	5.4	6.8	27.2	5.5	8.2	11.8	7.3	15.4	1.2
Masaka	15	1.2	-	1.4	2.4	-	1.5	2.1	0.7	-	0.9	-	1.2	2.4	1.4	-
Mubende	24	1.9	3.4	3.1	2.4	3.5	4.0	-	0.4	-	0.5	-	1.0	-	1.4	-
Buganda Province	150	11.7	24.0	11.3	16.7	12.2	11.3	7.5	7.9	27.2	6.9	8.2	14.0	9.7	18.2	1.2
Busoga	60	4.7	10.2	7.5	14.3	13.9	3.4	10.8	3.2	-	3.2	4.1	1.2	2.4	1.4	-
Bugisu	17	1.3	6.8	1.2	4.8	0.9	0.6	2.1	2.2	9.1	1.4	4.1	0.5	-	0.7	-
Bukedi	98	7.6	6.8	10.4	7.2	3.5	12.9	11.8	7.1	-	9.7	-	3.7	4.9	4.7	1.2
Teso	15	1.2	3.4	1.2	-	1.7	0.6	3.2	0.4	-	0.5	-	1.5	7.2	0.7	1.2
Eastern Province	190	14.8	27.2	20.3	26.3	20.0	17.5	27.9	13.4	9.1	14.8	8.2	6.9	14.5	7.5	1.2
Acholi	41	3.2	-	4.7	2.4	7.0	4.3	4.3	1.4	-	0.9	4.1	2.5	4.9	1.1	6.2
Lango	10	0.8	3.4	0.5	-	-	0.6	1.1	0.7	-	0.5	2.0	1.0	-	1.4	-
Karamoja	4	0.3	-	-	-	-	-	-	-	-	-	-	1.0	-	1.4	-
W. Nile	47	3.7	-	6.9	-	0.9	11.3	2.1	1.1	-	1.4	-	1.0	-	1.1	1.2
Madi	19	1.5	3.4	0.5	2.4	2.6	-	-	0.4	-	0.5	-	3.7	-	5.0	1.2
Northern Province	121	9.5	3.4	12.6	2.4	10.5	16.2	7.5	3.6	-	3.3	6.1	9.2	4.9	10.0	8.6
Bunyoro	60	4.7	6.8	6.4	11.9	1.7	8.6	2.1	1.8	9.1	1.4	2.0	4.0	4.9	5.0	-
Toro	11	0.8	3.4	0.9	1.7	1.7	0.3	2.1	-	9.1	-	-	1.2	2.4	1.4	-
Ankole	71	5.5	-	5.0	2.4	16.5	2.1	2.1	0.7	-	0.5	2.0	10.0	4.9	2.2	39.5
Kigezi	18	1.4	-	1.0	-	1.7	0.9	1.1	0.7	-	0.9	-	2.5	2.4	2.8	1.2
Western Province	161	12.4	10.2	13.3	14.3	21.6	11.9	7.5	4.2	9.1	2.8	4.0	17.7	14.6	11.4	40.7
Uganda Total	622	48.4	64.8	57.5	59.7	64.3	56.9	50.3	28.1	45.4	27.8	26.5	47.8	43.7	47.1	51.7
Kenya	528	41.2	34.4	35.6	26.2	31.3	38.9	33.3	68.5	54.5	68.6	71.5	30.7	36.6	30.1	29.6
Tanzania	35	2.7	-	2.6	14.3	-	-	9.7	0.7	-	0.9	-	4.5	17.1	3.2	2.5
Sudan	71	5.5	-	2.4	-	-	2.4	6.4	1.1	-	0.9	2.0	13.5	2.4	15.4	12.4
Congo	6	0.5	-	0.7	-	1.7	0.6	-	-	-	-	-	0.5	-	0.7	-
Rwanda-Burundi	23	1.8	-	1.2	-	2.6	1.2	-	1.4	-	1.8	-	3.0	-	3.2	3.7
All areas number	1,284		29	577	42	115	327	93	277	11	217	49	401	41	279	81
All areas %		100.0	100.0	100.0	100.0	100.0	100.0	100.0	100.0	100.0	100.0	100.0	100.0	100.0	100.0	100.0

SOURCE: EARH Administration, Kampala: Returns for Labour Enumeration 1965 to Government Statistician at Entebbe, Uganda. PWI omitted

calculated the pattern again remains consistent, i.e. those from particular areas tend to cluster in particular organisational units. This also occurs in the Kenya EARH labour force (Grillo 1969a : 302).

The distribution at the Kampala Depot may be accounted for in various ways, none of which are as satisfactory as the explanation by reference to chain migration which has already been suggested. It might be argued that not all Railway jobs are open to the Kampala labour market, which is certainly true. In the Nsambya sample only 36% of employees actually signed on in Kampala. Even allowing for this the relative distributions vary considerably. Another type of explanation is proposed by Elkan who, in discussing Kampala wages, argues: ' Why do employers have to pay more to get their heavy work done? The main reason is that men with the requisite physique are scarce. . . . That is why the Luo, for instance, are heavily represented in building and construction in the petrol depots, the brewery and the railway goods yard ' (Elkan 1960: 86–9). If this explanation by reference to physical type is correct then present figures suggest a number of anomalies. For example, one of the greatest concentrations of Ganda in the EARH depot is in the IW section, which is responsible for all railway construction. Likewise in the Kampala City labour force there is a heavy concentration of Ankole and Kigezi – two ethnic groups whose members have slight physique – in local government, especially in the health department where they are employed as dustmen. Moreover, why do those from Kigezi, but not from the neighbouring area of Ankole, form an important section of construction workers? And why is the reverse true on the Railways?

Elkan has proposed another explanation which accords more closely with present findings – ethnic restrictive practices (Elkan 1960: 88). Although it may be agreed that ethnic enclaves in industry indeed exist, it does not necessarily follow that they arise through the operation of tribal rivalries and hostilities, a point I have argued elsewhere (Grillo 1969a). Such clusters are generated by the operation of networks of kinship and friendship among people from within the same ethnic group. At the same time the effect is to produce groupings and associations which may be interpreted in ethnic terms, for example, by other workers or by members of management. For the observer to follow such local interpretations and to explain the clustering by reference to ethnic hostility is to overlook the significance of the specific mechanisms which are in operation.

If it can be agreed that the relative distribution of ethnic groups within the industry may be explained largely by reference to chain migration two problems remain. First, what attracted the group to the industry in the first instance? Most discussions of chain migration seem to ignore this issue, assuming that the original pioneer chose his location by chance. Unsatisfactory though this is, until we know much more about the historical development of the Uganda and Kenya labour force, in particular the different points at which each ethnic group was drawn into the labour market, we cannot even begin to tackle this question. The second problem, similarly intractable, is this. Given that a group establishes itself in a particular urban neighbourhood or industry, what prevents their complete domination in the area, allocating all the housing and jobs to their own people? In some respects, in the EARH, ethnic domination of an enclave may be greater than the figures sometimes suggest. This is because in many cases the effective recruiting unit is not the section but the subsection. For example, Ankole in the Station are almost all concentrated in the Carriage Cleaning subsection and similarly the subsection of the HI responsible for clearing up the Nsambya Estate – the Compound Cleaners – consisted in 1964/5 of eleven Ankole, one Rwanda and one Luo headman. The Parcels Office at the Station was almost entirely Luo, while the gangs of Loaders in the Goods Shed were predominantly Acholi, and so on. By no means all subsections are as homogeneous as these, and in recent years at any rate the groups seem simply to have maintained their existing share of jobs rather than expanded their position. A kind of self-regulating rationing system seems to exist, though details of this must remain for the time being obscure. The part played by recruiting policy itself in generating these ethnic enclaves and in maintaining the ethnic balance is also unclear.

The main points that this chapter has so far produced may be summarised briefly. In comparison with other East African workers for whom we have information railwaymen in all occupations are highly committed to industrial employment. They are also highly urbanised in the sense that they themselves have spent long periods resident away from their homes, and frequently maintain large urban households. Their degree of urbanisation may also be seen in their adherence to the social forms that participation in the industrial milieu generates, a feature that will be examined in subsequent chapters. At the same time almost all retain links with their homes in the rural areas, where they build houses, keep farms and send gifts. They frequently visit these areas and receive visitors from them whom they help with jobs and accommodation. The existence and persistence of these active rural networks contribute to the formation of ethnic boundaries in the urban areas by generating ethnic clusters in local neighbourhoods and industry. In my experience very few indeed maintained no extra-town ties, and this is supported by evidence from the Nsambya sample which produced only one respondent who had no land, never visited his home, never sent gifts, had not built himself a house, kept his wife in town, and whose parents were dead. The material raises two problems: why the high level of stability and why the continued commitment to the rural areas?

WHY DO THEY STAY IN WORK?

For many years it was standard procedure in African labour studies to ask informants why they came to work. Whenever railwaymen were asked a question of this kind they usually gave an answer which, while polite, threw doubts on the perspicacity of the questioner, a response which became so predictable that the question itself was withdrawn from the investigator's repertoire. For them there was only one reason, the need for a cash income. The need for a cash income has been discussed in Chapter 1. Most railwaymen come from the relatively poorer areas of Kenya and Uganda where there is no real alternative to labour migration. Even where alternative opportunities exist for gaining a livelihood from cash crops the returns in this sector have in recent years been poorer than those obtainable in employment. Outlets in trade, or say fishing, are limited and usually require capital which can only be acquired through saving other earnings. Employment opportunities locally are few and far between, and so they are thrown on to the migrant market.

It may be taken for granted that nowadays almost all Africans are in a situation where there is a continuing need for cash. Railwaymen, in particular, are not satisfied with accumulating savings sufficient only for a bike, a radio or a bride. They want, and as far as they can, obtain, a standard of living far above the subsistence level, including the whole range of goods characteristic of a modern consumer society. See, for example, the evidence of Chapter 5, Table 33. They also want a decent future for their children, which many of them see to be linked with education. Apart from a few scholarships at the secondary level, education in East Africa is (or was) not free and school fees are a major item on the family budget. The reasons for the stability of the labour force follow from this.

The continuous supply of cash that the desired standard of living requires can only be guaranteed through employment, as we saw in Chapter 1. Moreover, the fact of having an income, especially a high income, is in part a measure of a man's social standing, as we shall see in Chapter 5. Railwaymen are committed not only to a high level of consumption, but to conspicuous and competitive consumption. Given the background of poor opportunities outside the employment sector coupled with the short supply of jobs, for most railwaymen, leaving the EARH would be a disastrous step. In that they are dependent on employment for their livelihood, railwaymen are in the same position as any member of the industrial proletariat.

This argument suggests that the reasons for the stability of EARH employees are to be found in the social and economic changes that occur outside industry. Undoubtedly the industry itself has made a contribution to this stability. EARH wages are highly competitive and the fringe benefits – free housing, travel, welfare services, the Pension Scheme, all add to its attractiveness for employment. Important, too, is the fact that in recent years the EARH has offered many opportunities for advancement within the industrial hierarchy. Nevertheless managerial techniques of this kind are largely irrelevant unless there is a prior commitment to the cash economy or there is competition between firms for scarce labour. This would seem to suggest the futility of what might be termed the 'canteen' theories of labour stability that were popular some years back.

WHY ARE RURAL TIES MAINTAINED?

I argued earlier that for purposes of long-term security the urban worker needs to maintain a rural foothold. In the short term the farm may provide a number of benefits and subsidies to urban income, but the cost in travel, gifts to relatives and so on may outweigh these advantages. The worker is, however, maintaining more than just a farm or rights to land. Through his rural network he keeps alive his status as a member of the rural community. The necessity for this derives in part from the economic system. By making regular visits home, presenting gifts to kinsmen, marrying a locally approved girl, by assiduous attendance at funerals and other ceremonial occasions, by building a house, he is making an investment for his future return to the rural area, paying in advance for the goodwill and co-operation he may at some time require, or which through his death his family may need at any moment. There is more to it than this, however. Correct performance of all these transactions has the positive benefit of adding to his immediate prestige and reputation both at home and in the town. This prestige may extend to his whole family or kin-group. Conversely his failure to fulfil his obligations to those in the rural area is shameful both for himself and for them. A break with the rural areas is tantamount to a break with kin and ethnic ties, an act which may have both long-term economic consequences and immediately adverse results in both the rural areas and the town, a point which I have discussed briefly in previous publications and which is elaborated in Chapter 5.

Technically the urban and rural areas must be seen, following Epstein, as sub-systems within a single social field. Informants themselves tend to conceptualise the two areas as socially and morally apart, but it is clear that several sets of apparently distinct relationships must be considered as forming a single group. Thus reputation in town reflects and is reflected by reputation in the rural areas. Both are dependent upon the state of relationships between an individual and his fellow townsmen and between him and the people from his home area, which are in turn interdependent. Information on all these sets of relationships is readily available in the public domain and travels rapidly. For example, gossip about a young man who consorts too frequently with bar girls in Kampala will soon reach his rural home. If this is a Luo or Luhya area from which workers go out to other urban centres he may find himself the subject of comment in Nairobi, Mombasa or Dar es Salaam. This should be shameful for him, and would certainly be held to be so for his family. It would directly reflect on his suitability as a future son-in-law, affecting his chances of an approved match. Similarly, as we shall see, the man who neglects to send gifts to his family is soon known. He may be poorly regarded not only at home or within his own ethnic group, but in the urban community generally, for he breaks an obligation which is inter-tribal.

Superficially it would seem that the advantages of this system are more obvious for the unskilled and semi-skilled workers than for the better-paid clerks and skilled men. The latter are more likely to have at least the chance to save enough to sustain themselves independently after retirement. Although the economic benefits for these, too, should not be underestimated, a more significant factor is the element of prestige and standing. The man who fulfils obligations to homespeople becomes in some sense a patron. The extent of his dependants is an element in his reputation both at home and in the town. Moreover, as we shall see in Chapter 7, many in this group are heavily involved in competition for positions of prestige and power in urban associations, their success in which depends in part at least on the nature of their reputations both urban and rural. The number of those who are prepared to forgo both security and the competition for prestige is inevitably very small. Thus a whole series of relationships and activities are linked into a single social nexus. A man who breaks off relationships at one point, for example, by failing to build his house at home, is in danger of losing his position in the system as a whole. The option of doing so is always open, but for most people the benefits of staying in far outweigh the advantages of contracting out.

The evidence from the Railway labour force contrasts with that of earlier Kampala studies. Elkan (1960) divided the city's African workers into two categories – 'Migrants', short-terms workers who traditionally circulate between the labour market and their rural holdings, and 'Proletarians', mainly Ganda with small farms in the peri-urban areas who form the more stable element in the labour force, usually in skilled and white-collar occupations. Railwaymen fit into neither of these categories, a point discussed further in the Conclusion to this volume. Taking the African labour force as a whole we have to distinguish between several types of workers: (a) the short-term migrants (or 'Migrants' to use Elkan's term); (b) those with life-styles similar to Elkan's 'Proletarians' who are still to be found in some industries in the city (cf. Gugler in Grillo and Parkin (eds.), manuscript); (c) the fully-committed 'proletarians' who have severed all rural contacts; (d) the type of worker more frequently found in West Africa (cf. Peil 1972) who uses the labour market to achieve entry into private enterprise; and (e) workers like the majority of railwaymen in the present study, committed to industrial careers, but retaining their rural base. It is the latter who are perhaps most typical of the contemporary African worker in Uganda and Kenya.

CHAPTER 4

SOCIAL RELATIONSHIPS AND THE INDUSTRIAL FRAMEWORK

Long ago Mitchell (1956a : 693ff.) argued that the concepts of stabilisation and urbanisation are used with two frames of reference, a demographic and a sociological, which may heuristically be treated as distinct. A similar point is made by Moore and Feldman in discussing the concept of commitment which, they say, ' involves both performance and acceptance of behaviour appropriate to an industrial way of life. The concept is thus concerned with overt actions and norms. The fully committed worker, in other words, has internalised the norms of the new productive organisation and social system ' (Moore and Feldman 1960 : 1). Chapter 3 has largely concentrated on the demographic component of stability, showing that railwaymen stay in employment and in the urban area for most of their working lives. This tells us only by inference of the values with which they operate. It is this component with which the next three chapters are concerned. To echo a phrase of Gluckman's we are now interested in railwaymen as railwaymen! (Gluckman 1961 : 69).

As was stated in the Introduction this monograph does not deal primarily with what happens at work, though that aspect too will be mentioned. Nor does it consider whether railwaymen are *efficient* workers, though given that efficiency can be defined and measured it would presumably be taken as one of the indices of commitment. Much of the evidence to be discussed relates to relationships between railwaymen outside the work context. This has a significance of its own, for it argues that the members of this community have so internalised the norms and values of the industry as to use them as a basis for relationships in their everyday off-duty lives, a situation not unlike that implied by some of the Copper Belt studies, notably Epstein. It is the extent to which the industrial framework structures relationships that justifies the application of the term ' industrial community '. Finally, as the evidence of Chapter 3 suggests, although the relationships and values derived from the industrial system may be separated from those of other systems for the purposes of analysis and exposition, this is only a heuristic separation. For we are dealing with a single social field and it is the relationship between the sub-system within the field which forms the principal sociological issue.

RAILWAYMEN AND THE WORK PROCESS

Chapter 2 outlined the framework of the industry in terms of its organisational and occupational structure. How each of these elements structure relationships between railwaymen both outside, and as far as possible, inside work will be examined in this and subsequent chapters. Some introductory remarks are appropriate.

The operation of the organisation is controlled by a set of rules – the Staff Regulations – which define the spheres of competence of each organisational unit and of the occupants of each post. Each railwayman has, therefore, fairly comprehensive and explicit instructions on how to perform his job. The regulations also prescribe the form of the relationship that should prevail between the occupants of any two or more posts associated in the work process. As a consequence, if workers follow the code precisely, their behaviour at work is exceedingly formalised, not to say ritualised. They are perpetually acting out particular roles in highly structured situations. Moreover, the regulations governing behaviour have the force of a legal code since their breach is an offence which may be punished by a standard procedure. In theory, therefore, the EARH, through those officers responsible for the operation of the work process, maintains a rigorous control over its workers. All industry is authoritarian; on the surface the EARH, like an army, is more authoritarian than most.

The comprehensiveness of the regulations has the function of ensuring that, should an operational failure occur, an enquiry may determine and apportion responsibility. The necessity for the close control of the work process may be judged to exist in the complexity of the operations that the EARH performs, and the co-ordination required to bring them to a successful conclusion. Loading, marshalling and despatching a train from Kampala to Nairobi requires the participation of several departments and sections at various depots along 400 miles of track, involving directly several thousand workers, and indirectly many more. This happens every day, many times a day. The regulations attempt to ensure that everyone will do the right thing at the right time.

The existence of these regulations raises a number of questions, not all of which can be considered in this monograph. Are the regulations generally followed, and are offences usually punished? Are they supplemented or replaced by unofficial codes which order interaction at work? Are they relevant outside the work process? Conversely, do codes of behaviour pertinent outside work modify the norms required by the industry? In other words, are the work and non-work milieus two discrete social worlds? Some of these questions will be answered in the succeeding sections of this chapter. We begin by examining the organisational structure.

THE CORPORATE ETHOS

In a precise legal and economic sense the EARH is a corporation consisting of a body of assets owned, eventually, by all the citizens of East Africa. Each employee is a public servant subject to a stringent set of rules. The EARH is also in a sociological sense a corporate group, which limits membership, and has an 'order' enforced by a hierarchy of specific functionaries (Weber 1947 : 145). In turn it consists of a hierarchy of organisational units – departments, sections and subsections – which are themselves corporate groups, each with its own order, leadership and membership. Any railwaymen, therefore, is a member of a hierarchy of interlocking corporations. Our discussion will consider each level in turn, beginning with the EARH as a whole.

There are two main questions. To what extent does membership of the EARH generate among its employees a sense of belonging to a corporate body? In other words, is there a corporate ethos, an *esprit de corps*? Secondly, how far does the outside world view them as a corporation? The second question will be dealt with first. There are undoubtedly in Kampala certain occupational groups and organisations which have a clearly-defined image or stereotype in the public mind. Since these stereotypes are frequently accompanied by conventional behavioural reactions, they involve what Mitchell calls 'categorical relationships' (Mitchell 1966: 52). In Kampala such relationships seem to exist in the case of the police, the special force, the army, and the staff of Makerere University College. For example, one friend, an African police inspector, confided that he preferred to be introduced as a 'civil servant' rather than a policeman since if people knew his real job they were 'afraid'. Similarly, my own fieldwork was made easier because I was able to announce myself 'from Makerere', thus being placed in a harmless but respected category. There does not seem to be a stereotype of this kind for railwaymen. Mitchell says that 'it is an essential of categorical relationships that the internal divisions within a category should be ignored' (Mitchell ibid.), and this would seem to imply the existence or perception of a single easily-recognisable characteristic which expresses the essence of the category. In the railway case the public could apparently find no such feature. Few railwaymen in fact come into direct contact with the public, though this would seem not to be a crucial factor, *vide* Makerere staff, but when they do it is usually as workers performing particular tasks, as porters, ticket clerks, guards, stewards, that is to say, in specific rather than diffuse roles, and this perhaps detracts from any corporate image. Outside Kampala, in the rural areas, especially in western Kenya, there is some indication that railway workers *qua* railwaymen are viewed as 'big men' because of their high levels of pay. Informants sometimes argued that it is the local prestige of the occupational group that attracts people into the EARH. In the same way, it was said, correctly or not is irrelevant, that people from one area of Kenya regularly take jobs as lavatory cleaners in Nairobi, because such employment back home is considered prestigious. As far as Kampala residents are concerned, however, EARH workers have no substantive image.

What of railwaymen themselves; do they have a corporate identity? It is certainly management policy to attempt to foster such an identity. The EARH operates a public service, for individual customers and for the three East African countries, and railwaymen are continually reminded of this both by management and politicians. For example, at a meeting of the Central Legislative Assembly of EACSO one minister was quoted as saying, 'a "don't care" attitude by some railway workers [is] reducing efficiency and spoiling the railway's reputation' (*Uganda Argus*, 19 November 1964). Compare here the quotation from an exhortation by the GM which is given below, and his statements to workers at the time of the 1964 strikes which are discussed in Chapter 5. Many railwaymen are indeed aware of their contribution to the public weal, and are proud of it, but there is not the close identification of personal and corporate interest that the management would perhaps like. As we shall see in Chapter 5, many employees see a fundamental distinction between railway management – *Bwana Relwe* – and railway workers – in Swahili, *wafanya kazi wa Relwe* – stressing the divisions that exist within the labour force rather than the factors that unite them. In so far as the corporate interest is seen to coincide with that of the management, there is unlikely to be a strong identification with it on the part of the ordinary worker. Objections by workers to a strike expressed more concern at the damage a work stoppage would do to their private interests – themselves and their families – than at the harm it might cause to the image of the EARH. It follows from this that the corporate ethos is likely to be strongest among those on the management side, and perhaps from those who aspire to management positions, a point which will be illustrated in subsequent discussion.

So the corporate ethos, *esprit de corps*, is less a social fact than an ideological theme stressed and responded to in what are essentially political debates. In daily life it is the internal divisions within the labour force, rather than its overriding unity, which are more significant. Nevertheless, there is a certain pride involved in working for a corporation, whose interests transcend national allegiances. Ugandans, Kenyans, and Tanzanians recognise they are working for an *East African* enterprise. This emerges, for example, in the extent to which all railwaymen, whatever their national background, are willing and able to use fluent Swahili as a means of communication – even Ganda, who in Kampala tend to ignore other languages except English.

THE DEPARTMENT

Each department is a corporation with its own leadership, staff and function, and the workers in each share a common interest which distinguishes them from others. At the same time departments are functionally interdependent. For example, at Kampala the work of assembling a train involves several sections in the DTS and DME. The Control Office, estimating the demand, books the required waggons and carriages, and advises the Loco Shed on the engines that will be needed. The Loco Shed and the CxR service the vehicles and shunt the waggons to the Goods Shed for loading. Thence they are taken to the Yard where the train is assembled. It then moves to the Station to pick up passengers and parcels and is finally despatched, once more by the Control Office. Two questions are raised. To what extent is there a departmental solidarity derived from common interest and shared experience of the work process? And, as a corollary to this, do there exist departmental rivalries and hostilities?

That departmental rivalries of a kind sometimes occur is acknowledged in the following statement made by the GM, Dr G. N. Gakuo, in the Railway newspaper, *Sikio*. The relevance to our earlier discussion of the corporate ethos will be noted. After outlining some of the problems facing the EARH through pressure on resources, he says:

> We on the EAR & H are one big team: there should be no jealousies amongst us: no attempt to blame someone else or some other Department for poor performance. We are a very closely knit body and very dependent on full co-operation between the various departments into which the organisation is broken down. If we regard ourselves as a team and strive to achieve the goal of even better performance we shall win through provided that the fullest co-operation extends amongst us. Let us then think of ourselves not as members of the Engineering Department or the Chief Mechanical Engineer's staff or of the Operating Department, but as members of the EAR & H in which each of us, whether he be working in the Dar es Salaam Port, or in the Running Shed at Nairobi or in the Goods Shed at Jinja, has but one object in view – a better traffic performance by the EAR & H.[1]

Against this exhortation to solidarity must be set the various attempts to encourage activities which might increase departmental rivalries, particularly interdepartmental athletics and football matches. A description of the Athletics Match held at Kampala in July 1964 is given later. In fact this was one of the few occasions when people acted together outside the work context as members of departments *per se* or manifested any degree of departmental solidarity against others. Solidarity of this kind is rare. The idea that departments are like 'houses' in an English public school is perhaps a legacy from colonial days which has little relevance to the real world.

At the higher levels of the organisation rivalry and even hostility may not be unusual, particularly when there is competition for scarce funds for new machinery or buildings or additional staff. Among ordinary workers there would be less direct concern about this, though there is considerable awareness about developments affecting the various departments as perhaps the Foreman's memorandum, discussed in Chapter 6, will show.

The GM's statement implied that members of different departments may blame each other for mistakes and failures. In fact, at the lower levels of the organisation this kind of hostility tends to be expressed in other than interdepartmental terms. A brief example. Since the permanent way in East Africa is for the most part single track it is obviously necessary for the responsible staff in the DTS departments to ensure that two trains do not approach each other from opposite directions on the same stretch of track. The lives of all depend on the Control Office passing an order to a local Station Master to direct one of the trains into sidings until the line is clear.

On one occasion, owing to the failure of a Station Master to carry out this manoeuvre, two trains nearly collided. Fortunately both crews realised in time and pulled to an emergency stop. Whatever the official enquiry said about this 'averted collision', as it is called in railway jargon, the footplate staff at Kampala had no doubts. Interestingly their criticisms were couched not in departmental terms, but in terms of occupational hostilities, skilled men against white-collar workers, a point we will return to subsequently.

In several senses the department is a political unit. At a local depot, such as Kampala, representatives of workers and management meet together in the departmental staff committee, an arena in which common problems can at least be discussed. Since, moreover, the department is the unit within which the chain of authority is located, problems of discipline which originate at a lower level, say between a section or subsection supervisor and his workers, may rapidly become the concern of the departmental head and thus all members of the department. Thus the state of industrial relations in one part of a department affects members in co-ordinate sections.

In general, however, the department is not as important in relationships as it might be. In the first place, at a depot like Kampala, still more at Nairobi, the constituent sections and subsections are spatially separated. Members of one departmental section are as likely to be near and interact with those of a section in another department as of their own. Secondly, each department is composed of functionally distinct sections which consist of staff in a wide variety of occupations. The heterogeneity and the opportunities for the growth of cross-cutting ties created by these factors diminish the solidarity of departmental units.

THE SECTION

At Kampala sections vary considerably in size (see Table 15). For the most part they occupy a single area of the depot, the geography of which is referred to by section names: the Station, the Yard, the Loco Shed, and so on. Some sections are, however, dispersed and since the office sections of each department are placed in a single building near the Station, though on different floors, they form in some respects a single unit. For most staff the section head is the nearest and most important representative of management, the district department head being a relatively remote figure who can only be approached through the mediation of the section head. One junior employee who wrote directly on some matter to his department chief invoked the wrath of his section head who charged him with 'not using the proper channels'. It is the section head who is responsible for discipline within the section and all disciplinary charges, including those emanating from lower levels, must go through him. Requests for promotion or transfer must likewise pass through his hands, and his opinion naturally carries much weight with higher authorities. Finally, recruitment into Group C posts in the section is his responsibility, though this is usually delegated to the section clerk.

There is considerable variation between sections in their organisation of work. The Loco Shed and the CxR work twenty-four hours a day, seven days a week in three shifts: 'morning shift' from 8.00 to 1600 hours, 'broken shift' from 16.00 to 24.00, and 'night shift' 24.00 to 8.00. Most staff at the Station and the Goods Shed, and all Office staff work a five-and-a-half-day week, with hours from 8.15 to 16.30 with a lunch break. Thus the amount of time and the actual periods of the day spent at work or at leisure may vary from section to section. Since members of a section generally work in the same part of the depot it is usual to see them leaving or returning to the estate in a group.

Since the section is a relatively specialised unit there is less occupational differentiation than in the department as a whole. Some certainly exists with each section having its supervisors, clerks and unskilled workers. However, the majority will be either clerks – all Offices and the Control Office – or skilled workers – the Loco Shed and the CxR – or manual workers – the IW, PWI, Goods Shed. Those in different occupations in a section may have different hours of work, e.g. the clerk in the Loco Shed does not work shifts. In some respects, therefore, sectional *esprit de corps* may be a reflection of occupational homogeneity and interest.

For the majority of railwaymen the section a worker joins on first entry to the EARH will be that he stays with all his working life, irrespective of how often he may be transferred. The real membership of a section includes all those working in similar units throughout the network, and it is these who form the closest work associates throughout their careers. In the sections which have relatively few local branches, for example, Loco Sheds, CxRs, Control Offices and high transfer rates, a worker may become familiar with large numbers of those who work in the same section at each depot, and thus have a network of ties scattered all over East Africa. When a railwayman is asked where he is working he invariably gives both the depot name and the section, e.g. 'the Loco Shed at Voi', or 'Kasese Station'. This combination provides the grids of a map of the railway world. This is not, of course, the only map available, but it may be employed by railwaymen who are otherwise strangers to establish common points of contact – friends, relatives, experiences – which may serve as the basis for a relationship. This close-knit texture of ties between those in the same section has several consequences. First, the worker establishes numerous relationships of friendship and hostility which may survive repeated transfer and separation. Secondly, the nature of these relationships is likely to be known to other workers in the section. This in turn is a manifestation of the interest in and knowledge of the activities of section mates throughout East Africa. This applies particularly to the reputations of section heads and other supervisors. Information on their attitudes usually precedes them to any depot where they may be transferred. Finally, this reinforces the identification with the common interests and problems particular to those working in a section and which may be of little concern to outsiders.

Sectional solidarity is often expressed through a *rite de passage* performed when a respected member of the section is transferred or leaves the EARH –

71

the farewell tea, in Swahili *chai ya kwaheri*. A ' list' is sent round on which are recorded signatures of those who subscribe for food, drink and a present. The process is illustrated in the following episode.

The Shedmaster's farewell party

One Saturday I found Joseph O., the RSF at the Loco Shed, drinking beer in the Railway African Club with two Asian fitters, also from the Shed. They said they were planning a party in honour of the Shedmaster, a European, who was going to the UK on long leave. They would make a small presentation. Someone in the bar pointed out that it was unusual to make a presentation to a man who was only going on leave, but the Loco Shed men replied that the Shedmaster was much respected and, anyway, it was their business. I arrived early at the party which was held in the Railway Gymkhana Club. and found John M., another African foreman, drinking with some Asian artisans. As the guests arrived they were seated at the table by Joseph who acted as master of ceremonies. Food and drink – beer, Coca Cola, rum, crisps, sambusas – were brought out and consumed. Then Joseph made a short speech saying how much they all appreciated the Shedmaster. The AME, a Superscale African, followed this by declaring what a happy place the Loco Shed must be, and that he wished he worked there. He then presented the Shedmaster with a gold ring for which the staff had subscribed. The seating plan of those at the party is given in Figure 7.

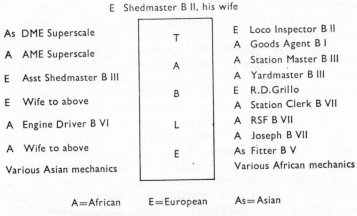

Fig. 7. The seating arrangements at the Shedmaster's farewell party

The episode illustrates a number of issues, some of which must await discussion in Chapter 5. The point here is the sectional *esprit de corps* which may occasionally override or at least temporarily submerge racial distinctions and hostilities. In a similar way if a section member dies, or is in some trouble, his mates may subscribe to a list, to help out with the cost of transporting the body back home, for example. They will also be prominent at the wake traditionally held in the deceased's home on the estate. In this respect the section parallels the activities of the ethnic associations.

Relationships between section mates are as important outside work as at work. People may associate together, visiting each other's homes, going out drinking, in part at least because they are in the same section. Nevertheless the homogeneity is once more affected by the existence of cross-cutting principles of organisation – occupation, grade, subsection. Here, however, we are concerned more with solidarity than heterogeneity. A number of other factors are relevant. At Kampala, and at other large depots, the Railway African Union base its branch organisation in part on the sections since each elects one or more representatives to sit on the branch committee. Similarly the section chooses a representative for the departmental staff committee. The representative's job in both cases is to formulate the case of the group which elects him, raising matters which affect them, and report back developments. He is also responsible, if he sits on the branch committee, for generating support for union policies. This form of organisation both recognises and encourages an identification of a common interest. It also turns the sections into political arenas in which, as we shall see in Chapter 7, aspiring leaders cut their first political teeth. Occasionally sectional solidarity may lead a group to act on its own in the case of an industrial dispute, as happened in November 1964 when a disagreement between an employee and a supervisor led the whole Loco Shed to down tools. Not surprisingly the *esprit de corps* of the non-management workers in a section appears greatest at times of industrial crisis when opinions are reported as from a collective body –' the Loco Shed thinks . . . ', ' the Goods Shed will . . . '

Sometimes a section as a whole may develop a reputation, an image, which is held to characterise its members. Some, in both union and management, held, for example, that the Loco Shed was the most troublesome, or militant, depending on the point of view, of all sections at the Kampala depot in industrial matters, and that the highest number of disciplinary charges originated there. The Loco Shed had a further reputation, perhaps not un-related, as a ' terrible place for witchcraft ' and that members were ' always bewitching one another ', an issue we examine in Chapter 6. Whatever the justice of such beliefs the point is that public opinion was recognising and expressing some idea of sectional unity.

The section, then, rather than the department, is a major principle of industrial organisation which generates the form of relationships between railwaymen. For the worker it defines a narrow field of interests and a specific set of people with whom he frequently interacts, and toward whom he may feel he has certain obligations of friendship and solidarity. As we shall see in Chapter 7 those aspiring to leadership in trades unions make use of these factors in their bids for power.

THE SUBSECTION

Figures 4 and 5 list the subsections in two departments at Kampala. The principal features of subsection organisation are that it is often, though not always, the primary work unit, that its functions are highly specific, and that occupational differentiation is low. The authority structure is usually simple, involving only one super-ordinate post – a headman, a head clerk, chargehand or supervisor. Generally its members work together at the same time, at the same place, on the same job. There are some obvious exceptions to this. For example, where work is undertaken in shifts there are three work units in each subsection which rotate and each has its own foreman. Frequently the unit is divided on an *ad hoc* basis into groups performing different tasks, as with artisans maintaining different engines. Sometimes a work unit may be formed of men from different subsections, including some from different departments. Take, for example, ' train crews '. Each long-distance passenger train is manned by two drivers and fireman, footplate staff who come from the Loco Shed, two guards from the Yard, and two TTEs from the Station. Each of these groups has its own distinct sphere of competence in running the train, and although they form in some respects a single unit, their paths need not cross in the work process. There is no sense in which ' train crews ' form a socially significant category who recognise each other as having a common identity. Indeed the reverse is the case.

The homogeneity of the subsection is reinforced by other factors. The grade difference between members is usually minimal. For example, the Carriage Cleaning Subsection consists of a Grade B VIII supervisor, and some twenty unskilled Group C men. The Parcels Office, another Station subsection, of a clerk/supervisor B X, three junior Group C clerks, one for each shift, and twenty to thirty Group C. The Compound Cleaners have a Group NC 1 headman, and a dozen unskilled workers. One of the few subsections to contain wide variations of grade is that of the footplate staff which is discussed later. Since occupation and grade tend to be similar, basic salaries and opportunities for overtime roughly the same, subsection members occupy the same income group. They will also be allotted the same house class on the estate. Since they will all have entered the EARH at the same level they are likely to possess the same standard of education. They may also have similar levels of technical skill, physical capabilities and so forth. Exceptions may occur when members of the same subsection have widely varying lengths of service, i.e. when they have been recruited at different times when different standards prevailed. The homogeneity among subsection workers may be further emphasised if, for reasons discussed in Chapter 3, they come from the same homeland or ethnic group.

Subsection membership frequently occasions relationships of friendship and solidarity, including covering up when someone is in trouble with authority, supporting the ' list' for a deceased workmate, and helping out with small loans. These relationships cut across ethnic lines, as when a young Luo, discovering that a Teso workmate had been arrested for a breach of the peace, went to the gaol to pay his 20s. fine so that the man could report in time for work. Sometimes members co-operate on relatively ambitious schemes. For example, the workers at the Parcels Office operated for a time a club with the following purpose. Once a week one member was sent to buy meat ordered by the rest from a butcher's shop near the Station. The meat, bought in bulk, was cheaper and on credit. At the end of the month the club 'treasurer' collected what each man owed as he received his pay packet and paid off the butcher. This neat system eventually foundered over accounting difficulties.

Like the department and the section the subsection also plays a part in depot politics. Although a contender for union power makes a bid for section support, he has to be assured of the backing of his own subsection, which is in a sense his primary constituency. For example, the supervisor of the Carriage Cleaners was reputed to maintain a block vote of his subordinates who were known as 'Alexander's men'. The representative from the HI on the branch committee came from among the Compound Cleaners who gave him their full support. In Chapter 7 the discussion of the internal politics of the Parcels Office shows the way in which affairs at this level are integrated into the wider arena.

Some subsections, like sections, are accorded a public image which it is difficult to dissociate from what are also occupational stereotypes. For example, the Carriage Cleaners consisted mostly of Ankole, though their supervisor referred to above was a Luo. By many people, including Luo, carriage cleaning is reckoned a low status occupation since it is associated with the cleaning of toilets, with the impure. The Luo supervisor, who always dressed for work in an immaculate white suit and solar topee, was nicknamed by his fellow ethnics *Ja-chieth* – a Dholuo word which can only be translated 'shitman'. The Compound Cleaners were similarly treated as performing polluting occupations, or were referred to as 'grass cutters', with a sneer.

In a number of ways, then, the organisational structure provides a framework for relationships between railwaymen both at work and outside work. The extent to which it is one of the principal factors delimiting the range of an individual's social contacts may be seen in Table 34. The departmental arrangements are by no means the only, or even the principal features of the industrial framework which perform this function. The rest of this chapter explores another of these, occupation.

OCCUPATIONAL DIFFERENTIATION

Hitherto the term occupation has been employed in a loose sense. We must be more precise, for in the context of the EARH there are several concepts involved. As we have seen all railwaymen are assigned a particular post involving specific function and task. The task, the job, is frequently similar to that done by the occupants of other posts. Take, for example, the post of Accidents' Clerk in the Kampala Control Office. The occupant, who writes reports on all accidents in the Uganda District does a unique job. There are, however, others – at Nairobi, Eldoret, Mombasa and so on, performing a similar job in those districts. 'Accident clerks' might therefore be considered an occupational group or category. Such people are also clerks, white-collar workers, whose jobs are similar to office staff throughout the EARH and further afield. 'Clerks' in this general sense are another occupational group. The post of RSF at Kampala gives four occupational points of references – to the other Shift Foreman at the depot, to those at other depots, to foremen of all kinds and to skilled workers with whom this category see themselves as having much in common. In considering the jobs that railwaymen do, their occupations, we have therefore to distinguish a number of aspects : (a) a specific post and its attendant role-set; (b) specialised occupational groups consisting of those in similarly-titled posts throughout the network; (c) non-specialised or general occupational categories, i.e. those performing similar tasks however the similarity is defined. Any railwayman, through his post, thus possesses a set of reference groups indicating others both in the EARH and outside with whom he may identify and from whom he may differentiate himself.

POSTS

In sociological jargon each post is a status which involves a set or constellation of roles (Merton 1957 : 364). This will be illustrated in two examples, the second of which will be given extended treatment.

The Estate Overseer at Nsambya

At Kampala this post is graded B IX. There is only one Overseer whose job it is to supervise the affairs of the estate and to allocate housing in classes 6 and 7. Higher class houses are the responsibility of the District Housing Committee whose chairman is the DE, and secretary the IRO. The Overseer notifies the IW when repairs are needed and in conjunction with the HI ensures the estate is kept clean. His work also brings him into contact with the Welfare Officer and his staff. He has one clerk under his control. Figure 8 shows the constellation of role relationships which his involvement in the

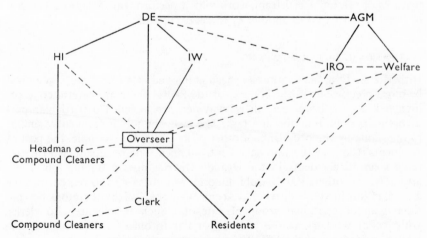

Fig. 8. The role-set of the Estate Overseer

work process entails. In the diagram unbroken lines represent formal links in the chain of authority, broken lines those posts which are associated at work.

No single characteristic defines all his relationships. To some he is subordinate formally in terms of the departmental hierarchy, to others superordinate. With others his relationships are bounded less strictly by the departmental structure but nevertheless involve degrees of super- and subordination. He is thus integrated into a hierarchical system, and this is reflected in the deference he shows to his superiors and the respect which is in turn accorded him by others, both in work and non-work situations. In some respects the Overseer is never off duty. Among his responsibilities is that of ensuring order on the estate. If a disturbance, say a fight, breaks out, it should be reported to him. In fact on the infrequent occasions when a fight occurs the hullabaloo alone is enough to bring it to his attention. If the matter is serious and injuries sustained he usually hands the affair to the police, but if it is trivial, a scrap between two women, for example, he attempts to settle it himself. This he does by summoning the disputants to his office, which is on the estate, cross-examining them and any witnesses, and making a judgment. Since he controls access to some of the housing he has the power to expel individuals from the estate or separate two quarrelling neighbours if that seems the best solution. In this way he becomes an arbitrator and a mediator in disputes between residents. Since trouble may occur at any time he is on call twenty-four hours a day, though his office is open only from 8.15–16.30. The roles entailed by his post, therefore, extend into his private life. Because of his power to allocate housing he is sometimes put into a difficult situation, for quite a few people seem willing to offer a gift in return for a better house, or indeed access to the estate.

The constellation of roles which the Overseer's post entails is perhaps more complex than average. For the Compound Cleaners, for example, there are only two basic relationships; equality among themselves and inferiority in respect to others. With each other relationships are easy-going. They work in a friendly atmosphere from which they exclude others by speaking their own language, Ankole. During their breaks they sit around in a group smoking home-made pipes and chatting. Their headman never joins them, but goes off alone to his house for tea, emerging later to harass his charges back to work. Invariably he has to order them to get moving again. They defer to him with a mixture of respect and defiance, indeed with the classic response of the low ranks in an authoritarian system known in Britain as 'dumb insolence'. Inevitably the flavour of the relationship extends to non-work situations. This will be illustrated in the following extended study.

The RSF at the Loco Shed

The role-set of the post increases in complexity the higher the grade and the more significant the position in terms of the hierarchy of authority. This is certainly the case with a position such as RSF at the Loco Shed. Of the several men who occupied these posts in Kampala, I take, as an example, Joseph O.

Career history. Joseph was born at Maseno, Kenya, *c.* 1914. He received a brief formal education and in 1930 joined the Post Office in Nairobi. After a short time he was dismissed for unpunctuality and went on to the Public Works Department. Later, on the advice of some friends, he signed on with the then Kenya Uganda Railways and Harbours Service for whom he worked continuously from 1932-52, first as a fireman, then as an engine driver. In 1952 he left, because of the emergency, and sat at home for three years. He rejoined the EARH in 1955 and continued as a driver until 1960 when he applied for and was given an RSF post at Kampala. He underwent supervisorial training at the RTS. He has been married three times and has several children. He is a Luhya, from Ebunyore Location.

The job. His main task is to assign footplate staff to their engines and to list repairs needed for each locomotive. He takes charge of one of the three shifts, changing weekly. His basic salary is 800s. per month, which is increased through overtime worked on Sundays and public holidays. If the foremen are one short, as happened when one of their number died and could not be replaced for some weeks, Joseph finds himself working twelve hours a day, seven days a week. A full month's work at this stage can, and did, bring him over 1,500s. earnings. The constellation of relationships with which he must operate is shown in Figure 9. Basically he is subordinate to the Shedmaster, co-ordinate with his fellow RSFs and other Loco Shed foremen and chargehands, and in charge of a group of firemen and drivers.

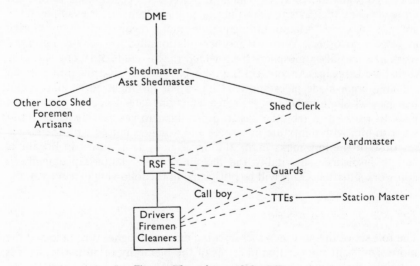

Fig. 9. The role-set of the RSF

Relationships with subordinates. Joseph claimed to be respected by his sub-ordinates both at work and on the estate and indeed it was observable that for the most part their attitude and behaviour towards him was character-ised by deference. They would address him as *mzee*, a Swahili term used respectfully to an older man, but which is also employed towards someone in authority. Another RSF, only thirty years old, was also greeted in this way by men twice his age. Similarly an older driver once commented apropos the Shed Clerk that ' he is close to the Shedmaster and should be respected. He is like our father '. In this connection the following comment by Joseph is interesting: ' Sometimes my workers say to me, " Joseph, come to drink ". I may take one small beer with them, no more. If they know me too much! I don't drink with children. If I want to accuse them, how can I accuse them? They will say, " this man drinks with us ".' By ' accuse ' he means send them to the Shedmaster to be charged. Sometimes he lends his subordinates money at the end of the month if they are short, but would on no account appear in their debt. Occasionally he got them to do small favours for him. Once a young ' light-up' (see Chapter 6) who was a handy carpenter was brought round to his house to make up a crate. On the other hand, with some of his drivers, formally subordinate to him, but with whom he himself had worked for many years as an equal, he is on much closer terms and they can often be found drinking together. This does not prevent him criticising their work if the record demands it.

Should problems arise at work he prefers the man involved to come directly to him, say at his house, and ask for the matter to be settled. If two men, a driver and a particular fireman, do not get on together, he assigns them to separate engines, but only if he accepts the reason for the bad feeling. Thus one driver who couched his complaints about another in ethnic terms was given short shrift. If two men are related he assigns them to different jobs, for it is felt improper that a man should be in a subordinate position to another he calls ' father ' or ' mother's brother '. It is also felt an especial tragedy should the engine crash and two members of the same lineage be killed at one blow. In disciplinary affairs he goes out of his way to settle a case out of court, as it were, or as he puts it, ' square the matter '. On numerous occasions (cf. Grillo, forthcoming 1974, Ch. 7) he could, had he wished, have sent some man to be charged, but chose instead to talk to the man in private or upbraid him publicly. Once when drinking with a group of senior drivers and others from Kampala and Eldoret, he made some pointed remarks, manifestly directed at one or two of those in the group. Many footplate staff, he complained, get drunk and then report sick, or report sick simply because they do not want to work. He contrasted their behaviour with that of one of the older drivers present who had never reported sick ' in all the time I have known him '. On another occasion one of his drivers was drunk and making a nuisance of himself in the bar. Joseph told him to calm down, but when the man persisted he escorted him out of the bar and took him home. Another man, a Station clerk, who had been drinking with Joseph, commented that he could not have done as

Joseph did, because he was not the driver's 'boss', i.e. he had no legitimate reason to discipline the man. A man's superior at work is felt to have a right, even a duty, to exert control over 'his' men even outside work.

Relationships with equals. Relationships between the three RSFs are always cordial. If one has something that he needs to do, then another might exchange shifts with him. If one is a little late coming on duty, he may make up the time of the man he relieves on another occasion. The Shedmaster does not mind so long as the work gets done. If one falls down on his duty the others might cover up for him. One night one of the RSFs came on duty drunk and incapable. The man he should have relieved sized up the situation and sent the offender home to bed, carrying out the duty himself. Although the matter was not reported to the Shedmaster, the other two RSFs made it clear to the drunkard that he should mend his ways. A sign of the relationship between the RSFs was the genuine grief felt by the other two when one of their number collapsed and died.

Joseph is keenly aware of his status in relation to the foremen in charge of other subsections, and when one of them tried to interfere in his own work was quick to put him in his place. Outside work he rarely associates with these foremen as they are for the most part Asians who keep to themselves, except on occasions such as the Shedmaster's party. Very infrequently Joseph does meet them for a drink, usually at the Gymkhana Club, which is still run by an Asian. With the small but growing number of African leading artisans and chargehands Joseph is on friendly terms.

Relationships with superiors. On all occasions when I saw him interacting with those above him in the hierarchy he treated them with deference. Then his manner is quiet, almost reverential, in contrast with the strength and authority with which he asserts his views under other circumstances. He claims to have a certain influence with his superiors, and indeed they respect his opinion. At one time he had a special relationship with one man, an Assistant Shedmaster newly arrived from the UK. Joseph took him under his wing, as it were, advising him on how to handle Africans. For example, he pointed out that some words, innocuous or nearly so for a European – such as 'silly', 'naughty', 'stupid' – are taken as highly insulting by many Africans. He once invited this man and his wife to drink with him at the Gymkhana Club. Since most of his superiors are Europeans or Asians the racial factor is one obvious influence on his relationships with them. On the other hand, the same style of deference also appears in his manner towards those Africans who have achieved senior positions, especially when they are younger than him or unfamiliar to him. When they are men whom he has known for many years at various depots he tries to insert a measure of equality and solidarity into their relationship.

Attitude to status. He says he is not *really* a foreman, he does not have a responsible job, he is not 'separated from other people'. He is anxious to achieve promotion, in common with many others in the labour force, as we shall see in Chapter 6, and wants to become either a Shedmaster at a smaller depot, such as Kasese, or RSF at a larger, such as Eldoret, Nakuru or Nairobi. He complains sometimes about the 'younger, less experienced men' being promoted over the heads of the older staff like himself. He says he has thought a lot about the role of the supervisor, and indeed appears highly conscious of the problems involved in such a job, though his views are not always consistent. At times he is in favour of extremely close supervision of work, each man being given a work sheet explaining in detail what he should do, at others he advocates greater freedom, saying 'many things should be left to the discretion of the workers'. He cites as an example, the unofficial tea break. He is not in favour, as some are, of abolishing the freedom of workers to make tea when they wish.

In the period leading up to the proposed strike of November 1964 (cf. Grillo, forthcoming 1974, Ch. 5) he was in a quandary as to what his attitude should be. If he were Shedmaster, he said, he would not support the strike, but as RSF he has to, through fear of the consequences. He is not quite on the Management's side. Nevertheless, when the EARH issued a leaflet appealing to the workers not to strike Joseph actually helped with the distribution. His attitude had changed in recent years since formerly he had been Chairman of the Kampala branch of the Railway African Union, and was at the time still one of the union trustees. Some people, in fact, described him as a 'changeface'. Joseph's changing orientation, away from the workers and towards Management, was consistent with the new circumstances in which he found himself. The implementation of Africanisation policy had opened avenues of advancement into higher echelon positions but it was apparent to Joseph and others that to achieve this advancement it was necessary to demonstrate a new allegiance. There is an important issue here which we will examine in Chapter 5. It should also be noted that Joseph's job as RSF placed him in an intercalary position between management and workers, which was at once his strength and weakness.

At all levels of the industry railwaymen identify with and are identified by their post. There seems little variation between posts of different kinds, and between the social backgounds of different occupants. Ethnic differences, educational standards, rural–urban orientation, age, length of service, seem to be of little relevance. Even new recruits are inducted rapidly into the behavioural expections of the post to which they are assigned. It must be remembered, however, that the status an individual acquires by virtue of his post is only one item in his status-set. Each of his statuses involves a range of appropriate behaviour, and it may happen that the behaviour expected from him in one status is not consistent with that expected in another. As Goffman (1957: 280) has shown, such inconsistency is especially important when roles are not segregated, that is to say when individuals are operating with multiplex relationships in a close-knit community. At Nsambya many railwaymen have a choice as to which role they will use in a relationship, or which aspect of their status they will attempt to implement. Some important differences emerge when we consider how various people make such choices. This issue, however, will be left to the next chapter.

So far we have examined the specific constellation of relationships within which the post-holder is embedded. Each post, however, carries with it a potentially wider, less specific, set of relationships. Joseph is a foreman and a skilled worker. He is also, as an RSF, a member of a specialised occupational group, and it is to this category we now turn.

SPECIALISED OCCUPATIONAL GROUPS

This category includes those performing the same jobs in posts with the same or similar titles throughout the EARH. Usually the jobs are peculiar to railway work – pointsmen, ticket examiners, Station Masters and so on. Men such as RSFs will usually have much in common besides the fact of being engaged in the same work situations. They will often have the same standard of education and skill, have followed the same career paths and have similar future prospects. They will have attended the same course at the RTS where they may even have been classmates. All these factors add to their solidarity. As examples two groups are considered among whom there appeared to be particularly strong bonds of unity.

Footplate staff

Footplate staff – locomotive drivers and firemen – are found in one sub-section only of Loco Sheds. Their jobs are, of course, unique to the railways and involve many special problems: responsibility for the safety of the train, the dangers inherent in their work, the particular skills and know-how they require; factors around which their *esprit de corps* is built. As one of them put it: ' A driver's work is very hard. Sometimes he can't sleep at night thinking about his work. Last year a train crashed and the driver and fireman were both burnt up completely. They never found the bodies.' Joseph, the RSF, told me that he had known drivers who had refused to go out because they had noticed ' a single nut loose in the engine '. The fear of accidents, and the belief that in their job they are particularly vulnerable to disciplinary charges will be shown in Chapter 6 to be related to an apparently high incidence of accusations of witchcraft and sorcery.

In compensation for these dangers drivers and firemen have a relatively privileged salary position. They are given special pay scales in which a driver B VIII, for example, receives £60 per annum more than other workers on the same grade (for details see Appendix III). The additional amount consists of a ' consolidated' sum, which varies with grade, and which re-placed allowances for ' mileage ' and ' stabling out ' (spending nights away from the home depot) which were formerly calculated individually. In addition they have good opportunities for overtime. In the Nsambya sample it was found that the take-home pay of firemen was 16% above the basic, and that of drivers 29%. Senior drivers can regularly earn more than £100 a month, which in 1965 placed them in the top bracket of African workers.

Some shifts, or assignments, are better than others in this respect and foot-plate staff are well aware of this as they are of the detailed problems in-volved in driving over particular sections of the track. Such topics are the staple of any bar-room conversation among this group.

The interest in and concern about their work turn them into a tightly-knit group which may include those, like the RSF, who are in allied occupations. In addition many of the senior drivers, those at the top of the career struc-ture, have been with the railways for more than twenty-five years, in the course of which they will have served at many depots, forming friendships in the way described earlier. Besides this, the very nature of their work enables them to keep in contact with others in the network. One day a driver may be assigned to the overnight train to Kasese, spending a day there before returning with the next down train. The next assignment may take him to Jinja. The through trains from Nairobi are manned by crews from Eldoret who likewise stay overnight in Kampala. During their leisure periods on these visits footplate staff invariably pass the time with their colleagues, drinking and gossiping. Consequently they are well informed about events and personalities in their world, and also carry information of a more general interest. They also operate an unofficial postal service between depots. It is always possible to send a letter or parcel to Nairobi by way of the drivers.

Footplate staff form such a strong interest group that it is not surprising that they had plans to form their own trade union, to be called the 'Enginemen's Association'.[2] As we will see in Chapter 7 the Railway Unions in Kenya and Uganda are dominated by white-collar workers, and some drivers believe that their own interests are insufficiently represented. They often feel that the union leadership is concerned solely with power and, 'anyway, the clerks despise us'. The move to found the association eman-ated from Kenya with representatives from Mombasa, Nakuru and Eldoret attending a meeting at Nairobi. Footplate staff in Uganda were sympathetic but awaited developments, which never occurred.

Relationships between footplate staff and other occupational groups were often said to be hostile. Drivers claimed that they worked hardest of all and were paid accordingly, but that others were envious of them. In connection with the 'averted collision' mentioned earlier one driver commented that when station staff were found responsible for an accident, 'then we are happy. They abuse us, say we are illiterate and earn too much money. But when they are guilty, we say " All right ! "'. A remark like the following is not untypical. 'Clerk's work is ladies' work. All they want is to sit in an office and wear a white shirt and tie.' Hard, dirty, skilled work comes to have connotations almost of virility. Conflict between footplate staff and clerks is not apparently confined to Africans, for European drivers voiced similar complaints. This is not to suggest that Africans are simply taking up a European response. Irrespective of race the structural situation generates this type of occupational hostility.

Although footplate staff do exhibit a high degree of solidarity the group is by no means structurally homogeneous. Grading differences are considerable, as we shall see in Chapter 6, and there is a major distinction between drivers and firemen. The relationship between the two is characterised by three factors. Drivers are much further advanced in terms of the occupational career structure and therefore much older on average than firemen. Secondly, firemen at work are subordinate to their drivers. On both counts, therefore, the former owe respect and deference to the latter. It is also considered that firemen are apprentice drivers and that part of the driver's job is to pass on the accumulated skills of the profession to the next generation. Sometimes special relationships develop, with a driver having a favourite fireman whom he persuades the RSF to assign him. As with the RSF and his subordinates, a driver may get his fireman to perform small favours, as when one Luo driver had his Luyha fireman provide sleeping accommodation for his eldest son.

Running staff

There are a number of similarities between running staff – guards and TTEs – and footplate staff. In both cases their jobs are unique to the Railways. Both are on consolidated salary scales and have good chances for overtime. Among running staff in the Nsambya sample take-home pay was 33% more than basic salary. Both groups travel around the network in their work and act as carriers of information and goods between depots.

Running staff in fact consist of two distinct groups, for guards and TTEs are in different subsections, and at work they have two quite different jobs to perform. Outside work they form two separate cliques who keep themselves apart from each other and from other workers. Each clique has its own favourite bar where they can usually be found in leisure periods. They tend to patronise one bar for a few months and then move on as a group. Their relative affluence creates ill-feeling between them and others. Both clerks and footplate staff regard them collectively as 'thieves', for it was rumoured that each group operated a racket by which they improved their own financial position at the expense of the EARH. The TTEs were said to organise the following ramp. Often, especially at wayside stations, passengers can board the train without a ticket. The TTEs job is to collect the appropriate fare. It was alleged that they simply collected the fare, or part of it, and issued a ticket for a shorter journey, pocketing the surplus. They were even said to bribe station booking clerks to close the booths early to boost their custom on the trains. The guards, whose job it is to look after parcels, were said to arrange for them to be 'lost' so that they could steal the contents. On one occasion a guard was in fact charged with such an offence and suspended from duty pending the court case. The other guards rallied to his support with money and help. One of the principal witnesses alleges that he was approached by one of them and told, 'Do you think a young man like you can trick us men of 20 years' experience. We will teach you a lesson you can't forget.' The guard was acquitted.

Most of these allegations are gossip and rumour, but they were widely held to be true. Other workers pointed to their undoubtedly extravagant spending on clothes, drink and women as proof. Once, for example, in a bar quarrel a Luhya driver abused an Acholi guard, telling him 'you are a thief at your work'. He tore the man's shirt, a symbolic gesture. The guard calmly replied that he would not retaliate since he was insured, and his insurance company would sue the driver for damages, a remark which was deemed to have won him the argument.

Footplate staff, guards and TTEs are by no means the only railwaymen who form specialised groups of the kind dealt with here. For example, industrial relations and welfare officers are both strongly identified with their posts, and have a strong sense of unity derived from the particular problems and interests of their work. This unity is reinforced in both cases by the fact that they are all relatively young, highly educated, ambitious men who have been picked out for rapid promotion, being among the first to benefit from the Africanisation of higher-level posts. They all receive training on specialist courses, often abroad in the case of IROs, and they maintain frequent contact by attending conferences at Nairobi HQ.

Each specialised group is in turn integrated into one of a limited number of broad occupational categories which operate both within and outside the EARH.

MAJOR OCCUPATIONAL CATEGORIES

When sociologists, especially those concerned with Western societies, discuss occupational groups they are frequently referring to a few inclusive categories such as manual workers, artisans, white-collar workers, professional men. In what ways are these broad distinctions used as frames of reference or rallying points for social aggregates or are otherwise relevant in a study of railwaymen?

All the particular jobs performed by workers in an industry may be reduced by reasonably objective criteria to a small number of categories. Sociologists, economists and collectors of industrial statistics usually employ level or type of skill required to perform the job as the principal criterion for achieving this reduction. It can then be shown that objectively the members of each group exhibit common characteristics differentiating them from each other. Parkin (1969a: 23ff.) follows this method in his discussion of occupational differentiation on the housing estates of Kampala East, and in the first instance a similar method will be used here.

Taking the respondents in the Nsambya sample it was found possible to divide them into five main categories which are listed here together with the particular jobs that each includes:

Supervisorial: station master, assistant station master, yard foreman, train inspector, estate overseer.

White collar: clerks, welfare assistant, train guards.

Skilled: locomotive and other drivers, mechanics, electricians, turners, stewards.

African railwaymen

> *Semi-skilled*: loco firemen and cleaners, electricians' and masons' mates, gardeners.
> *Unskilled*: headman, pointsman, trolleyman, checker, watchman, porter, etc.

The distribution of particular occupations within the groups is not dissimilar to Parkin's in the reference cited. Some information on differences between members of each group in respect of education, pay, age and other factors is found in Table 30. (The discussion here also ties together a number of points that have been made previously.)

TABLE 30. *Occupational groups at Nsambya: a comparison*

	Super-visorial	White collar	Skilled	Semi-skilled	Unskilled	All
Number in sample	5	14	14	13	13	59
% of sample	8.5	23.7	23.7	22.0	22.0	99.9
Mean basic pay [a]	787/–	496/–	445/–	209/–	191/–	378/–
Mean take-home pay [a]	841/–	565/–	569/–	238/–	200/–	437/–
% increase take-home/ basic pay	6.4	13.9	27.8	13.9	4.7	15.5
Age [b]	42	30	37	35	42	37
Length of service [b]	22.6	8.5	15.6	10.8	13.8	12.9
Schooling [b]	9.8	9.5	4.4	4.5	1.5	5.4

[a] Shillings per month.
[b] Mean years.

The career patterns and prospects of those in each group differ widely. Unskilled workers enter in Group C, and there they must remain unless they change their occupation. The best grade they can attain is NC 1, and the most important job that of headman of a gang of loaders or cleaners. The low average level of education within this group (see Table 30) makes a change of occupation difficult if not impossible, since so much weight is given to formal educational achievement. Semi-skilled and most skilled workers also enter in Group C, but their career structure often includes the possibility of promotion to Group B posts. Semi-skilled workers in fact comprise two categores – those in jobs such as firemen, electricians' mates, etc. which are really apprentice levels in the skilled worker's career, and other jobs from which there are no formal promotion channels. Almost all white-collar workers enter in Group B and have, at the present time, considerable opportunities for advancement. They are younger than average, with high standards of education. The older workers in this category, with greater lengths of service, are likely to be found in the fifth group, the supervisors.

Basic salaries differ considerably between groups, supervisors earning four times as much as unskilled workers, a differential which is slightly greater when take-home pay is considered. As we have seen, chances for overtime are greatest among skilled workers. If running staff are excluded from the white-collar category the average increase in take-home over basic salary in this group is 9%, compared with 28% for skilled men. The fact that those in different occupations are assigned different places in the grading system is reflected in the evidence of Table 31, which compares occupation and

TABLE 31. *Occupation by class of house*

Class	Unskilled	Semi-skilled	Skilled	White collar	Supervisorial	All
7 (i)	6	9	5	–	–	20
7 (ii)	7	4	3	2	–	16
6	–	–	2	4	–	6
5/4/3	–	–	4	8	5	17
All	13	13	14	14	5	59

class of house. There is on the estate a rough polarisation between the un-skilled and semi-skilled in classes 7 (i) and 7 (ii) and between supervisors and white-collar workers in class 6 and above. Since the house classes are located separately on the estate we may say there is a tendency towards occupational zoning at Nsambya. Skilled workers are, however, found in all classes. Many of these are undoubtedly living in quarters below their entitlement. In the sample 86% of skilled men should have been living in class 6 or above, where in fact 43% did so. This reflects partly the result of a general shortage of middle-grade house units, and some white-collar workers do have to suffer the rigours of class 7 accommodation. The disparity appears, however, to be substantially higher for skilled men, which may reflect either the extent to which clerks are given priority over others in the allocation of housing or their greater inclination to agitate if they are relegated to a standard of housing beneath their entitlement. Both are probably true, as a case to be considered in the next chapter will perhaps show. One consequence of this is that since there is an association between house class, family size, and the extent to which married men maintain their wives and children in town, unskilled and semi-skilled workers in the lowest house classes are less likely to be found leading normal family lives.

Among the more obvious differences between occupations we may include the fact that the jobs of unskilled and skilled men involve dirty, manual work for which special clothes are usually worn, whereas clerks – as the other term 'white-collar worker' indicated – work in offices in much better physical conditions where everyday clothes – shirt, jacket, tie – are *de rigueur*. Working hours vary, with unskilled and clerks generally having a fixed schedule and regular lunch break, while others work shifts which change weekly and also work Sundays and public holidays.

All that has been so far documented is that the labour force may be divided into several categories between which there are some important differences from the observer's point of view. What has not been demonstrated is the extent to which these categories are significant from the point of view of the workers themselves, though this is strongly implied by evidence already presented. The occupational groups discussed here are hardly groups in the strict sense. They are better described as categories, using that term to mean not an item in a classificatory system but a set of people who fall short of forming a corporate group (Cohen 1969: 4, Williams 1964: 18). They are also reference groups which provide a set of people with whom the individual may identify, the key factor in the identity being the common situation in the work process. If this sense of identity were of a certain degree of intensity we might expect it to be given some institutional expression. In the case of the footplate staff something of this kind was indeed mooted – the Enginemen's Association. Their grievance that the unions were dominated by white-collar workers was reflected to the extent that the principle behind the proposed association was supported by other than drivers and firemen. Their complaint that the 'clerks hate us, because we are illiterate and earn large salaries' could be made by any skilled worker, and indeed frequently was.

Although the organised expression of common occupational interest did not go very far, it is clear that broad occupational categories are used as frames of reference. This was seen in some of the statements made by the drivers which we recorded earlier, and is also demonstrated in the following remarks collected from a range of informants.

Joseph, the RSF. Joseph maintained that when he joined the Railways in 1932 he preferred to go into a mechanical rather than a clerical job because the pay was better. At any rate he did not have the expense of spending large sums on shirts, collars and ties. He sometimes grumbled about the present generation of workers who 'only want to work as clerks'. He felt people should learn technical trades, and praised one young Acholi in the Loco Shed who although he had a high standard of education had preferred to train as a boilermaker rather than become a clerk.

A small group at the tailor's shop on the estate. The group was discussing the news that a train had crashed at Kasese, a passenger killed and the crew injured. The tailor commented that his brother had recently joined the Loco Shed, despite having a good standard of education. He now wanted to go for training as a driver, but the tailor was advising him to become a clerk and forget about the extra money. A by-stander declared that he would not be a driver, even if they paid him 'thousands of shillings'.

A clerk at the Station. He came from Rusinga Island. Opio (see Figure 6), who had been one of the pioneers from Rusinga on the Railways in Kampala, had advised the young men from home to avoid skilled trades. Did they, he had asked, want to go around with greasy clothes, their hair covered in oil? So no Rusinga men ever went into skilled jobs, but 'always' became clerks or porters.

From these and other statements we may isolate a number of general occupational categories. If it were possible to undertake this fieldwork again, I would consider a more systematic method of eliciting categories of this kind. A simple card-sorting technique of the type which has been used in the study of stratification in European peasant societies would seem relevant (cf. Silverman 1966). In this informants are presented with a list of items – in this case specific occupations – and asked to form them into as many groups as they wish. Failing the availability of such evidence in the present survey one must rely on unsystematic data. Three categories emerge at once, viz. unskilled or manual workers, in Swahili *wapagazi* (literally 'porters'), skilled workers, *mafundi*; and white-collar workers or clerks, *makarani*. The distinction between skilled and semi-skilled which appears necessary and useful from the observer's point of view seems to be lacking in the cognitive categories. Above these three classes may be located the 'officers' (*maafisa*) which includes what I earlier termed 'supervisors', and above them a fifth category of 'senior officer'. Within each group there are a number of finer distinctions, e.g. between drivers and artisans among skilled men, and among unskilled workers between those engaged in cleaning work – carriage cleaners, compound cleaners, 'grass cutters' or 'shamba boys' – and other manual labourers – loaders, checkers, porters and the like. The association of the work of cleaners with latrines places them virtually in a separate category, not unlike the untouchables in the caste system.

Analogies with the caste system are always suspect, but here they are not entirely inapt since it is clear that the occupational categories mentioned above are ranked in a hierarchical order. That occupations are ranked in order of prestige or preference is well known in Western society and a similar tendency has been noted in Africa.[3] Once again I must regret the absence of more systematic evidence of the kind available in other studies, but time and resources prevented the application of the sort of techniques that are available. Once more, reliance must be placed on unsystematic observation.

There seems general agreement among all workers, whatever their occupation, as to the rank order of the categories. Skilled men, by their very objections, recognise that the public places them below white-collar workers on the prestige scale. The views of informants on the nature of the categories may be summarised in a series of thumb-nail sketches:

Unskilled: dirty, illiterate, ignorant, poorly paid. They waste their money on the cheapest drink. They dress in rags and are not interested in improving their condition.

Skilled: dirty, greasy, oily, illiterate. Highly paid, but waste their money on drink.

White collar: educated and well-paid. They dress well, but waste their money on fine clothes which they flaunt about. As a result they are always in debt.

Officers: similar to white-collar workers, but these are 'big men' in responsible jobs who deserve respect. They ought to ensure that their private lives measure up to their public positions.

One of the major functions of occupational differentiation, then, is to provide a system by which members of the community may be ranked. It is, however, not the only ranking system which is available to railwaymen. In the argument between clerks and skilled men, for example, both income and education were used as measures of relative status. In fact it is the inconsistency between the two groups' ratings on these measures that apparently causes the conflict. This is one of the themes that will be discussed in the next chapter.

Some final points. Within the Railway community both specialised and broad occupational categories are relevant in the structuring of relationships and attitudes. In the urban context as a whole the finer distinctions, as between, say, guards and TTEs, engine drivers and boilermen, are largely irrelevant. In that case railwaymen are fitted into an urban-wide system of ranking which consists of a set of general occupational categories similar to the ones discussed here. That such a system exists in Kampala may be seen in the work of Parkin, and in the extent to which the relative prestige of various occupational categories is a constant theme in Swahili and Luganda popular songs.

CHAPTER 5

STATUS, REPUTATION AND CLASS

Modern Western industry is in its very essence hierarchically ordered. In the system of authority, in the differential allocation of rewards it mirrors, indeed moulds, the culture and values of the society in which it is situated. Whether large industrial enterprises could ever be run otherwise is an important political question which, perhaps unfortunately, is beyond the scope of this monograph. Here we are able only to document how the structure of a particular industry generates alignments and oppositions among its workers of a kind which are usually described as those of status and class.

These two terms are among the most discussed in the whole of social and political theory. There is an enormous literature, the relevance of which for the material to be presented here would itself need a whole monograph. Consequently the theoretical significance, if any, of the findings, can be dealt with only cursorily, and largely in parentheses. Some initial discussion of one issue – the definitional problem – is, however, unavoidable, for as has frequently been shown the concepts that are involved are often given widely varying meanings (cf. Lasswell 1965: 53ff.). One of the more lucid analyses of the issues is to be found in the work of Ralf Dahrendorf (1959). Broadly speaking I accept the distinction he draws between 'class' and 'stratum', and my use of the term class largely follows Dahrendorf's recension of Marx. In traditional Marxism classes are groups whose members are defined by their relationship to the means of production, e.g. owners of capital. If this definition is applied to railwaymen then there are clearly no classes since no worker, not even the GM, owns the EARH. However, if as Dahrendorf (and others) have suggested the criterion 'relationship to the means of production' is extended from ownership to control, and classes defined in terms of power and authority, then the concept once more becomes useful. The growth of class relationships in this sense in modern Africa has been little documented outside of the specialist Marxist literature. On the other hand we have considerable information on the increasing importance of modern status systems which give rise to what Dahrendorf refers to as 'social strata'. The ancestry of this concept is not Marx, but Weber. Status and status groups or strata are terms used in the discussion of relative rank, honour and prestige, and not the distribution of power as such (Weber 1948: 187).

In this study alignments of status and class are considered separately. The discussion of status raises a number of issues. First it will be found necessary to distinguish between status or 'standing' and 'reputation'. An individual's standing is his formal rating within the systems by reference to which prestige is accorded. In urban Africa this usually means his occupation, his income and his level of education.[1] 'Reputation' refers to the esteem in which he personally is held by other members of the community. Differentiating the two concepts simply underlines the obvious point that an individual can have high status, but be held in low esteem, and perhaps *vice versa*. Secondly it will be noted that relative status is measured by several distinct criteria – not only income, education and occupation, but also grade, and to some extent age and length of service. It follows that for some individuals or groups their ratings according to different systems of status allocation may not be consistent or congruent. We will examine the extent to which status 'crystallisation' as Lenski (1954) has called it, actually occurs and what happens when it does not. Thirdly, it will be necessary to consider the relationship between alignments created by the systems of status and class and those which derive from outside the industrial framework, particularly from kinship and ethnic identity. Finally, we will raise the question whether this is a *stratified* community, or at least, in what sense it may be said to be stratified, and what constitute the social strata.

THE CATEGORIES OF SOCIAL DIFFERENTIATION

We have seen already that various occupational groups – manual workers, skilled men, clerks, officers – are ranked in terms of their prestige. A local word which accords most closely to our concept of prestige is the Swahili *heshima*. A popular Swahili song goes: 'We came to Nairobi to find work, to find work to earn money and to become *watu wa heshima*' – men accorded prestige or status. The form *mheshimiwa* is used in the titles of ministers in the Kenyan and Tanzanian government to mean 'the Honourable'. Another related term is 'big man" – an important person. The obvious Swahili phrase here is *mtu mkubwa*, but there also exist a number of slang terms which change with some rapidity. In Kampala and in parts of Kenya in 1964/5 two phrases in particular were frequently used: *watu wa juu* and *watu wa chini* – men of above and men of below. Many of the comments recorded below relate to these terms.

Officials of the Railway African Union

I first heard the terms *chini/juu* used by the Chairman of the union's Kampala branch when at a committee meeting he was rehearsing what he would say to a supervisor with whom one member was in trouble. He would begin 'Sisi watu wa chini . . .' 'We men of below'. Later he told me that the phrase meant the same as the 'common man', which was at that time popular in political circles. He also said that it was used to refer to different Groups in the grading system. Thus Group B was *chini* to Group A, Group C to Group B. The clerk to the union branch, not a railwayman, said that *sisi watu wa chini* would mean in the first place Group C, but Group B used the term as well, Group B grades XI–IX referring to IX–VI as *juu*. As far as he knew the phrases had been used by railwaymen before he was associated with the union, viz. 1960. A Luhya fireman (Geoffrey) who was a Loco Shed representative on the branch committee said that *chini* meant Group C plus Group B grades XI–VIII. He himself was opposed to the phrase and tried to tell his fellow workers in the Loco Shed not to use it, for they were all equal.

A Luo Group C labourer in the Yard. Chini were Group C like himself. All 'graded staff' (sic) i.e. B XI and above were *watu wa juu*. He also wanted to distinguish between *juu kwa kazi* and *juu huku nyumbani*. By the former he meant those who because of their jobs were wealthy, well dressed, with big houses, with cars, who speak English, and by the latter important men in the rural areas, old men with many cattle and wives. As examples of big men 'at work' he cited the union President, the Welfare Officer and the Carriage Cleaning Supervisor.

An Ankole Compound Cleaner. He, too, classified the union President and the Welfare Officer as big men whom he defined as having important posts (Sw. *daraja*) and a high income and possessions such as a car. With regard to the union President he qualified his statement by saying, 'but he works for the people'.

A Luo Clerk, B XI. He complained that if a man goes home wearing a clean shirt people will think him *juu*. They don't understand town life. If a man owns a radio worth 300s. or 400s. people in the rural areas see this as representing more than they earn in a whole year. They don't appreciate that the townsman has a lot of expenses. The people at Nsambya are ignorant, too, because they think of him as *juu*, whereas in fact he, too, is poor and there are people above him, e.g. in Grade V and above, who are really *juu*.

A Luo Group C Clerk (Francis: see below). He thought that the *chini* phrase was used when people got angry. As a Group C man he considered himself *chini* and Groups B and A as *juu*, but at work he, as a clerk, was considered *juu* by the men under him. He once asked whether I thought that men who were *juu*, e.g. the Station Master, objected to my friendship with him, a low grade man. This was in the light of a remark he subsequently made about other Group C envying him because of this friendship. Once he became angry with someone who commented on this and replied: 'Why can't people stop being envious. Some of us are *juu*, others are *chini*, and there are others who are *chini* who try to be *juu*.' There is in fact a Luo verb – *okaore* – which fits the latter category and means roughly someone pretending to be better than he is. This informant also stated, in a discussion of sorcery, that if a man who is *juu* catches his wife in adultery with a man who is *chini* he would dismiss the wife. If the reverse occurred, the *chini* man would get his own back through medicines.

Some 'big men'. There is considerable range in the complexity of ideas about social differentiation. On the one hand, for example, an Acholi B XI boilerman who thought that *chini* were simply Group C and *juu* the foremen and such in the Loco Shed where he worked. On the other hand, take the following discussion which formed part of a general conversation in a bar. Most of those present were in grade VI and above and of mixed ethnic background – Lango, Soga, Luo, Luhya. At one point someone broached the question ' What does the phrase " the common man " really mean? ' No one was quite sure. The IRO said ' all voters ', while a clerk suggested 'all men whose fathers were not important'. The Kabaka of Buganda, by his definition, was the opposite of the common man. All, however, agreed that the phrase had no connection with *chini/juu*, the IRO declaring that those terms were purely relative : ' I have people above me.' At this juncture the clerk began describing, in Swahili, though the rest of the conversation had been in English, the typical *mtu ya juu* – with his house, his car, his big job and salary. At this the IRO became nettled and said, ' You are talking about me.'

The Welfare Officer (James), who it will be recalled was often cited as an example of a big man, made some interesting comments while discussing his job. When he had first arrived at Kampala he was accused in an anonymous letter to his Head at Nairobi of not spending enough time with Group C men. He had tried to change this and now some people said he met with them too often. His work, he felt, demanded constant contact and cooperation with all kinds of people. He claimed he felt free to invite all grades to his house and go to theirs. Group C looked upon him as a friend, and he paid more attention to their complaints than those of Group B, since the former had less understanding about what was wrong. He thought that at Kampala it was easier for him to keep in touch with Group C because his house was on the estate. At Nairobi, where house classes are separated, he found that his principal associates both at work and at leisure were people of his own grade.

A propos attitudes towards Group C and others, I once asked an African officer why third-class train passengers were not allowed to use the dining car or buffet. He said it was because they were usually drunk through consuming too much *waragi* – an illicitly-distilled alcohol – and would make a lot of noise and disturb other passengers. The stereotype of Group C is virtually the same as that of manual workers. Joseph, the RSF whose career we discussed in Chapter 4, said that he would never drink with those in Group C : ' Such a man has low pay and low grade, why should we go to drink? ' Describing how Group C men took no part in running the affairs of the union, he asserted : ' They are not interested in learning. They don't know what a union is. They drink *waragi*, come to meetings drunk, and want to fight.' This attitude is underlined by the existence of the two Railway Clubs. The Railway African Club has a low membership fee and is unrestricted. The Gymkhana Club has always been restricted in different ways, first by allowing Asian members only, then by barring entry to those in grade VII and below, and finally by fixing an entrance fee of 5s. per month, a sum large enough to deter the lower-paid workers.

The following comments show that the terms *chini/juu* and the associated attitudes are not confined to railwaymen. Nearby the estate there was a Kikuyu who ran an open-air barber's shop. Once when I was talking to him a senior police officer went past in a chauffeur-driven car. Such, he said, was the way of *mtu ya juu*. He himself he described as *mtu ya chini kabisa* – ' the lowest of the low '. The Luo owner of one of the Nsambya bars claimed that the distinction originated when Africans began to obtain promotion to well-paid posts. *Watu wa juu* can be recognised because they are well-dressed and fat. The Welfare Officer, the RSFs and the senior drivers were *juu* because of their pay. A friend of the bar-owner commented that the men in government in Kenya and Uganda would do nothing for the poor of the country until they themselves had first become ' fat '. I also heard the phrases in Nairobi and in the rural areas of western Kenya where I was told that they had come into use since independence. Another phrase was also in use in Nairobi in 1965, when the word *mzungu* – literally European – was coming to mean anyone who was a boss. In Dar es Salaam another pair of concepts appeared to mean much the same thing with *nisesheni* being used for *juu* and *kamchape* for *chini*. *Nisesheni* is short for *ndugnisesheni* or ' brotherisation '. *Kamchape*, according to informants, has no real meaning. However, it seems to be the same word as that which at that time was being used as the name of an anti-witchcraft movement in southern Tanzania (cf. Willis 1968). How this came about is obscure.

The statements recorded here show that the terms are used in a variety of analytically distinct ways. First they simply provide a way of stating the relative positions of Groups and grades in the grading system. Secondly they refer to super- and subordinate position in the authority structure. Thirdly they are used as synonyms for particular sets of grades, with *chini* referring to Group C. Finally they are used as general terms for those in the upper and lower echelons in society as a whole. The statements also imply a range of attributes attaching to those in different social positions – wealth, jobs, possessions, habits, attitudes. Each statement, each usage, illustrates one or more of the class and status models with which informants operate. The wide variation in the models may be reduced to three basic types, implying three kinds of social structure. In one of its applications the *chini/juu* distinction represents a two-status model – the rich and the poor, the big men and the common men. This model relates to a second in which *chini/juu* refer to differential distributions of power. It then becomes a two-class model, in Dahrendorf's sense. The third model is an expansion of the first and instead of just two there is a multiplicity of status groups. This model is built up with elements from the grading system, though the number of strata, and the precise boundaries between them vary considerably.

The multiple strata model derived from the grading system may be compared with that derived from the perception of occupational differentiation. The two are interlinked but do not completely overlap. Although the number of strata within the grade model varies with the perception of the informant there are some areas of agreement. Thus Group C as a whole is placed at the lowest level. When at the start of fieldwork I asked an unskilled worker his grade he would frequently reply: ' I have no grade. I am just a Group C man.' Note the word ' just '. The term ' grade ' in popular speech, especially in the phrase ' graded staff ', referred to Group B. To begin, therefore, we have two major categories: Group C, which includes unskilled and semi-skilled workers, and graded staff, which includes white-collar workers and many skilled men. Among graded staff themselves the category is frequently broken down into a number of sub-strata, e.g. B XI–IX, VIII–VI, and so on. The precise boundaries between the sub-strata are problematical. For those above a certain level in Group B, the terms used are the same as those that appear in the occupational model – officers and senior officers, though for both categories collectively some people, especially active trade unionists, had yet another term – *Bwana Relwe*. There is also a quite distinct set of categories which employ standards of education, with at one end of the spectrum ' illiterates ', and at the other the ' educated men ', with Cambridge School Certificates, who ' speak English '. The material raises some formidable analytical problems, which must for the moment be shelved. For the time being let us accept the existence of a general status differentiation which we may treat as a two-strata ideal model.

The attributes of status

Life-style. The basic components of status differentiation are grade, income, occupation and education. We may assume for the moment a congruence or crystallisation of ranking on each dimension, and that the community can be conveniently divided into two categories of high- and low-status individuals. In analysing the Nsambya sample I have in fact found it useful to calculate an average status score for each individual, taking into account his rating on each of the four dimensions,[2] with a maximum score of ninety, minimum ten. In Tables 32 and 33 referred to subsequently the sample has

TABLE 32. *Status and household composition among Nsambya residents*

	High status	Low status	Total
Number of households	27	32	59
Mean household size	5.3	4.1	4.7
% with 1–4 persons	33.3	75.0	56.0
% with 5 or more persons	66.7	25.0	44.0
% householders married	95.0	84.0	90.0
% with spouse(s) at Nsambya	85.0	56.4	67.9
% with children at Nsambya	81.5	50.0	64.5
% accommodating guests	55.5	25.0	42.4

been divided into two status groups, those with scores above fifty and below forty-nine. It may be interesting to note the average scores, measured by grade, income and educational level, of those in each of the five occupational groups discussed in Chapter 4: supervisors seventy-six; white-collar workers sixty-six; skilled forty-five; semi-skilled twenty-five; unskilled seventeen.

Throughout the comments recorded earlier runs the theme of differences in life-style in which three elements stand out: housing, possession of material goods, and patterns of consumption. We will look at each in turn.

Housing. Normally housing would be an item on the family budget and would be a useful source of information on wage- or status-related styles of life. We know from other Kampala studies (Parkin 1969a: 59ff.) that in the city the kind of house an individual occupies and the area where he lives are reflections of his status. There is, in fact, a recognised hierarchy of residential areas, and as status rises individuals move from one area to another, e.g. from the Nakawa Estate to Naguru. Railwaymen who do not live at Nsambya generally find accommodation in those areas appropriate to their status, for example the Ankole Compound Cleaners who live at Kibuli. At Nsambya the allocation of housing is directly related to one element of status – grade – and indirectly to other elements. The average status scores of individuals occupying each class of house is as follows: 7 (i) – 25.8; 7 (ii) – 31.2; 6 – 50.8; 5 – 65.7; 4/3 – 81. There is, therefore, as we might expect, a distinct status zoning on the estate. This is in turn associated with differences in the composition of households. Table 32 illustrates this for the high- and low-status groups in the sample. High-status people have larger households, are more often married, with children, and maintain their families and guests at Nsambya. The critical factor seems to be the class of house, and the amount of room available, since those higher-status individuals in low-class housing tend to have smaller households.

We noted in the previous chapter that some people were living in house classes above or below their entitlement. In the sample this included 24% of respondents, 7% above and 17% below the class appropriate to their grade. House allocation is a sensitive issue, and those in charge are frequently accused of all manner of malpractice, including the taking of bribes. Although such accusations are usually groundless they illustrate the amount of feeling centred on the distribution of housing. It is an index of the sensitivity towards status as the following cases show.

On one occasion I accompanied the IRO to a small depot outside Kampala. He had been called in to arbitrate a dispute that had arisen between the staff, represented by the local branch of the Railway African Union, and management. At that depot there were three EARH officers: the Shedmaster and Station Master, who were both African, and an Asian PWI. The Shedmaster had taken charge of local house allocation and the dispute arose because of an allegation that he was guilty of ' tribalism ' – handing out the best quarters to his fellow Luo. The IRO summoned a meeting between the Shedmaster and the union branch officers, heard their complaints and called witnesses. It emerged that there were indeed a number of workers living in house classes both above and below their entitlement, though the circumstances under which this had arisen were contested. The Shedmaster claimed that the situation antedated his arrival and had arisen because at one time the depot had been in the unusual position of having a surplus of higher class and a shortage of lower-class units. Some of the former had accordingly been given to Group C men with large families. When they had been transferred their successors had moved into their quarters. Group B staff arriving subsequently had found the higher class housing full and had to go into class 7 units. The union, some of whose officials were in this position, had taken up their case. The IRO solved the problem by ordering a reallocation of housing, but successfully managed to ignore attempts by the leading union spokesman to get himself assigned better quarters. The accusation of tribalism is standard form in these disputes and may in this case be discounted.

Naturally railwaymen are anxious to receive in full those perquisites to which their status entitles them, and become annoyed when they see those with the same or lower rank than themselves receiving something they are denied. For example, Joseph, the RSF, who occupied a class 5 (i) house, one day told me that he wanted to move into the class 4 unit which had been occupied by a colleague of his until the latter's death. He had, he said, already put in an application but had been told over the 'phone that he was not eligible. He complained that this was not true since he knew of several people with the same grade as himself, but with less seniority, living in higher class units. He wanted to move because the house was bigger and there would be room for him to build a small shed for his car. If he moved he would give up drinking at the Railway African Club or the bars at Nsambya and use the ' Asian Club' which was near the house he wanted. He was not in fact entitled to a higher class house and though the authorities reviewed his case the application came to nothing.

The statement by the Welfare Officer cited earlier implied that in Kampala, compared with Nairobi, the arrangement of housing gave more opportunities for himself and others to come into contact with each other irrespective of grade. In practice such interaction is limited to specific situations and specific forms as we shall see. This is even the case when, as happens, people of different grades or status are neighbours. Among those living next door to each other or in a cluster of houses there is a general assumption that they will become good friends, and relationships of friendship and solidarity between neighbours frequently occur. Wives gossip together, help each other with babies, and let their children play with one another. The men accompany each other to bars or to football matches, and if one gives a party he is expected to invite those living around him. Failure to do so is taken as an expression of social distance and hostility. If one man has a car he is expected to offer lifts, to hospital, to town, to fetch and carry visitors from other parts of Kampala. If, as occasionally happens, one family has a television set, then all the neighbouring wives and children have to be invited in to watch. Sometimes neighbours drawn together by such informal ties associate more formally in cliques of the kind I describe later. The fulfilment of neighbourly obligations, however, depends as much on social as spatial proximity. When neighbours are of different status, interaction tends to be minimal, as infrequent as is consistent with living at peace with people with whom one may have to share a lavatory or washing or cooking facilities. On the part of those living in houses below their status there is always the hope and expectation of a rapid move, by hook or by crook. Those in housing above their entitlement are almost always supposed to have got there through some malpractice, and not through a freak of the allocation system. They are avoided because of this and because of differences of occupation, grade or income, and therefore look outside their circle of neighbours for friends and associates. The situation is not unlike that reported by Parkin (1969a: Chapter 3) for Kampala East.

Possessions. That status may be expressed through the possession of material goods goes virtually without saying. Among railwaymen and other urban workers the acquisition of consumer durable goods eats up a large part of earnings. Certain items, in particular suits, sofa sets and sewing machines, are accorded especial status and increasingly the classic status symbols of Western civilisation – the refrigerator, the car and the TV set – are becoming of interest to well-to-do urban Africans. For railwaymen the days when a man's prestige could be enhanced by owning a bike or a radio are gone forever. This is illustrated in Table 33 which gives the percentage owning

TABLE 33. *Possession of household goods by status*

Item	Percentage owning item among		
	Whole sample	High status	Low status
Bed	100.0	100.0	100.0
Stove	81.0	89.0	74.1
Watch	66.0	89.0	45.2
Suit	64.0	89.0	42.0
Radio	60.5	74.0	48.5
Sofa set	41.5	74.0	12.9
Clock	36.2	44.4	29.1
Bike	36.2	41.6	32.4
Sewing machine	27.6	41.6	16.2
Record player	13.8	18.5	6.5
Motorbike/scooter/car	12.1	22.2	3.2
TV/fridge	3.5	7.4	–

each of several items within two status groups in the Nsambya sample. The average number of individual items possessed by those of low status was 4.3, of high status 8.8.

The significance of clothing as an item of expenditure and its relationship to status may be seen in the fact that 89% of high-status men owned at least one suit, and many more than one. There is a Swahili proverb – *mwanamke ni nguo* – a woman is her clothes – which is often quoted in contexts where it is clear that men are included. The emphasis on clothing as a sign of social pretensions is often satirised in Swahili and Luganda popular songs. In the quarrel between the driver and guard referred to in

Chapter 4 the former tore the latter's shirt. The meaning of this gesture was clear in another quarrel between a man not apparently wealthy and another dressed smartly in white shirt and tie. The former shouted, in Swahili, 'Who do you think you are lording it about (*kujivuna*). Do you think that I don't have a shirt and a tie like you?' Even those who do not have a suit have a best outfit consisting of a good pair of trousers, a white shirt, tie and black leather shoes. Few railwaymen when off work wear khaki shorts, vests or tyre sandals – all items which figure largely in the official 'African cost of living index' published annually.

Clothing is associated with a particular style of behaviour – being a 'gentleman', in Swahili *gent*, plural *magent*. Connected with this are two other terms, *smart* and *style*, which are used even by those who have little English. A gentleman dresses smartly in style. Style means something of unusual design or quality – it can also refer to outstanding, even odd, behaviour. Railwaymen are well aware of the varieties of quality available in clothing and it is considered more prestigeful to wear something imported from the UK than similar, cheaper articles manufactured locally or in Japan or Hong Kong. A gentleman is judged not only by his dress, however, but by his behaviour. He does not engage in bar brawls over women, for example. The emphasis on personal appearance extends to the use of cosmetics – powders, expensive after-shave lotions, and face-lightening creams which claim to make those with black faces browner and, it is believed, more attractive. It may well be thought that the stereotypical association of high status and cleanliness is not unfounded in reality.

Food and drink. The higher income of high-status people naturally allows them a more varied diet, including more protein foods – milk, butter, eggs, meat and fish – and a wider range of starches with bread, rice and potatoes supplementing maize, millet and plantain. There is some tendency to prefer 'European' foods, a habit which is again satirised in one song: 'The clerks at Nairobi at the end of the month [i.e. payday] eat European food, but by the middle of the month they are in debt and eating African style again.' Since at Nsambya many can now afford non-African food, there is perhaps less prestige attached to this tendency than there may have been formerly.

We saw earlier that *watu wa juu* are sometimes described as 'fat' or 'well-fed'. It follows that the external characteristic is taken as a sign of status. Fat men are, almost by definition, believed to be rich men. A food metaphor is used to describe a big spender – he 'eats' his money. A big man is also judged by the lavishness of his hospitality, and by the kind of meal he prepares for his guests. There is a traditional hierarchy of animals: in ascending order, chicken, duck, sheep, goat, bull. The preparation of one rather than another indicates both the host's wealth and the value he puts on his guests.

A wide range of items are judged in status terms, including tobacco and alcohol. In the lowest echelons smokers appear content with a manufactured cigarette with black tobacco, such as 'Kali', which retails at 50 cents for twenty (1965 price). Higher up they smoke 'Sportsman', and there are yet more expensive brands. The quantity consumed and the amount bought at one time also varies, for cigarettes may be purchased singly or in packets. A man with aspirations to social status would not buy one 'Kali' with a few cents change. Drinking, or rather social drinking, is the major leisure-time activity indulged in by the majority of railwaymen. Only 25% of the Nsambya sample claimed not to drink regularly, equally distributed in each status group. There are some religion sects which forbid both smoking and drinking, e.g. the 'Saved Ones', but their influence is small.

Alcoholic beverages available locally can be divided into four categories: African home-brewed spirits (*waragi*); African beers made from maize, millet, banana and virtually any other argricultural product; European factory-bottled beer, mainly lagers; and European manufactured spirits and fortified wines. The categories represent a progression of both cost and status. In the sample the proportion of high-status people drinking *waragi* was 22%, but European beers 74%. Among the low-status the figures were 50% and 46.9% respectively. Those drinking African beers were: high-status 40.6%, low-status 69%. It is clearly an over-simplification to state that high-status people never indulge in African beers, though few risk the rigours of *waragi*. To understand this we must digress to consider the organisation of drinking in the urban area.

African beer such as *malwa*, a millet beer, is usually brewed by the wife in the home. The husband may then invite his friends in to drink with him. Some unskilled workers actually brew on a commercial scale, using their homes as unofficial, and illegal bars. Their clients are usually members of their own ethnic group, especially those working in the same section. Higher-status people either brew privately or send out to buy the stuff prepared by the lower-status workers. Sometimes they monopolise one brewer. For example, a group of Luhya trades union officials used to gather on Sundays at the house of the permanent clerk to the branch who lived nearby the estate and who ran a small *malwa* business at weekends. In this way higher-status individuals and cliques indulge their taste for African beer, which they may justify by reference to the 'traditional African way of life', and at the same time maintain social distance from others.

There are a number of full-time and legal bars selling African beer in the vicinity of Nsambya, only one of which is at all popular with railwaymen. There are also four 'European' bars. The analysis of bar visiting involves several considerations – the choice of bar, the people who go drinking together, the people who interact in the bar, and the relationship between customers and the bar-owner. The second and third aspects will be dealt with later. As to the first, it may be recorded that the bars in Kampala as a whole are graded in terms of a rough hierarchy. At the lowest level are the 'local bars', so-called because they draw their clientèle almost entirely from the neighbourhood in which they are situated. Outsiders rarely have occasion to use them. Then there are 'high-class bars', mainly to be found in the city centre, though some local bars, e.g. 'Superjet' at the Kiswa Estate, have graduated to this level by attracting important customers from outside. 'Superjet' had the advantage at that time of being owned by two professors from Makerere. Beyond these are bars in the centre which were formerly restricted to Europeans and Asians, and at the very top two exclusive clubs frequented by politicians, leading businessmen and others. In a slightly different category are the several nightclubs which give Kampala the reputation of a city of pleasure. The difference between the various levels exists in the facilities, especially the type of building, the quality of the furnishings, the presence of a juke-box and by the number and beauty of the barmaids, though at the higher levels these are replaced by barmen. They are also characterised by the quantity and range of the stock, and by their prices. The real significance for our present purpose is the variation in the social statuses of the clients. Among railwaymen the lower-status workers tend to get their beer at the Railway African Club, only occasionally using the bars at Nsambya market. For people of middle status – most clerks and many skilled men, for example – the practice is reversed. Some of the latter also roam farther afield. Attendance at bars beyond the local neighbourhood generally requires transport, a car of one's own or to which one has access, or money for a taxi. The need for transport derives not from the distance to the nearest high-class bar, but from the fact that it is the usual practice to be seen at several such bars in the course of an evening. There is what one might call a high-class bar circuit.

We may briefly mention here the position of the bar-owner, for the relationship between the publicans at Nsambya and their clients is of some significance in the local community. Since the bar-owner is able to give credit or to perform other services such as introducing customers to his barmaids he is able to place many of his clients in his debt. These are frequently ' paid ' in the form of services. Since the bar is a place to gossip he is also at the centre of a complex communications network. I found that

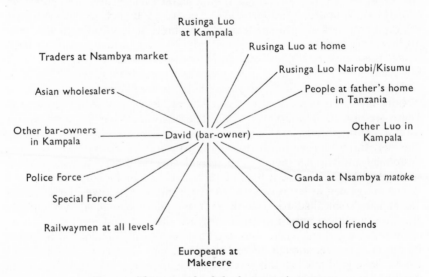

Fig. 10. The network of the bar-owner's contacts

the owner of one bar, a Luo who had been born at Nsambya, was one of the best-informed men in the area. His position is illustrated in Figure 10 which shows the extent of his contacts, through which he is, as it were, ' plugged in ' to a wide range of social groups at Nsambya and elsewhere. Individual customers can use his facilities in a variety of ways. For example, a railway-man requiring a service from a policeman, or a Luo from home looking for a railway job. Thus, one young man became friends with the owner's young brother. The latter persuaded his brother to approach the recruiting clerk of one of the sections for a job. The clerk was willing to oblige, partly because at the time he had political ambitions and saw the move as helpful to his cause. We will return to this episode in Chapter 7.

THE PROTOCOL OF GRADE

So far we have seen how high status defined in a general way as having a high rating according to such criteria as education, occupation, grade and income, is associated with a certain life-style. The grading system, however, in certain contexts, acts in a more specific way. This will be illustrated by reference to two episodes. The first was described in Chapter 4, viz. the Shedmaster's farewell party. Figure 7, which outlines the seating arrange-ments for this occasion, demonstrates the protocol which the grading system imposes. This extended at this event to the order in which the food and drink was distributed and to the matter of who was and was not invited. Those present included the senior staff of the Mechanical Engineering Depart-ment at Kampala, plus all those Africans at that time section heads at Kampala. Among Loco Shed workers almost all those in grade VII and above were invited and duly attended if only for a short time. No Group C men were there, and few of those in grades B XI–VIII, although both cate-gories had subscribed heavily for the occasion. Among the middle grade staff those principally excluded were the locomotive drivers, only one of the eight grade VI drivers being present. When I asked one of the guests why certain people whom I knew to be off-duty and available did not seem to be at the party, he replied that the organisers must have restricted invitations to keep out ' undesirables ' (*sic*). The example shows that while the grading system may impose an order of rank among a group of people it is by no means the only social consideration. It may be noted that two guests, myself and a station clerk were outsiders who joined the party on the strength of our respective relationships with one of the principal organisers.

The second example occurred relatively early in my fieldwork and estab-lished vividly the emphasis placed on relative status in this community. In theory every year, in practice less frequently, the EARH organises in each district athletics competitions between the departments. The following is an account of arrangements for the sports held at Kampala in July 1964.

The committee set up to run the event had as its chairman the District Welfare Officer with his principal Assistant as its secretary. The committee itself consisted of eight members, all Group B, the lowest grade X, the highest grade VI. The programme for the sports carried an impressive list of 'officials', the ranking among whom corresponded roughly with their relative positions in the EARH hierarchy. The chief umpires were the AGM and the DTS, both Superscale Europeans, and the Welfare Officer, African B III. The chief field judge was the Shedmaster, chief track judge the IRO. The time keeper was the Goods Agent, the official photographer, appropriately enough, the Public Relations Officer. The last three named were Africans in Group B, Division I. There were eight assistant field judges, mixed Asian and African, in the lower grades of Division I and upper grades of Division II. There were six assistant judges, six first aid attendants, two announcers and one prize steward, all Africans from Group B Division II. This does not complete the count, for on the day there were many more people wearing 'Official' badges than were listed on the programme. In fact the Estate Overseer was going round handing them out to such Group B staff as thought they should have one. I was offered one myself. All the competitors were Group C, though the team captains were Group B, and the only Group B who actually took part were a number of artisans summoned at the last moment from the Loco Shed to add weight to their department's side in the tug-of-war.

Both these events, though outside the work context, were very much in its shadow. They were also occasions of some formality, organised not to say stage-managed. To what extent does the protocol implied by such formal occasions extend into more informal, less heavily-structured situations? The answer to this question has been foreshadowed first in the discussion of the roles emanating from the occupancy of a post and secondly in the analysis of neighbourliness. In both contexts, it was implied, railwaymen are highly conscious of status factors. In the latter discussion it was suggested that sometimes a set of neighbours would formalise their relationship to the extent of becoming a clique. This aspect deserves a more thorough investigation.

CLIQUES AND NETWORKS

Network and small group analysis has already proved to be a fruitful source of data and hypotheses in urban African studies.[3] Network analysis in particular has been pursued with great rigour, for example in the theoretical contributions of Barnes and Mitchell, and in the application of certain techniques to ethnographic data as in the work of Kapferer.[4] Nevertheless it poses a large number of as yet unresolved, and perhaps insoluble, problems. One of the difficulties, as a leading practitioner has noted, is that of distinguishing qualitatively between the different kinds of relationships that 'ego' maintains with different individuals in his network (Epstein 1969: 124). A social network can provide us with a map of the range of ego's contacts and the extent of interaction between those in the network – its density, and there are methods available for the measurement and comparison of both range and density. More frequently, however, it is the content of relations that are our chief concern, and network analysis as yet has been unable to apply rigorous methods to this. In attempting to understand the significance of status factors in informal interaction, therefore, it is perhaps more useful to concentrate on small groups of individuals who maintain frequent contact with each other, rather than the full range of ego's social contacts. What I mean by these small groups or cliques appears to be similar to what Epstein calls on one occasion an 'effective network' which consists of 'clusters of persons fairly closely knitted together' (Epstein 1961: 57). In a later publication he refers to 'sets' of people among whom 'the exchange of gossip denotes a certain community of interest: it marks off the "set" from others of whose intimate affairs they are ignorant' (Epstein 1969: 125). The term 'gossip set' is in fact used by Parkin, though primarily with reference to small, regularly interacting groups of women neighbours (Parkin 1969a: 67).

Any railwayman maintains a wide range of social contacts both in town, and as we have seen, in the rural areas. At Nsambya he selects from these a small number as close associates and friends who in turn often associate with each other, forming a clique. People on the estate are very conscious of the existence of these cliques, and they are often referred to by the English word 'group', or the equivalent in other languages. There is, for example, a Luo word *gikwanyore* which describes those who set themselves apart as a clique. The solidarity of a clique's membership is expressed in a number of ways, not least by self-identification as 'our group'. Clique members often take up certain words, phrases and gestures and incorporate them into a private language, their conversation being frequently allusive and elliptic. Among small groups of Luo the private language is developed into a fine art by a series of linguistic devices which transform the orthodox language into something incomprehensible to outsiders. I once sat with a Luo overhearing a conversation between two other Luo which continued for about half an hour during which time my friend did not understand a single sentence spoken. This was in rural Kenya, and I never came across such an example in Kampala where, as we shall see, many small groups are interethnic.

Among the members of a clique there is frequently a complex network of debt, and perhaps 'common property', e.g. a car owned by one but used by all. Often the clique becomes a decision-making unit with the strategy and tactics of social interaction – either of the group as a whole or of an individual member – discussed in great detail. Their approach to this resembles contingency planning in that a wide range of possible combinations of response and counter-response are worked out in advance of any social event, as was shown in part in the discussion of David's search for a wife recorded in Chapter 3. The military analogy is not inapt since one kind of activity, the seduction of a woman, is often referred to as a 'campaign'. Since the discussion of what action to take in a social situation involves the consideration of right and proper as well as effective behaviour it is perhaps in the clique that the relevance of general principles to particular instances is most frequently formulated. Moreover, although a clique member can expect support from his friends if he is in conflict with others he has to make out a case for their support, i.e. demonstrate that he is in the right. He cannot expect them to follow him in any action he decides to take.

The clique can apparently veto any course he proposes to follow and should he ignore them they may expel him permanently or temporarily. In so far as he wishes to retain his membership the clique can therefore exert some control over a member. In this way it becomes one of the informal mechanisms through which social control operates in the urban area. Much of this control is directed towards behaviour in public places such as bars and dance halls, and this may be one of the reasons why they are less boisterous than they might be.

Table 34 gives particulars of some fourteen cliques at Nsambya on which I have detailed information. The numbers in each vary from two to six, with an average of between four and five. The period of duration of a clique is variable, and is effected by such factors as the transfer rate. Cliques (x), (xi), (xii) and (xiii) lasted for shorter periods than the others which had considerable continuity during fieldwork. Occasionally an individual belongs to more than one clique, but this poses a problem for one cannot have more than one set of 'best friends'. Members of one clique, of course, have contacts with others, for example, (iii), (iv), (v) and (vi) are linked with each other because of their jobs, (ix) and (iii) and (x) and (xiii) through pairs of kinsmen, and so on. Figure 11 shows how each clique is linked to others, though no attempt is made to distinguish between ties of kinship, friendship or neighbourhood or those which derive from interaction in the work process. If further information were available it would be possible to show how most railwaymen are integrated into a fairly dense network of cliques of the kind illustrated by Figure 11.

Turning to the factors underlying clique composition, Table 34 shows that all are composed of men who are of roughly equal status in terms of education, occupation and grade and hence income. Many of the cliques are also based on a work unit – subsection or section and sometimes department. Clique members are also usually within the same age group, a factor not shown in the table. This is consistent with activities since much discussion centres around sexual matters and in accordance with custom men feel great diffidence in broaching such topics in the presence of others much older or younger than themselves. Table 34 also shows the average status score of the members in each clique and a measurement of average status crystallisation. This value, which is discussed further below, measures the degree of consistency between an individual's rating on each of the main status variables. Ten of the fourteen groups contained members whose crystallisation of status attributes was absolute. In the case of three other groups (engine drivers, TTEs and guards) the individual members shared a mutual incongruence of statuses, for example, all the drivers have high pay and grade but low educational and occupational status.

It seems that the selection of friends is determined largely by reference to status factors. In another publication (Grillo forthcoming) where the composition of clique (x) is discussed in detail, I show how members use status arguments and criteria to include and exclude potential members, and that a claim to equality and friendship by reference to an ethnic tie may be rejected if the claimant is of a lower status. However, among those of equal

TABLE 34. *The composition of cliques at Nsambya*

Number	Occupations	Grade	Education	Ethnic composition	Status score	Status congruence
(i)	Labourers in Goods Shed	Group C	Illiterate	All Acholi	10	100
(ii)	Compound Cleaners	Group C	Illiterate	All Ankole	10	100
(iii)	Firemen	Group C	Primary	Luhya (Wanga)	30	100
(iv)	Firemen	Group C	Primary	Luhya (Samia)	30	100
(v)	Firemen	Group C	Primary	Luo (Alego)	30	100
(vi)	Drivers	B VI–VII	Illiterate	Luo, Luhya, Ganda	55	41
(vii)	TTEs	B VII–VIII	Intermediate	Soga, Toro, Acholi, Tanzanian	70	72
(viii)	Guards	B VII–VIII	Intermediate	Soga, Toro	70	72
(ix)	Clerks, all unionists	B VII–IX	Intermediate/Secondary	Luhya, Samia, Toro	65	79
(x)	DTS Clerks	B VI–VII	Secondary	Luo, Luhya, Samia	70	100
(xi)	CxR, IRO	B II–IV	Secondary	Taita, Gisu	90	100
(xii)	Another IRO, an ATS, a Clerk	B II–IV	Higher	Lango, Tanzanian	90	100
(xiii)	Welfare Officer, PRO	B II–IV	Secondary	Luhya	90	100
(xiv)	Goods Agent, Station Master	B I–III	Secondary	Luo (Gem)	90	100

High Status

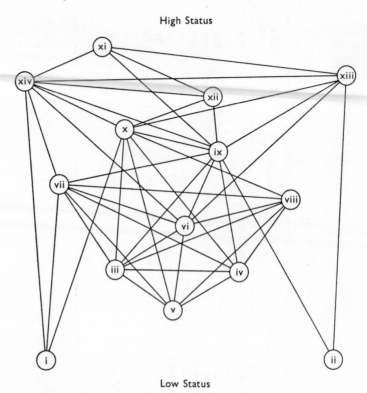

Low Status

Fig. 11. Clique linkages among railwaymen (for clique identities, see Table 34 on p. 107).

status ethnic differences do emerge as criteria differentiating between cliques. For example, among firemen there are three cliques listed, each based on a different area of origin. Common ethnic identity in this respect does not link individuals across the status boundaries.

STATUS INCONGRUENCE

Throughout the previous discussion of the life-styles of high- and low-status individuals it was assumed for convenience that there is a high degree of consistency or congruence between the individual's rating on each of the four status variables, viz. grade, income, occupation and education. As we have already seen this is not necessarily the case. The theory of status incongruence, or its converse crystallisation, has been extensively discussed by sociologists, particularly by Lenski, who noted: 'The structure of human groups normally involves the coexistence of a number of parallel vertical hierarchies which usually are imperfectly correlated with one another' (Lenski 1954: 405). Lenski devised a method by which an index of the degree of status crystallisation for any individual could be calculated. This has been applied to the respondents in the Nsambya sample.[5] A score of 100, representing complete congruence of status ratings, was achieved by only 15% of the sample, but 69% had scores of 80 or more, a figure which in terms of the sample may be taken to represent a relatively high degree of crystallisation. Those with low crystallisation scores who included both high- and low-status individuals could be divided into two main categories: those whose educational attainments were much higher than their grade, occupation or income (28% of those with crystallisation scores below 80) and those whose income and grade were much higher than their educational level (61%). The latter category consisted almost entirely of skilled workers, the former of unskilled and semi-skilled.

The average scores for each occupational group were: supervisors 83; white-collar 78; skilled 69; semi-skilled 77; unskilled 86. This quantitative evidence which shows that skilled men as a whole have a relatively low degree of status crystallisation merely underlines what we learned in Chapter 4 concerning the position of the skilled worker and his relationship with white-collar men. The disagreements and conflict between the two groups may be understood in terms of status incongruence. The language of their arguments illustrates this with the white-collar workers emphasising that element of status on which they score heavily, education, and underlining this by pointing up the ' illiteracy ' of skilled men. By suggesting that the latter ' waste ' their money on drink they undermine that aspect on which the skilled men rank higher. In turn the latter downvalue the occupational prestige of the clerks by questioning the virility of those performing office work.

The small number of workers, 8.5% of the sample as a whole, whose educational qualifications are higher than their other status attributes, do not emerge as a distinct group in the community. They are individuals who are in many respects the victims of changing circumstance. Their length of service, about four years, is much lower than average and they for the most part joined the EARH during the period of educational expansion and falling job opportunities. In most cases had they joined five years earlier they could probably have obtained significantly better positions. As an example of their situation we will consider the case of Francis. In 1965 he was in his early twenties having left school some four years earlier just before he would have taken his Cambridge School Certificate (CSC). He had joined the EARH as a Group C clerk and had been posted to the Parcels Office. His post had previously been established in Group BI grade XI, but had been downgraded. Francis was one of the very few clerks in Group C, a fact which naturally affected his income and place of residence relative to the majority of his occupational group – he earned 210s. per month and lived in a class 7 (i) house. He was continuing his education by correspondence course with a view to improving his position and did eventually succeed in obtaining the CSC. All these factors placed him apart from other workers in his subsection and his neighbourhood on the estate as did his private interests. For he was fond of European music – he had a considerable collection of long-playing records – and of art, he painted in his spare time. The pursuit of these interests took him outside the community, bringing him into contact with the fringes of artistic and literary circles in Kampala. He believed, as we saw in statements by him cited earlier, that his fellow workers in the Parcels Office resented his pretensions, as they saw them, and were envious of him. He for his part mostly avoided their company, never drinking with them, and had few close friends on the estate. Others saw him as a 'proud man' (see below) acting above his status. At work he strongly urged his own views and interpretations against those of his superiors and deprecated what he considered to be their lack of intelligence. This naturally led him into conflict with his section head who complained that Francis paid him no respect or deference. He commented that Francis considered himself superior because he spoke 'Indian English', i.e. with more fluency than most Africans. Francis in his turn felt that the section head picked on him, and indeed found himself with several 'letters of explanation' to answer.

The admittedly somewhat extreme case of Francis illustrates a point made by Lenski who refers to the individual with a low degree of status crystallisation as a 'particular type of marginal man' (1954: 412). In the short run, at any rate, the number of individuals in a similar situation to Francis is likely to increase as educational standards rise. There could in consequence emerge a considerable group of individuals who have higher educational attainments or, as they would perhaps see it, 'intelligence', than most of their superiors. How they deal with this situation could make an interesting study. This point relates to an association found by Lenski, though contested by others, between low crystallisation and 'political liberalism' – Lenski's interpretation of support for Democratic candidates in presidential elections in the USA in the early fifties. It is tempting to test this hypothesis in the African context, though the definition of 'political liberalism' poses many problems. It could be argued, for example, that support for independence in Uganda and Kenya was strongest among educated white-collar workers, i.e. among men whose status on two dimensions was inconsistent with their status as third-class citizens. Within the Nsambya sample itself the only possible measure of 'liberalism' which appears to be available is membership of the trade union. As will be shown in Chapter 7 union membership is greatest among low-status workers, but holding status constant there appears to be a slightly greater tendency towards union membership among high-status workers with a low degree of status crystallisation. This in turn seems to be associated with occupational group, for while union membership among clerks and supervisors is a relatively low 32%, among skilled men, including those in high grades, it is 71%. As we saw in Chapter 4 skilled workers certainly felt strongly that organisation through a union or association was necessary for the advancement of their interests, and in Chapter 7 we will see how this emerges as a theme in union politics. In a tenuous way Lenski's hypothesis seems to hold. In another respect, however, this finding runs counter to what occurs elsewhere. For Lenski and others have noted a tendency towards withdrawal from associational activity among respondents with low crystallisation scores. Nevertheless where there exist institutions which seem able to ameliorate their status, such people might also become active in them. Interestingly, those in the sample with both high status and low crystallisation scores seem to be more actively involved in the leadership of urban associations in general. Some 50% of those in this category were so engaged compared with 23% of other high-status people. As we shall see in Chapter 7, in Kampala prominence in associations is one of the ways in which an individual can enhance his status. It also seems that at Nsambya, as we saw in an earlier section, those with low crystallisation do not always withdraw completely from interaction, though Francis was perhaps an example of this response, but cluster together in small cliques consisting largely of those whose status situation, including degree of crystallisation, is similar.

The concept of status incongruence would seem to have something in common with another theoretical concept, relative deprivation, since both relate to the perception and evaluation of self and others in status terms. Though both may be treated as analytically distinct, the same response – for example Joseph's attempt to acquire a better class of house – could be treated as an example of either. Discrepancy between house entitlement and actual allocation is indeed a frequent source of status incongruence for skilled workers, as we have seen, which simply adds to the load they must already bear.

STATUS AND REPUTATION

At the beginning of this chapter it was stated that it would be necessary to draw a distinction between an individual's status, his standing as measured by his rating on the prestige variables, and his reputation, the respect he has in the eyes of others in the community. This distinction relates to a central issue, the relationship between alignments of status generated by the industrial framework and those which derive from the ethnic system. In Chapter 3 we saw that continuing involvement in extra-town ties forces the individual to maintain active relationships with people from his area of origin and by extension with those from his ethnic group. Given that the assertion of common origin is a claim to solidarity and equality (cf. Grillo forthcoming) and that the assertion of a difference of status implies inequality and social distance, what happens when two individuals are in a multiplex relationship in which either principle may be asserted? We will examine this by reference to a number of cases in which this appears to happen. Some of these refer to an important concept which we have already seen applied to one person, Francis, namely, the concept of ' pride '.

The first case involves a man, Wellington, who, at the time of the following episode, had recently been transferred from Kampala to a larger depot in Kenya where he held the post of RSF Grade VI. He was a Luo, about fifty years old. One day at Nsambya the drivers up from Kenya brought the news that Wellington was dead. He had apparently collapsed one night when alone in his house and his body was discovered the following morning. These were held to be suspicious circumstances, and soon opinion crystallised around the view that he had been killed, probably by witchcraft. It was

rumoured that during the Kenya Emergency he had denounced many people
to the authorities as Mau Mau and had in this way earned his promotion.
He was said to have been worried about his transfer to a depot in Kenya
where there were so many Kikuyu. Gossip also revealed that his behaviour
in recent months had been that of a ' man who would die soon '. He had
treated his subordinates very badly, banging his desk with his fist and
abusing them. Some of his drivers apparently refused to contribute to his
collection. One of the RSFs at Kampala commented: ' They say he was
prouding. He was a *lonely* man. If you don't mix where people are they say
you are proud.' In the end, among those who accepted a belief in witchcraft,
there was agreement that Wellington had been bewitched by one of his
subordinates as a consequence of his performance in the post to which he
had been promoted. Since he himself had formerly been a driver he was
accused of abusing those with whom he had previously worked on terms of
equality.

Some of the issues raised by this case will be discussed in the next chapter;
here I want to concentrate on the themes of ' pride ' and ' loneliness '. The
word ' pride ', which in Luo and Luhya has the same root *sung*, was frequently used to describe the behaviour of those maintaining social distance
in the face of some claim to equality or solidarity. Take, for example,
Jeremiah, who was a section head at Kampala. He had been recently
promoted to this position, a fact of which he was very conscious, saying:
' I was sent by the EARH to be the first African —— at Kampala, and I am
determined to do my job properly.' He kept his word to the extent that his
staff complained bitterly, especially on the hard line he took over disciplinary matters. He insisted on the strict protocol attached to his position.
On one occasion a junior supervisor of one of his subsections, who was also
a fellow clansman, wandered into his office. Jeremiah shouted at him to get
out and not come in without permission. On another occasion he ordered
a man from his own ethnic group to get on with his work. The latter ignored
the order and continued chatting to his girl friend. Jeremiah charged the
man and had him dismissed. In this way he built up a reputation as a
' proud ' man, and added to this by boasting about the prowess of his
children, one of whom had gone to study in the UK. In fact he had some
sympathisers, for on the two occasions noted above it was felt that he had
been provoked. That is, the two recipients of his wrath were thought to have
overstepped the line of tolerable behaviour.

People such as supervisors are, of course, in especially difficult positions
so far as their home people are concerned, and both sides realise this. There
appears to emerge a compromise in which neither party strays too far from
solidarity or too close to equality in the handling of their relationship. It is
the strong denial of solidarity and the assertion of inequality which pro-
vokes the accusation of pride. This happened in the case of a Luhya from
Ebunyore Location who achieved promotion to the post of Welfare Officer.
This man, James, whose views on social differentiation were cited earlier,
did not always follow his precept of keeping in contact with Group C
workers. In particular he seemed to avoid former friends and relatives from

his home area of whom there were several on the estate. When James attained his high status he became, as one of them put it, ' a lonely man, a man who walked alone ', who no longer drank at Nsambya but ' went up there, to the bars in the city '. Unfortunately James' enjoyment of the good life ran him into debt, he was tempted by the Welfare funds which he held, stole them and was arrested. He was tried and sentenced to eighteen months' imprisonment. At the time of his arrest he was approached by a delegation of his home people who asked if they could help. He replied, ' only if you have money to get me a lawyer '. This remark so offended them that they lost all interest in the case, and though his father came up from Kenya to rally support, and actually got a small committee going, they provided only desultory assistance.

A relative of James, Jackson, whose problems are considered in more detail in the next chapter, was also an example of a man thought by the lower-status members of his Location and ethnic group to be lonely and proud. He was a Grade VII clerk and he very rarely joined with them in drinking and never invited them to his house. Sometimes he failed even to greet them when they met in passing on the estate. He had, moreover, married outside the ethnic group, taking as wife an educated Ganda girl, and the children of the marriage could speak more Ganda than Luhya. Unfortunately one of their children died as an infant and although the mother wished the baby to be buried at her home Jackson accepted the advice of an old and respected railwayman from his home area to hold the funeral at Nsambya cemetery. This man organised the funeral, persuading several people from the home Location to act as gravediggers, and engaging the services of another man from home, who was active in the Africa Israel church, to say prayers. At the funeral hymns were sung and a short speech made in which Jackson was urged in future to pay more attention to those from his home area.

It is significant that one of the accusations levelled at Jackson was that he never supported his close relatives at home and that he had not even sent ' ten shillings to his mother '. His behaviour may be contrasted with that of a number of other people. For example, Joseph, the RSF, was a man who, for the most part, commanded immense respect from his subordinates at work and from members of his ethnic group on the estate. This derived in part from the care with which he handled problems of discipline at work – it will be recalled that he preferred to ' square matters ' outside work – and the extent to which he was willing to help people from his home area, getting them employment, sending money for local projects such as a school, and so on. Yet they deferred to his superior status and allowed him to main- tain his closest friendships among men of equal status to himself. Similarly there was Graham, a Luo Grade VI clerk, who was a neighbour of Jackson, who was said by many to be ' the most respected Luo at Nsambya ' who at one time had been a senior official in the RAU(U). Yet Graham had married a girl from Toro and he, too, maintained a close circle of friends of his own status. On the other hand, he was known as a man who made every effort to support his relatives at home and who was actively involved in the affairs of his Location, being a prominent member of his association which used to meet occasionally in his house.

Another much respected man was Christopher, a Luhya Grade IX clerk who was a prominent union officer. Many people from his home area, Wanga Location, worked at Nsambya, including his younger brother, Geoffrey, who was a semi-skilled worker in Group C. Each had his own circle of friends, Christopher being a member of clique (ix) in Table 34, and Geoffrey in clique (iii), and their activities frequently took them into separate social circles. There was, however, apparently no conflict between them. Christopher had fulfilled all the obligations expected of an elder brother, paying Geoffrey's school fees, letting him have a bed in his house, finding him a job on the railways. At the same time, he, Christopher, never stressed his distance either from his brother or other Wanga people. For example, on one occasion when drinking in the Railway African Club he was approached by an engine driver up from Kenya, still in his work clothes and the worse for drink, who turned out to be his ' mother's brother ' and who requested a dance. As they waltzed around the bar Christopher explained loudly that this was an example of the ' African way of life '. Interestingly Christopher was later given a scholarship to study ' industrial relations ' in the UK for a period of three months. Prior to his return there was considerable speculation on what this would do to his behaviour which was in the event watched very closely. It was noted at once that he arrived at the estate sitting in the back of a large white taxi from which he produced several new suitcases, filled with clothes and books that he had bought abroad. In his first days at home he went around wearing a new suit and carrying an umbrella. He went to the bar for a drink, but kept looking at his watch and asserted that he had to go quickly to an important meeting. All this provoked the immediate comment among both Luhya and Luo that the trip had made him ' very proud ', as they expected it would. However, after a short while he dropped what was seen to be pretentious behaviour and reverted to his more usual style.

Christopher's behaviour on his return from the UK was not categorised as just an example of pride, however. For it was felt to indicate a status higher than that which he had acquired. As we saw earlier Francis was the subject of a similar accusation, as was Alexander. The latter, it may be recalled, was the supervisor of the Carriage Cleaning subsection who because of his work was nicknamed the ' shitman '. His habit of going to work in a white suit and solar topee was described by the Luo word *okaore* which it will be remembered Francis himself paraphrased as a man who is ' *chini* trying to be *juu* '.

If a man in a high status wishes to have a good reputation he must avoid the pitfalls of pride and pretension. Pride is more than an attitude, however, since in many of the cases we have considered it emerges as the converse of maintaining obligations to kinsmen and friends from the home areas. It may be asked why high-status individuals should concern themselves with their reputation among lower-status members of their own ethnic group. This question has already been answered in Chapter 3, for it comes to the same, in this context, as the question why individuals maintain links with their rural areas of origin. More than this, as we shall see in Chapter 7, many of those at least in the middle-status regions, especially clerks in grades IX to VII, need a good reputation to further their chances of advancement in urban associations such as ethnic unions and the trade union, advancement which in itself is a means of acquiring prestige and power in the urban situation and fame in the rural areas.

In sum it may be said that many people both of high and low status agree to operate in terms of a compromise between solidarity and distance. Respect goes to those high-status people who do not impose their superiority in relationships and who fulfil what might be thought of as their patronal obligations. It is the content of their transactions with those of lower status, particularly from their own ethnic group and especially from their home locations and sublocations, which comes under scrutiny. It may be added that a similar ideal model of appropriate behaviour applies to any relationships in which distance is tempered by some form of solidarity. For example, Wellington was criticised for abusing those who had formerly been his colleagues, Joseph was praised for his relationships with his subordinates at work, irrespective of their ethnic group. In so far as individuals follow this ideal model the structural consequences are that those in high and low status are in a kind of patron-client relationship, though the analogy should not be pressed too far, and thus those at different social levels are linked in mutual interdependence.

CLASS

The final category of social differentiation that we shall consider here is that of class. Classes, which may be defined as sets of people in a similar relationship to the distribution of power, are potentially conflict groups since the interests of each class in a society are usually incompatible. The theory of class is complicated, subtle, and replete with specialised jargon, and the material to be presented here will no more than scrape the surface of the issues. We will concentrate on a single problem : to what extent is there among railwaymen any indication of a recognition of a class interest?

In Chapter 4 it was mentioned that a distinction is often drawn, especially by union officials, between management (*Bwana Relwe*) and railway workers. The boundary between the two is not clear-cut, indeed in some respects the concepts are best considered as rallying cries rather than as social categories. Nevertheless the identification of those in each category is a problem both for the union and for management. This problem was in 1964/5 rendered pressing by the changing situation. In the years before independence the lines of industrial conflict had largely coincided with those of racial and anti-colonial conflict. With the coming of independence and the implementation of Africanisation policies Africans began to move into positions in the industry previously occupied by Europeans. Both unions and management, therefore, were faced with finding an alternative frame of reference for determining loyalties in disputes and conflict. The unions were presented with the specific problem that some of its own officers were being promoted to posts in the EARH where it was thought that their loyalty to the union might conflict with their loyalty to the administration. As a result it was suggested, though never officially incorporated into the constitution, that while any African might become a union member, those in grade B V and above might not hold office. Note that they drew the line between Division I and Division II of the grading system, thus defining a class model by reference to a status system. In general terms the management followed the same principle, as we shall see, though drawing the boundary at a different point.

Some consequences of the union's position may be noted. Among the criteria which differentiate posts in the industry is relative position in the chain of command, and there is a *prima facie* case for supposing that the workers whose interests come closest to those of management are the supervisors and others responsible for order and discipline, whose job it is to ensure that the work process is carried out in accordance with the regulations. Such workers are found at all levels, including Group C, where they are usually called headmen, and in the lower grades of Group B, for example, Carriage Cleaning Supervisor, Grade VIII. The union clearly expects such people to have a primary loyalty not to the management, but to the workers. On the other hand, those in grade V and above not in supervisorial positions, and this includes many clerks and other workers such as engine drivers, are expected to be in the reverse position. We may recall here the comments by the RSF Joseph who said that in his present post he would have to join a strike or suffer the consequences, but if he had been Shedmaster ('really a foreman') he would stay at work. Thus the union, and others, would seem to define classes not just by reference to the distribution of power. They distinguish, at least, between those with more or less powerful and important positions.

The management, too, used a similar framework for defining loyalties as the following will show. During 1964 the three African Railway Unions in Kenya and Uganda had been pressing their demands, including a pay-rise, on the administration. By November negotiations had broken down and the unions prepared their members for strike action. The administration responded with appeals in the press, over the radio and in leaflets, two of which were issued, one in English addressed to Group B, another in Swahili addressed to Group C. Extracts from both follow.

To all Group B staff: a message from the General Manager:
The Railway African Unions in Kenya and Uganda have stated that they are calling their members on strike on the 5th November 1964. This strike will be unconstitutional because it contravenes the Industrial Relations Machinery Agreement. Many of you in supervisory positions will be anxious to know to whom you should be loyal. You should be loyal to East Africa and the EARH which serves the public. All Group B staff are expected to show a high degree of responsibility and loyalty. They are not expected to strike. If they do their suitability as supervisors and managerial staff is doubtful. I should be very sorry indeed to see any of my

Group B staff on strike because a major stoppage of the . . . service would have very serious adverse effects on all East African people . . . A very fair offer has been made to increase the wages of Group C staff but it will not be possible to [increase] Group B salaries which already compare favourably with those of [other public services] . . . I appeal to you to continue to do your utmost to ensure that our essential services to the public are maintained.

To all workers in Group C: a message from Dr. Gakuo, General Manager: I wish to give you my opinion on the strike . . . The strike will be un-constitutional . . . For this reason, any man who leaves his work will do so without permission and might lose his job. Why leave work and lose money? Five million shillings are being offered to increase your wages. This will give many of you a big increase. No more can be offered. Even if you strike we cannot increase the amount offered. If you strike all you will do is be without wages for the whole period in which you strike and you might lose your job. For this reason I ask you to think of the EARH and all our fellow Africans. Take my advice and do not stop work.

It would be illuminating to reconstruct from these leaflets the images of Group B and Group C with which the GM and his advisers are operating. To Group B he appeals unambiguously and at length to their sense of *esprit de corps* and their sensitivity to the role of the EARH in the public service, while in the case of Group C such sentiments are mentioned but briefly. Both groups are threatened: Group C openly and simply (strike and be sacked), Group B more subtly. The threat to their aspirations (a strike on their part would reflect on the suitability for promotion) is devastatingly accurate in its assessment of the weak spot in Group B's defences, as we shall see in the next chapter. The strike threat of November 1964 was in the end averted (see Grillo forthcoming 1974, Chapter 5), but the expectation of industrial action forced many individuals in Group B to choose between two sides: management (and thus their class position) or the union (and hence the African labour force). For the most part they opted for manage-ment. It is perhaps only at times of industrial crises that class differences begin to emerge openly, and individuals have to demonstrate their allegiance. On the other hand, as the example of Jeremiah shows, differentiation in terms of power and authority within the African labour force is implicit in the day-to-day relationships between workers and supervisors. This, how-ever, raises questions beyond the scope of this monograph.

IS THE COMMUNITY STRATIFIED?

We have seen how differences of status are associated with distinct life-styles and how status structures relationships in both formal and informal interaction. In the preceding section it was also shown that under certain conditions the labour force begins to divide into two classes with divergent interests and loyalties. Leaving aside the issue of class differentiation, and concentrating on status, can we now answer the questions: is the community stratified, and if so, what are the strata?

This is far from being a simple problem since even to pose it implies a certain view of the nature of social structure and even if it may be agreed that it is a meaningful question very different answers might be obtained depending on the criteria employed. For example, should we take cognitive categories as the determinants of strata or interactional boundaries? If the categories, then whose perception and which principles of status should we accept? Figure 12, which is a composite model which attempts to integrate

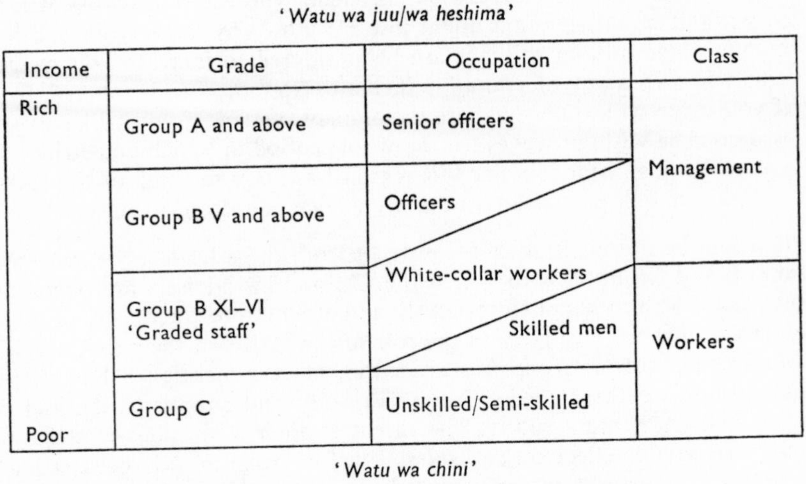

'Watu wa juu/wa heshima'

Income	Grade	Occupation	Class
Rich	Group A and above	Senior officers	
	Group B V and above	Officers	Management
	Group B XI–VI 'Graded staff'	White-collar workers / Skilled men	Workers
Poor	Group C	Unskilled/Semi-skilled	

'Watu wa chini'

Fig. 12. Class and status groups among railwaymen

all the variables we have considered, except education, into a single system, underlines some of the difficulties. Supposing the primary variable determining the strata is taken to be occupation, we might then conclude that there are four or five status groups. If grade is taken, then perhaps there are four, with boundaries which do not coincide with those derived from the occupational system. Then again, as the statements cited earlier in this chapter show, there is considerable variation in terms of the perception of the internal lines of stratification within the grading system particularly within Group B. For example, the category 'graded staff' may sometimes be stated to be divided into two or three subdivisions. If we take income, which unlike grade and occupation is a continuously distributed variable and not divisible into neat categories, we find a general distinction between 'rich' and 'poor' with little or no conceptualisation of any intermediate group. There seems to be, from the cognitive point of view, not one system of stratification but several, not one structure, but a multiplicity of structures.

It is clear that the community is *perceived* as stratified and individuals act in terms of models of stratification which vary according to the criteria relevant to a particular context or relationship or according to the position of the individual. Thus among clerks in Group B minute differences as between grade VI and grade VII, invisible or irrelevant to a man in Group C, are taken up as critical. Similarly when occupational or grade interest are at stake it is stratification by references to these criteria which are emphasised.

If interaction on the basis of equality is taken as the principal criterion in some respects a clearer picture emerges. For example, taking the cliques in Table 34 and Figure 11 there would seem to be a number of distinct social levels. At the top are the highly educated, high grade, well-paid officers – cliques (xi) to (xiv), while at the bottom are the unskilled illiterates in Group C, cliques (i) and (ii) with above them the semi-skilled apprentices, the firemen in cliques (iii) to (v). In the middle are numerous groups between whom there is equality in some respects, inequality in others. It must, however, be emphasised that the picture drawn here is relatively easy to perceive simply because only a few cliques have been enumerated. With a larger number of cliques the distinction between levels, the interactional boundaries, would become much more blurred. What can be said, perhaps, is that if any clique is taken it would be possible to isolate other cliques with which its members interacted in terms of equality and yet more which they would consider to be of higher or lower status in varying degrees. The community as a whole could be conceived of a series of overlapping fields of status equality. Unfortunately the demonstration of this would require more data than is available.

SOCIAL MOBILITY: STRATEGIES FOR SUCCESS AND RESPONSES TO FAILURE

So far our discussion has been largely synchronic in that it has analysed the position of a railwayman, his status and the groups with which he identifies, at one point in his career. That through time this position may change has been largely ignored, as has the fact that conditions within the industry itself are changing. Perhaps the most important change the individual experiences in the course of his working life is promotion from one post to another, which is frequently accompanied by transfer between depots. The significance of promotion as a channel of social mobility needs little emphasis after the discussion of status in the previous chapter. Railwaymen accept both that grade, occupation and income provide measurements of relative rank and that the individual can and should advance his social standing relative to others by upward mobility within the industry. Since the opportunities for such advancement are limited, a competitive element is built into relationships at work, and this spills over into the extra-industrial context. A ' big man ' has achieved his status by competing successfully against others, and those who have not attained promotion when opportunities exist are deemed to be failures. Since the rewards, both material and social, are considerable, it is not surprising that competition for advancement is usually aggressive and sometimes violent. Throughout the history of the labour force promotion has been available in some form for at least some Africans, but as we have already seen, during the period of the present study political and social changes created a novel situation in which the opportunity for rapid advancement became available to thousands of workers. Here we will document some of the consequences of that change.

In the first half of this chapter we will examine the careers open to various groups of railwaymen, and how advancement may be attained. This is followed by a discussion of responses to success and failure. Since post, grade and occupation place the individual in a nexus of relationships of equality, subordination and superiority, a change in his standing as measured by reference to these variables entails a change in his position within the community and calls for a restructuring of his personal relationships. Much of the material relates directly and indirectly to the problems posed by this.

For many railwaymen a normal working life involves a steady progression within a particular career. For most specialised occupational groups there is a recognised hierarchy of posts, spread over the railway network, which are linked in what I shall term a 'promotion ladder', a phrase which reflects the Swahili *daraja*, which literally means 'stairway', but which also means 'rank', and by extension, promotion. Promotion ladders vary in their length, their starting and finishing points, and their geographical spread. The concept is illustrated by reference to some examples from two departments.

PROMOTION LADDERS IN THE MECHANICAL ENGINEERING DEPARTMENT

Footplate staff

In the discussion of this specialised occupational group in Chapter 4 it was noted that one factor underlining their solidarity is their mutual experience of a common career structure. Their promotion ladder begins at the lowest level of Group C and ends in Group B grade V. Normally the completion of a career and the attainment of the highest point in the ladder takes a whole working life. All the drivers at Kampala in grades V and VI were men with more than twenty-five years' service. The career structure, which has changed little over the years, may be illustrated by reference to the progress of a hypothetical individual.

On entering the EARH the novice begins work in the Loco Shed at the depot where he joins as a *cleaner*, a job which involves crawling inside the boilers of the locomotives and scrubbing them out with a wire brush. As such he receives the lowest Group C salary prevailing at the depot. After a year or so he becomes a *light-up*, a promotion in status though not in grade or salary. In the days when the railways used wood-fired locomotives his job was literally to light the fire. He now has to initiate the fuel flow and warm up the oil-fired engines. He also assists the shunter driver in moving the locomotive from the Shed onto the sidings and thence to the Yard or the Station. Should his work prove satisfactory he is then sent to the RTS on the 'Fireman's Course' which if he passes will gain him promotion to *fireman* NC 2. This appointment may bring him back to his original depot or take him on an assignment elsewhere. He is then employed on engines used for shunting in marshalling yards. Further success will bring him to fireman NC 1 when he operates on main line engines of progressive importance. After this apprenticeship he is sent on the 'Driver's Course' to emerge as a *shunter driver*, Grade B X, who, as the title implies, operates locomotives in the yards or in the immediate environs of the depot. As he gains experience he is entrusted with various main line trains, which are graded in importance. In the network as a whole the most important train is the 'Number One Up' which goes from Mombasa–Nairobi–Kampala, and which is taken into Uganda by drivers from Eldoret. At Kampala itself, pride of place is given to the mixed passenger and goods train which hauls copper from Kasese in the west, and for this train are reserved the *senior drivers* in grades V and VI.

Table 35 shows the footplate staff in each grade at the three principal depots in Uganda. The number of posts at the lowest level, cleaners and light-ups, is relatively small compared with those in posts immediately above them. Anyone who starts as a cleaner would seem assured of promotion at

TABLE 35. *Staff in posts of firemen and drivers, Kampala, Tororo, Jinja, 1965*

Posts	Grade	Kampala	Tororo	Jinja
Senior driver	B V	1	–	–
Senior driver	B VI	6	–	–
Driver	B VII/VIII	9	1	–
Driver	B IX	11	13	2
Shunter driver	B X	11	10	10
Trainee driver	Division III	2	–	–
Fireman	NC 1	26	14	–
Fireman	NC 2	17	14	11
Light-up/cleaner	NC 3	6	–	–
Total		89	52	23

SOURCE: EARH Administration, Kampala.

least to fireman NC 1, provided his performance is satisfactory. After that, competition becomes stiffer and only a handful of drivers can hope to attain the highest positions.

Each step up the promotion ladder means that the worker has successfully completed a period of apprenticeship and training and acquitted himself to the satisfaction of his superiors, principally the Shedmaster. Those in line for promotion are under continual assessment. A bad mistake can mean a delay in promotion or even a demotion. As we acknowledged before, the career is a difficult one, but very rewarding. Each promotion involves not only a better basic salary, but better fringe benefits including chances for overtime. A shunter driver usually works only a normal eight-hour shift, but a main-line driver may be on duty for twelve hours at a stretch. Leaving aside overtime the salary differential between those at the bottom and the top of the ladder is about 8:1. Overtime may increase this to 15:1. In general the prospects for a young man entering this career are much greater than those available to him elsewhere. Recent recruits for posts as cleaners often have at least primary, and sometimes higher, educational qualifications, and although in the past such attainments would have guaranteed white-collar employment, changes in the labour supply have forced such people into unskilled work or even unemployment. In this respect the current intake differs from the older staff, for many of the senior drivers were recruited in the thirties and forties when lower standards prevailed. As we saw, these 'illiterates' now earn perhaps £100 per month. This gap in education and literacy between the older drivers and their firemen or between the former and drivers more recently promoted sometimes leads to ill-feeling and conflict. For example, recently the EARH has been changing from oil-fired steam to diesel locomotives and in Kenya (though not by 1965 in Uganda) the newer type of engine was in use for hauling main-line trains. Many of the older drivers failed to pass the special courses set up to train them for transfers to the new locomotives and so younger men have been given accelerated promotion to the plum jobs.

Although the promotion ladder entails a formal progression from status to status, the worker can informally gain experience of work at a higher level. There are often staff shortages caused by vacations, deaths and snarl-ups in the transfer system, and an experienced fireman, for example, may be called upon to work as a shunter driver, or a shunter assigned to a main-line train. Informally, therefore, the worker may begin to acquire a new status before he is fully entitled to do so. He thus gains useful experience of the social problems created by promotion. For each step up the ladder changes his formal relationship with other workers in the subsection, placing him, for example, in a position of equality with those to whom previously he was subordinate, changing the style of life which he can act out and giving him a different occupational interest. On the estate, as we have seen, small cliques among footplate staff are largely determined by grade and thus by position in the career structure. Reverting to Table 34, cliques (iii), (iv) and (v) consisted of firemen, clique (vi) of senior drivers, and there were other small groups made up of shunters and lower grade main-line drivers. On promotion the worker, therefore, inevitably changes his network of close associates. In fact he may do this if informally he is working at tasks above his official grade. Thus a top fireman who occasionally works as a shunter may associate with such men in off-duty activities. Since, however, promotion often means transfer, the immediate problem of dropping old friends is usually solved of its own accord. The worker moves into a new status at his new depot, and it is only when he is brought into contact with his old associates by further transfers that real difficulties arise.

Artisans

In Loco Sheds and CxRs the term artisan is applied to all classes of skilled men – mechanics, fitters, electricians, boilermen, etc. Most new recruits enter at a local depot on Group NC 3 and become artisans' ' mates ' who carry the tools and learn the trade. Locally they are called *boi-spanna*. Many artisans never rise beyond NC 1, but a number are sent to the RTS courses to become grade B workers. A limited number of Africans with secondary schooling are now recruited directly into training courses for Group B – Joseph, remember, praised such a person when lamenting the tendency for young men to become clerks. A further major step in an artisan's career comes after many years of experience when he achieves promotion to a post as *leading artisan*, grade VI, which is a junior supervisorial position. Further promotion would take him directly into the supervisorial hierarchy of foremen and chargehands. An artisan career, therefore, in theory at least, may lead directly into the upper echelon of railway posts.

The supervisorial hierarchy

In the Loco Shed at Kampala the lowest grade post given the title of fore-man is the RSF B VII, the highest the Shedmaster B II. In between are a number of subsection heads and others – Assistant Shedmaster, working foremen, chargehands, and so on. There are also a number of ' inspectors ' at or above the same grade as the Shedmaster whose responsibilities usually encompass more than one depot. At other depots similar posts may have a higher or lower grade, e.g. the Shedmaster at Kasese is B IV. In the recent past almost all posts in grade VI and above were restricted to Europeans and Asians, though for a long time Africans have been able to attain at least the lower ranking leading artisan and RSF positions. We have seen that the former are directly linked into the artisan promotion ladder, but there are no career structures which naturally lead on to the latter. This is perhaps because in the past the RSF was an early step in what was essentially a European career. For Africans in Loco Sheds promotion to RSF is not a logically linked stage of any particular career. A driver grade VIII still has opportunities ahead of him, and may be on the threshold of achieving a really lucrative position. Consequently a driver or anyone else who becomes an RSF may be said to have switched from one promotion ladder to another. A driver grade VIII who makes this switch appears at the outset to suffer a loss of pay since the basic salary for a driver grade VII is £498 per annum, compared with £402 for an RSF Grade VII, and though both jobs carry plenty of overtime the driver's position is superior in this respect too. This may, however, be only a loss in the short-term, for at the present time the career prospects for Africans in the supervisorial hierarchy are probably excellent. As a driver an individual can at best achieve grade V, as RSF he is in line for promotion to posts in grade IV or better which are presently being Africanised. Moreover, while there is a shortage of suitably qualified and experienced African personnel for supervisorial positions, there are many drivers competing for senior positions. Besides this the supervisorial post carries a status in the community which the drivers perhaps lack.

Among those in RSF positions both at Kampala and elsewhere are a number of former drivers, like Joseph and Wellington, who have made the switch onto a new ladder. They tend to be men who have acquired, largely on their own initiative, a rather higher standard of literacy than is usual among drivers of their generation. This is essential for the post requires attention to a certain amount of paper work. There are also some who have switched from other careers, particularly as Loco Shed or DME Office clerks. There are two major consequences for those who become supervisors. First, they are now operating at a level where many of the posts are still filled by Europeans and Asians with whom they may be in direct competition for promotion. They are often also, as far as work is concerned, in relationships of equality and sometimes superiority with those of other races. Their position in this respect is reflected in the degree of interest that Africans at this level show in the problems of Africanisation and its progress, as we will see later when we discuss a memorandum on this issue prepared by one of their number. Secondly, as the section on class in the last chapter suggested, their position in the industrial framework brings them closer to the interests of Management and they may experience a change of class allegiance.

Throughout the industry there are channels of advancement similar to those mentioned already, and they exist at all levels.

PROMOTION IN THE COMMERCIAL AND OPERATING DEPARTMENT

Watchmen in Goods Sheds

For footplate staff and artisans the promotion ladder begins in Group C and reaches the middle grades of Group B. Some ladders, however, are confined entirely to the lower level. Watchmen in Goods Sheds are responsible, in conjunction with the police, for guarding the vast quantities of material that accumulate at depots for on- and off-loading and for delivery to customers. They form a quasi-police force, having power to apprehend those acting suspiciously. Watchmen employed by the EARH and other organisations tend to be former soldiers or policemen, often middle-aged, with no formal educational qualifications. At Kampala they form a subsection of the Goods Shed, and are organised into gangs each with a leader. Over all is the Head Watchman, NC 1. Thus even those employed in such menial capacities can obtain promotion, though the number of senior positions available either at Kampala or elsewhere is very few. The same applies to other manual workers whether they be loaders, checkers, station porters or compound cleaners. There are opportunities for all, however limited they may seem.

Section heads

Just as some ladders are confined to Group C, there are others confined to Group B. As an example we may take section headships such as goods agents, yardmasters and station masters. The latter will be given extended treatment. Certain station masterships have been open to Africans for at least forty years, but only since 1963/4 have Africans occupied all posts carrying that title, with the first African station master at Kampala arriving in early 1964, and the post at Nairobi being Africanised at about the same time. The career structure for African station masters is, however, well established, and the procedure for moving up the promotion ladder has now become more or less traditional. The initial step is training on the 'Station Masters' Course' at the RTS. This may be taken either on entry to the EARH or subsequently by a worker, usually a clerk, who has decided to change his job. The first assignment will be as an Assistant Station Master, Grade X, at some remote wayside station. After serving his apprenticeship in this way the individual can expect transfer on grade IX or VIII as an Assistant, at a larger depot in a post which is often entitled *station foreman*. Then, after a further period of training, he is given charge of a small depot, and as he gains experience he will be transferred to successively more important posts. The Station Master Kampala, Grade III, is the highest attainable in Uganda, and the post at Nairobi, grade I, the highest in the entire network.

For station masters there is, then, a regulated promotion ladder with each step well established. By reference to this the individual can estimate his own achievements and compare them with those of others. The same applies to yardmasters and goods agents, though the number of posts in the latter category is small.[1] The post of goods agent at any depot is graded above that of the station master and yardmaster, and Africans promoted to the headship of goods sheds have usually been recruited from among those at the top of the other sections. The Goods Agent Kampala, for example, was previously Station Master Mombasa. Those near the top of yard and station sections, therefore, have the choice of waiting to obtain one of the senior positions in their sections' hierarchy or of applying for a position as an assistant goods agent. There is also the possibility of switching to yet another ladder, that of the train inspectors. In Uganda posts in this career start at grade IV and go on to grade I, with higher grades available in Kenya.

The ultimate goal of those at the top of section ladders is selection for training for administrative posts such as assistant traffic superintendents. Their chances of obtaining such positions in the mid-sixties was seen by them to depend first on the rate of Africanisation that the EARH would allow, and second on its policy. The EARH had two principal options – to promote what were generally called the 'old and experienced staff' or recruit younger men with Higher School Certificate or even university qualifications directly into administrative posts. As we will see later it was felt by the African section heads that most of the available senior posts were going to younger, better educated, but less experienced men, and there was considerable criticism of this policy. For section heads, therefore, promotion to higher positions involved competition with each other, with Europeans and Asians, and with this new generation of highly qualified Africans.

For most of the careers that we have considered so far there is a relatively well-ordered progression of posts making up the promotion ladder, and only at certain critical points does the individual have to make a strategic decision as to his next step. Not all careers are as regulated as this as the following discussion shows.

Clerks

What we have learned so far about clerks – white-collar workers – may be summarised briefly. Almost all are in Group B, and they enter the EARH at one of two levels, depending on their educational attainments, those with intermediate schooling traditionally coming into Division III, and those with secondary into Division II. At the RTS the trainees in each division live and work together and form a tightly-knit group. After training they are dispersed to any part of the network where the EARH needs them. This usually means to the larger depots, the district headquarters, where large numbers of office staff are employed. Table 36 shows the distribution of clerks by grade in each of the principal DTS sections at Kampala: 55% of clerical posts are in the Goods Shed and 32% in the Office. Since these two sections are found only at the larger depots it can be seen that few clerks

TABLE 36. *Clerical establishment, DTS Department, Kampala, by section,*
   1965 [a]

Grade	Goods Shed	Station	Office	All
Executive B	–	–	2	2
B III–I	–	–	–	–
B V–IV	5	2	5	12
B VIII–VI	21	7	18	46 (plus 1 in Yard)
B XI–IX	36	4	11	51
Total	62	13	36	111 (plus 1 in Yard)

[a] These are establishment figures.
SOURCE: EARH Administration, Kampala.

can expect to work in small outlying stations. In the Office clerks form a
majority (54%) of all employees.

In the past the promotion prospects for clerks were clearly defined and
limited. The ceiling attainable was set at a fairly low level, for posts in the
middle ranges were filled largely by Asians and higher positions by Europeans. From 1955 onwards the number of Africans employed at these levels
rose rapidly. In 1954, 2,445 Africans worked as ' clerical and station staff ' [2]
throughout the network and they formed 48% of all employees in that category. By 1964 the number had risen to 4,689 and they formed 83% of the
total. Although in 1955 the first Africans entered the service as Division II
trainees, it was between 1961 and 1964 that the greatest changes occurred.
During this period the number of African clerical and station staff rose by
nearly 1,700. Compare here the figures given for the proportion of Africans
in each occupational group in Table 9. Separate figures for a comparison of
the proportion of African clerks in each grade are not available, but some
of the impact of Africanisation may be obtained from the figures given in
Table 12. These show that between October 1962 and April 1965 the number
of Africans in Division II and above rose from 1,500 to nearly 4,000, and
their proportion of those grades from 24% to 62%. Although these changes
affected all occupational groups the position of the clerks was changed
most of all.

For the white-collar employees the sixties created a rapidly changing
career perspective. Among footplate staff and artisans the new developments
were likely to have a significant influence only in the long run, unless they
were already at the top of the existing career structure. The same applies
to those in the middle of careers as station masters. In each of these cases
the immediate future seemed to entail the long haul of steady progression
up an already established hierarchy. For the young clerk there was no such
certain path. In theory, of course, a clerk could have expected to make a
steady advance from, say, a post as Goods Shed Clerk Grade VII to a similar
post in grade VIII. In practice under the conditions prevailing in the mid-
sixties this rarely happened. The rapidity with which Africanisation of
middle range white-collar posts actually occurred, and the chain effect that
this produced, meant that a worker might be employed one month as Acci-

dents' Clerk Grade VII, Kampala, and the next be transferred as Oil Wag-gons' Clerk, Grade VI, Mombasa. A study of the career histories of clerks shows that during this period they were characterised by short periods spent at each depot, swift promotion, rapid transfer, and frequent change of job, subsection and section. Consequently, if a young clerk were to examine the records of those above him, he would be unlikely to be able to discover any consistency in the pattern of achievement of the kind that a fireman could perceive among senior drivers or a young station master among his superiors. It would be apparent, however, that advancement depended less on taking the long view, sticking to a particular job, gaining experience and seniority, than on showing immediate promise of success.

In this situation the clerk cannot rely on the promotion escalator to advance his position. He is thrown very much onto his own initiative, to hack out a career for himself as best he can. In this somewhat anomic context it is clear that some people are going to be markedly, and from the viewpoint of others, inexplicably successful. The consequences of this will be seen later. The clerk, above all, needs to be aware of the ways in which he as an individual can advance his own cause. The following sections discuss how he, and others, might do this.

STRATEGIES FOR ACHIEVING PROMOTION

Normal procedure

In theory all appointments to EARH posts are regulated by a formal pro-cedure. A vacancy occurs, the position is advertised, eligible applicants are assessed and a candidate appointed. As in any similar organisation the appointing officers take into account the applicant's past and present per-formance, his qualifications and character. In their assessment of EARH personnel they depend heavily on the candidate's personal files in which his various superiors record their comments and in which are retained details of any offence against regulations which may have been committed. An individual with a ' dirty file ', i.e. which lists numerous charges leading to a reprimand or other punishment, is reckoned normally to have little chance of promotion.

Besides being competent at their work and keeping their records clean, candidates for promotion usually reckon to maintain good relations with their superiors and ensure that they recognise their worth and ambition. They must also watch closely when vacancies occur so as to be ready should a suitable opening appear. When a choice of alternatives is open they have to consider both the long- and short-term advantages of each. For example, transfer to an outlying depot means absence from the eyes of higher authority, a prospect viewed with such apprehension by the ambi-tious that such a move is often seen as a punishment rather than a reward. I heard numerous people complain in these terms about promotions which took them to Pakwach in northern Uganda, or still worse, Rhino Camp on the Sudan border.

The preceding paragraph, and the discussion of specific techniques which follows, distils information obtained from a wide range of informants. Specific examples of those using the principles involved will occasionally be given here, but the main illustrations are to be found in the case studies of ' relative deprivation ' that are analysed later in the chapter.

Switching careers

Earlier we noted on several occasions the practice of switching from one career structure to another which occurs when the individual decides that his promotion prospects will be enhanced by a transfer to a different occupation or organisational unit. Frequently these switches are made between promotion ladders within the same section; the driver and the shed clerk who become RSFs come into this category, as does the guard who becomes a yard foreman, of which several examples are to be found. The highest posts for guards are in grade VII, while at Kampala Yard supervisors are found up to grade III, so once again the individual sacrifices present income for future prospects. He also exchanges a job which for reasons we discussed in Chapter 4 is held in low repute for another with higher status. While career switches within a section are commonly found among all categories of staff, moves from one section to another within the same department are rare except among non-technical employees in Commercial and Operating. As we saw clerks are frequently transferred between sections and many choose to make such a move, as do those at or about the level of section headships. Leaving aside the necessity for such transfers imposed by the implementation of Africanisation policy, the non-specialised and non-technical nature of many clerical jobs makes such movement more feasible. This possibly accounts for the impression that sectional loyalty and solidarity is perhaps less in Commercial and Operating than in other departments.

Moves between departments are rare, and the only instances encountered of this were of transfers into the GM's department, particularly into welfare and industrial relations sections. These sections were founded in the early sixties and had to recruit staff from a variety of sources, in particular from among clerks in Commercial and Operating. Since the sections were expanding rapidly this was a good move for those that changed. Besides the many who actually made a switch of some kind – and there is unfortunately no way of estimating their number – plenty of others contemplated doing so. Frequently their plans were objectively little more than daydreams; see, for example, Alan, the Stores Assistant, whose case is discussed later. Often young men in semi-skilled occupations aspired to white-collar jobs, estimating the financial advantages of their present career as inferior to the status attached to clerical occupations. Such workers would generally find their basic educational qualifications insufficient for such a change of career, though this disadvantage is not always insurmountable.

Self-advancement through further education

For those like the semi-skilled worker aspiring to a job as a clerk the improvement of educational standards is crucial. Many others also see this as a way forward. We noted earlier that certain older drivers would, because of their illiteracy, be unable to change to supervisorial work, and that now, since the change to diesel locomotives, it is becoming increasingly difficult for them to attain the highest posts on the drivers' promotion ladder. One of the drivers (Odhiambo), who had failed the diesel course, tried to improve himself by getting his son, aged nineteen, in his tenth year at school, to teach him how to read and write. Although the boy gave his father some instruction, the old man found it was too late for him to break new ground. Early on in fieldwork I was overwhelmed with requests for help of this kind which it was impossible to fulfil. Many workers also discussed the courses they were taking with one of the many correspondence colleges. So frequently were such courses mentioned in conversation that it came as something of a surprise to find that in the Nsambya sample only 10% of respondents claimed actually to have completed one. This need not have been surprising as the following episode showed.

After I had been in the field for some months I was approached by a number of railwaymen and requested to ask the authorities at the Makerere Extra-mural Department to lay on an English class at Nsambya. A notice put up in the Railway African Club attracted seventy-four signatures. About the same number, including many who had not signed, arrived for the inaugural meeting. In the event about fifteen people started the course, but their numbers dwindled so rapidly that the scheme had to be ended. It is not so much through active participation as through the expression of intense interest that the extent to which education is seen as the key to advancement is revealed.

One special kind of educational activity, which is not solely related to advancement in the EARH, is the subject of particular interest. It is termed locally 'going abroad for further study'. Consider the following case. Peter O. is a Luo, aged twenty, with standard 8 education. He works as an Electrician's Mate NC 3 in the Loco Shed. Since his father died he has been the main financial support of three brothers and two sisters. Formerly they had been helped by the husband of another sister but that source is now closed. One of his brothers had recently received a scholarship to go to Russia and when I first met Peter he had just received a letter from the brother asking for 150s. to buy clothes. This came as a blow since Peter had just sent 600s. out of his savings. Peter was at his wits' end; he just had not got the money. In talking about his own ambitions he said he could go to the RTS for training as an electrician, but would rather increase his proficiency in English and become a clerk. Most of all he wanted to follow his brother abroad. He then persuaded me to help him draft a letter to a prominent Luo politician in Nairobi, outlining his case and putting his name forward for a scholarship.

Many people could name someone, often a relative, who had gone abroad for training. Occasionally the EARH itself sends workers to the UK or to an East African university, particularly for technical training. Welfare and IROs almost all go on overseas courses at some time in their careers. Peter's request failed, but enough were successful in their applications for scholarships to arouse the hopes of others.

ALTERNATIVE CHANNELS OF ADVANCEMENT

An approach to a politician for a scholarship is an attempt to short-circuit the barriers to advancement found in the industry. There is no guarantee, of course, that the successful applicant will use the advantage he gains to further himself in the EARH. There are, however, similar channels which are used in this way. Almost all IROs, for example, are former trade union officers. Of the four IROs at Kampala in 1964/5 two had held positions in the Railway African Union (Kenya), one in the union in Uganda, and the fourth had been a permanent official with the Dockworkers in Tanzania. In a typical case the individual concerned had first been employed in the EARH as a Division II clerk. He had obtained prominence in his union, first at a local branch and then in the national executive. He then obtained a trade union scholarship to come to the UK to study 'industrial relations' and on his return applied for a post in the GM's department as an IRO. He was thus able to obtain rapid advancement to the upper echelons of Group B, a considerable jump in salary and status.

That the institutions can be manipulated in this way is widely recognised. One young man, Francis, whom we met before, was approached by the union to become a representative on his departmental staff committee. He accepted because, he said, if he joined the committee he might become well known in the union and work his way up to branch secretary or chairman. He might then be offered a scholarship abroad. At this point his imaginary career diverged from the pattern noted above. For he said, 'If I ever go abroad they won't be able to get me back in a hurry.'

One other possible avenue of advancement is to leave the EARH. Except in rare cases this is not an attractive proposition, and though many talked about this, few actually took the step. At least one person, however, used the device of applying for jobs outside the industry in order to attract the attention of his superiors to his ambitions for promotion within the industry (see case two below). Only those with high technical and administrative qualifications are in fact in a position to exploit a market shortage.

PROMOTION AS AN ISSUE IN INDUSTRIAL RELATIONS

Although Africanisation became a reality only in the 1960s, it had in one form or another been an issue between Railway unions and management since the end of the Second World War. The history of African advancement in Railway employment in East Africa and the development of the issue over the years 1946–65 when the unions hammered home their case in a succession of memoranda to commissions of enquiry is discussed extensively elsewhere (Grillo forthcoming 1974, Chapter 3). So, too, is the significance of the changes brought about by the implementation of African-isation policies for the structure of worker–management relations in the industry. The emphasis in this book is on the effect of such changes for individuals, their careers and expectations, and their relationships with others in the community. Two points may, however, be noted.

First, that Africanisation should have been seen as a key issue by the Railway African Unions is a reflection of the composition of union leader-ships. As we shall see in the next chapter, that leadership is largely in the hands of lower and middle echelon white-collar workers, one of the cate-gories to benefit most from the implementation of Africanisation. Since the majority of union members are in Group C, for whom the immediate benefits of Africanisation have been considerably less, if indeed they exist at all, it would seem that pressure for Africanisation was an expression of the interests of union leaders rather than the rank and file.

Secondly, the process of Africanisation did not affect all departments and sections equally. Although the replacement of expatriate clerical and ad-ministrative personnel proceeded apace during 1961–4 the lack of trained staff made it difficult to achieve the same progress with technical posts. This caused some dissatisfaction in the departments most concerned, parti-cularly Mechanical Engineering, and in Uganda led to criticisms of the union. One of the Loco Shed workers, Joseph, the RSF, reacted by compiling a memorandum on the subject which he circulated to the heads of his department in the district and at headquarters, and to several union leaders. Some extracts follow. It is addressed to the Chief Mechanical Engineer.

Africanisation in Mechanical Department

I would like to draw your attention to the above subject which appears to be escaping your duties towards ensuring that it has been achieved as has been laid down in the Udoji Africanisation report which the East African Common Services has accepted in full. Frankly speaking you have not changed your ideas of the past on which preference in your department has been accorded to Europeans and Asians. The following are the jobs in your department which you have delayed to Africanise and I call upon you to replace the suitable experienced and educated Africans in the places which are now occupied by Europeans on contract terms, and the Asian who should be retired to give room to the Africans who have suffered a long time without sound advancement. . . . The existing great changes of Africanisation in other departments and in all government services should not leave Mechanical Dept. to an isolated island of Europeans and Asians.

The memorandum goes on to list positions which the author believes should be Africanised at once, including loco inspectors, loco instructors in sheds, the RSF at Nairobi, working foremen, chargehands and shed-masters. In respect of the latter he says:

If you really had interest to serve in East Africa you should have promoted some suitable Africans to these jobs. You are working quite
contrary to the wishes of the citizens of East Africa. Regarding this issue
you are trying to block Africans to hold shedmasters' jobs which are
non-professional and non-technical. Every step should now be taken to
bring Africans to control these jobs.

The style of this memorandum is not untypical of many contemporary
East African political documents in the vehemence of its rhetoric and the
themes it employs, though a fuller analysis of the complete article (it runs
to over 2,000 words), would be required to demonstrate this. The document also shows that at least one railwayman has a very clear picture of
the structure of the organisation and of the events that occur within it. In
my experience such understanding is widespread among EARH employees.
Note also the departmental frame of reference which the author employs.
He is saying in effect, 'We in Mechanical Engineering, compared with
workers in other departments, have been poorly treated in the process of
Africanisation.' A comparison of this kind is an example of what has been
termed 'relative deprivation', a topic we shall examine in detail in the
next section. Finally, if one refers back to the discussion of Joseph's career
and present status described in Chapter 4, it may be seen that the memorandum reflects not only his concern for fellow workers in his own department, but his own position and ambitions. For he himself was most anxious
to obtain promotion to precisely those posts whose immediate Africanisation he is demanding here.

RESPONSES TO SUCCESS AND FAILURE

Relative deprivation

Consider the following extract from an interview with James,[3] the Welfare
Officer, whose attitudes towards status were noted in Chapter 5. During
the interview he gave me an outline of his career. At that time, April 1964,
he was just twenty-nine. He had left school in 1956, having gained his
Cambridge School Certificate, and had proceeded to the RTS at Nairobi,
where he had been one of the early entrants in Division II. He passed out
in March 1958 and was posted as a Grade VIII Clerk in the Rates Section
of the Commercial and Operating Department at Nairobi Headquarters. At
that time, he said, a European senior officer took an interest in his career
and advised him to gain experience at outside stations. Accordingly he
obtained transfers first to Mbale, then to Kampala in the Goods Shed, and
then the Control Office. In September 1961 he returned to Nairobi on grade
VII. In November of that year he applied for a post as Senior Welfare
Assistant, Grade V, at Nairobi, and was accepted. In 1962 he was transferred in rapid succession from Nairobi to Mombasa, to Kisumu and back
to Nairobi in grade IV. Then in June 1963 he was appointed District Welfare
Officer at Kampala on grade III. So successful had his career been that at
the time of our discussion he was about to go to Nairobi for an interview
for a cadetship which he expected to obtain.

In the course of some seven years this man had moved from being a schoolboy from a poor rural family to being within sight of an income of over £1,000 per annum. Yet during the interview he was able to cite several examples of men who had been in the same class as himself at the RTS who were already in higher posts, including one man in grade II, others who were cadets and one who had actually made it to ATS. He also indicated a man who had been in the EARH for only a year but who was already in Group A. On the other hand, he could also point to some, including two in grade VII at Kampala, who had not risen so fast. He felt that with such men, who had formerly been his friends, his relationships were now poor, but he admitted that those he disliked most were people on his own level. He claimed, for example, that when a fellow welfare officer, in fact the man who would succeed him in the event of his transfer, heard that he, James, was likely to get a cadetship, he became very resentful towards him.

James' position may be summarised as follows. He compared his performance in the EARH with a group of people with whom at one time he had been on equal terms – his 'contemporaries', principally those who entered the Railways at the same time and who trained together on the same course at the RTS. They provide a group by reference to which an individual may measure his own relative rate of advancement. They are like the runners who got down together at the same start line. Now, after a few laps of the track, James finds himself, if not among the leaders, then at least not trailing badly behind.

In analysing this interview, which I will call 'case one', and others which follow, a useful tool is the concept of 'relative deprivation'. This concept, which has its roots in American sociology of the twenties and thirties, was taken up and defined in the mammoth study of American forces personnel in the Second World War (Stouffer *et al.* 1949). The theoretical implications of the concept have been discussed by Merton and Rossi (Merton 1957: Chapter VIII), and more recently in Britain by Runciman (1966). The applicability of the concept to this study of railway workers in East Africa emerges from a discussion in the 'American Soldier' which notes that in army units where the objective chances of promotion were reckoned to be high the members of the unit were unhappier about their promotion prospects than those in units where chances for promotion were low. This response is very similar to that of certain railwaymen who, compared with many others in the EARH and with the population of East Africa as a whole, are objectively well-off, but who feel in some way or other that they have failed. For 'some way or other' one may read 'relatively'. For their dissatisfaction is invariably expressed in terms of comparisons similar to those used by James in his interview. The crucial factor here is the subjective selection of a reference group. As Merton and Rossi have shown, the process of selection can reveal much about the structure of the community from which such statements are drawn. In particular they shed much light on systems of status and on the problems of the individual in a rapidly mobile society.

Case two: Jackson, Accidents' Clerk Grade VII, Control Office, Kampala

Jackson was one of those referred to by the Welfare Officer as a contemporary who had not risen as fast as himself. They were, in fact, classificatory brothers who had attended secondary school together. Jackson had followed James to the RTS and had passed out a year later. The material used in this case study consists of statements made by Jackson and his friends, and episodes in which he was involved, over a period of about a year. They are recorded largely in chronological order. If the anthropologist appears to intrude into the case more frequently than might be considered proper he pleads that the relationship between the observer and his informant is in this instance an integral part of the data.

We first met at the Railway African Club, of which Jackson was then the secretary, when James, the Welfare Officer, asked him to see me safely home from the estate. We met again soon after, and he invited me to his office to meet his fellow workers and supervisors. On that occasion we were accompanied by a friend of his from RTS days who was now on a mature entry scholarship at Makerere University College. Subsequently I became a frequent visitor to Jackson's house. During our talks in this period he continually hinted at his past and what might have been. He wished he had taken the chance when younger of going to an agricultural college where he had been offered a place, instead of joining the EARH. If he had not married and had children he could have gone abroad for further study. When a young man at the RTS he had acquired a certain prominence as a footballer and had been a member of the famous RTS team; he showed me the photographs. Former friends from the RTS kept re-appearing in his life. Once at his house I met a former classmate and schoolfriend who had just arrived in Kampala to take over a grade VI post held until then by an Asian.

After some weeks when it seemed that a rapport had been established I decided to interview Jackson systematically. This was an error. We began well enough with his family history and background, how he went to a well-known secondary school in western Kenya, how he and others had heard about the EARH from local men who had already joined, how he had decided to apply and was accepted. In doing this Jackson now felt, 'I made my first mistake.' When he finished training he had first been posted as a Pier Clerk Grade VIII at Port Bell, on Lake Victoria, near Kampala. He was then transferred to Kampala itself, first to the Parcels Office, then the DTS Office, and finally to the Control Office at the same depot. At this point he claimed he was now on grade V. Unfortunately I knew this to be untrue as his promotion to grade VII had recently been listed in *Sikio*. When pressed on this he broke off the interview abruptly, saying it was a personal matter. To digress a moment: in each issue of *Sikio* there are two or three pages devoted to 'Recent promotions'. This is a very popular section and it is a reflection of the interest shown in promotion that a railwayman invariably turns first to read the recent promotions column. In this way they keep informed of the whereabouts and progress of friends and acquaintances.

Despite this setback we continued to meet. One day he showed me a piece of work which he had taken over from the man who shared his desk in the Control Office who was away on leave. It was the Train Guard's Report in which are recorded any train delays. Jackson complained that the responsible clerk, who has to follow up the reasons for each delay, had not done the work properly and that he, Jackson, was having to go over it again. Yet this man was in grade VI, a grade higher than himself.' How would you feel,' he asked, ' if you know you are more intelligent and better than the man in charge of you? ' Pressed on the word ' intelligent ', he said he meant with ' higher educational standard '.

A significant incident occurred when one Saturday afternoon Jackson and I went for a drink at a bar at Nsambya market. There we found sitting together the Station Master, the Goods Agent, the IRO and two non-Railway friends of the latter, one of whom was a Superintendent in the Prison Service, the other a chartered accountant. I was invited to join them and sat down. The IRO bought a round of drinks for all except Jackson, for whom I bought one, as promised. We talked for half an hour but no attempt was made to include Jackson in the conversation, though he was known to them, and he made no effort to bring himself in. The discussion soon got round to promotion and the IRO said that he was shortly going on transfer to Nairobi in a Superscale post, though at the moment he was in Group A, Segment I. After a while Jackson made signs that he wished us to leave, telling the others that a meal was ready for us at his house. When we arrived there, Jackson, who had been drinking steadily all day, complained that he had felt ' extremely uncomfortable ' sitting in the bar. All those men had been of high grade, and he was just grade VII. He claimed, however, in an aside, that the IRO was not Segment I but Segment III. Even so, ' he earns three times as much as I do '. Perhaps exceeding the brief of an impartial observer, I tried, naïvely, to console him by pointing to his job and his wife and children, saying that compared to the majority of Africans he was a lucky man. He totally rejected this, declaring ' If you say that you are my enemy number one.' He became increasingly maudlin. I was supposed to be his friend and should help him. How? He would say no more than that I should use the influence which it was commonly believed I possessed, to get him abroad for further studies. Then when he returned he would be a big man and people like the IRO would respect him and he could drink with them. He ended by saying that he was ' useless ' and would ' be better dead '.

A friend of Jackson's commented that since he had got his promotion to grade VII he had begun drinking heavily. He had also, under pressure from his wife, bought a refrigerator on hire purchase. The friend criticised him on both counts, saying that he ought to be saving his money, particularly since he talked of sending his children overseas to school. Jackson's view of himself as a failure was fed continually by reports of the progress of his contemporaries from the RTS. The man who had been transferred to replace an Asian, for example, once brought news from Nairobi where he had been on leave, mentioning several of their mutual friends who were now doing well, including one who had gone to grade II. Hearing this news, Jackson became very quiet.

It was about this time that Jackson began to show great interest in extra-mural classes at Makerere and arranged with a neighbour, Graham, to go in the latter's car to attend lectures on economics and industrial relations. He also obtained an application form for a mature entry scholarship. At the same time he began to look for jobs in other firms. He showed me a letter he was writing applying for a post in the East African Cargo Handling Service at Mombasa with a salary of £756 per annum. He said he would ask his superiors for a reference for this job in the hope that this would bring his dissatisfaction to their attention and they would promote him so as not to lose him. Soon afterwards he was in fact told that he would be transferred to Mombasa on grade VI, but for administrative reasons would not be posted for some months. He pressed on with alternative job plans, making enquiries, which came to nothing, with East African Airways and the district administrative service in Kenya. He also bought a TV set on hire purchase and claimed that he was giving up drinking so as to be able to save half his salary each month to buy a car. It was now December 1964 and the time of the celebrations for the advent of the Kenya Republic. Jackson refused to celebrate, declaring ' *Uhuru* has brought me nothing.'

Many of his resolutions were of short duration, the extra-mural classes were soon forgotten, and he took to drinking again. There followed another incident in the same bar. We were drinking together, this time in the Railway African Club, when we met the Yardmaster. The three of us then walked up to the Nsambya bar where we found the Station Master sitting with the PWI Gulu who was on a brief visit to Kampala. Jackson introduced me to this man who was one of the highest grade Africans in the District Engineering Department. The Station Master, however, complained that the introduction had not been properly made, and when Jackson and the Yardmaster left the bar for a moment, he brought the man from Gulu across the room to where I was sitting, and made what he termed a ' proper introduction '. When Jackson and the Yardmaster returned they found their seats occupied and moved to the other side of the room. After a while Jackson insisted on leaving and we went back to his house. There he said he had been very offended by my behaviour since I should have sat with the people whom I had accompanied to the bar. The Station Master, he said, despised him and liked insulting him. Later the Yardmaster commented that he thought Jackson had an ' inferiority complex '.

Several points can be drawn from this case history. In his career Jackson had passed through two educational institutions – his school and the RTS – which provided him with a number of friends, classmates, whom he used as a reference group. The level of education he had attained provided him with a further, more general, frame of reference. It is taken for granted that a major goal in life is success as measured in terms of progress up the industrial and social hierarchy relative to members of the selected reference groups. The comparison is, however, not with the average member but with the ' high-flyers ' and it is by reference to their success that Jackson considered himself a failure. That his salary was over £400 per annum in an area with a *per capita* income nearer £20 was quite irrelevant. Jackson, then, aspired to the kind of position that the most successful of his contemporaries had attained. All the jobs he applied for outside the EARH were in the £700–£800 range, twice his present salary but equivalent in the EARH to that received on grade III or in a cadetship, i.e. to the salaries now earned by his successful contemporaries. His life-style, the TV set and refrigerator, the desire for a car, was more in keeping with that of the status he aspired to reach than that which he actually had. The attempts to improve his education, to get to Makerere or abroad, may also be understood in this light.

The case also illustrates the kind of relationships that may prevail between those at different levels of the status system and how mechanisms of exclusiveness operate in social interaction. In this respect Jackson was the victim of the same mode of behaviour which he himself employed in his relations with those of lower status. For Jackson was said by lower status members of his own ethnic group to be a proud and lonely man, as we saw in Chapter 5. A final point: the Yardmaster's judgment in no sense represents a medical opinion, and no claims can be made here about the relationship between failure and mental disorder in competitive systems. To say that Jackson's case can be understood in terms of the concept of relative deprivation makes a sociological, not a psychological, point. Nevertheless the extent to which a particular structural situation generates 'abnormal' responses on the part of the individual is an important anthropological question which deserves fuller consideration than can be accorded to it here.

Although this case has been described at some length it was not an isolated one as other examples will show. Graham, Jackson's neighbour on the estate and contemporary at the RTS, felt himself to be in a similar situation. He, too, sought to enhance his status through further education and applications to other jobs, in this instance the Institute of Transport. He frequently compared himself with his neighbour. 'Both Mr Jackson and I have been overlooked,' he complained. Both had seen their contemporaries 'go ahead'. A similar complaint was made by others.

Case three: the Estate Overseer, Grade IX

He once called me into his office and told the following story. He had been on the same grade now for seven years, first at Tanga in Tanzania and then at Kampala. He was 'desperate' for promotion. He complained that he had been promised that his present post would be upgraded, since similar posts at other depots, with less responsibility, were in higher grades, but the regrading had failed to materialise. He had also been told that he was first in order of seniority for promotion within his section, but he had seen all his contemporaries 'going ahead' while he had been 'overlooked'. He had applied for several posts but had been turned down. What should he do? I replied that I had heard, as many people in fact said, that the chances of promotion were better at a larger depot, so why not apply for a transfer to, say, Mombasa, even if it meant taking a grade IX post? No, he replied, he could not acept a transfer to a post on the same grade, not after seven years. He must have promotion; he had twelve children to support and could not afford, on his present salary, to educate them properly.

The Estate Overseer was in fact one of those who pressed most strongly for English classes at Nsambya. Eventually he obtained his promotion to a grade VII post at Nakuru. It should be noted that the concept of a 'contemporary' refers not simply to those who joined the EARH at the same time, but carries the implication of those who joined at the same level, and in the same occupational group. This same frame of reference is used by those at all levels in the system.

Case four: the Station Master and the Goods Agent

Both these men, whom we have met in several situations, had been very successful in objective terms, each being the first African to occupy his post. Both had joined the then Kenya and Uganda Railways and Harbour Service in 1938 and had completed over twenty-five years' service. Both were now in Group B Division I, but both complained of their lack of promotion. In common with others at their level, their main ambition, as we have seen, was to become traffic superintendents, and they complained about EARH policy which, they said, was 'overlooking the old and experienced staff'. At the same time, and in a somewhat contradictory fashion, they also grumbled that several of their own contemporaries had achieved senior positions. There was a further comparative framework available to them which they also used. As youths they had both attended a famous secondary school in Kenya where they had gained Cambridge School Certificates. Among their classmates were some who had now attained national prominence as government ministers, civil servants and university professors. Compared with such men they may well consider themselves as relatively unsuccessful.

Just as two people may share a solidarity derived from mutual misfortune, so a relationship may be sundered by the success of one party. Jackson and James, classificatory brothers though they were, no longer associated with each other, as I have shown elsewhere. The next case illustrates this.

Case five: Loco Driver Grade VIII, Fireman NC 1

Both of these men, one (Benedict) a Luo, the other (Wanyama) a Luhya, had been born on a Railway housing estate at Nairobi, their fathers being Railway employees. They had attended the same school and had joined the EARH at the same time. They had served together as cleaners and light-ups and had attended the same fireman's course at the RTS. Thereafter their careers had diverged with their transfer to different depots. Some years later they had met again at Kampala, but in the meantime Wanyama had become a driver while Benedict had progressed no further than fireman. Their associations at Nsambya inevitably took them into different social circles and they rarely met outside work. Both men, however, used each other's position as a reference to compare their own careers, the one to illustrate his success, the other his failure.

In each case considered so far the individuals employed a specific frame of reference to judge their progress in the social system. They pointed to a specific, objectively defined, set of people – their contemporaries. They also used equally precise measures such as educational standards, though Jackson, for example, subsumed this under the more diffuse concept of 'intelligence'. The next case deals with a man who used a similarly diffuse notion, that of 'ability'. His assessment of his own ability, and of the individuals with whom he compared himself, far exceeded his actual educational attainments.

Case six: Alan, Stores Assistant in Loco Shed, NC 1

This man, Alan, was about thirty-four years old, married with several children. He had received five years' schooling and could speak a fair amount of English. On leaving school he had been employed first as a policeman and then in the GPO, both in Kenya. In 1955 he joined the EARH as a Storeboy at Nairobi, and after a spell at Kisumu had come to Kampala. He was one of a very few Group C men active in union affairs, being at the time a branch officer. One lunch-time, over a beer, he discussed his career.

He said that he had recently applied for the post of RSF in the Loco Shed, but had received a letter from the Shedmaster saying that he was not suitable for the job and was not in line for promotion. This offended him. Many times he had 'acted' as a grade X Storeman when the man who held the post went on leave, but his promotion to that level had never been confirmed. He had been to the Shedmaster and told him that with his large family he needed a better job. He had his wife, five children and two relatives staying in his class 7 (ii) house and promotion would give him larger quarters. He said he told the Shedmaster, 'If you see me right, I will help you in the future.' But people were against him in his efforts to obtain promotion. The job of RSF was 'simple' and it would take him 'just two weeks' to learn something about shunting after which he could do the job easily. 'John', he said, referring to one of the RSFs, 'was just a clerk before he got the job as running shift foreman'. Driver's work was '*bure*' – nothing, not hard at all. They earn high wages and dress up and don't want to know anyone', but they are usually 'illiterate'. If he were Shedmaster he would put into effect his own system of industrial relations. He would not be satisfied to be confirmed in grade X, 'I am at least grade VII, and could do work up to grade III.' The newly-arrived Assistant Shedmaster, a European, could not speak Swahili and did not want to learn it, whereas he, Alan, knew ten languages which he had picked up when in the police force. At this point in our conversation he looked at the time and found that his lunch hour was over, but he refused to go back on duty, saying he wanted to 'control my own work' and go where he pleased in his own time.

Since Alan entered in Group C it is unlikely that his contemporaries, in the sense that term is used here, would have moved very far up the promotion ladder. If they were his primary reference group, then he might have been less concerned about his own position. His frame of reference, however, is a subjective and diffuse notion of ability, and his assessment of his own ability places him on a level of equality with those far above him in the grading system. The RSFs, even the Assistant Shedmaster, are seen as people with less talent than himself but in higher positions, and the drivers – 'illiterates' – are far better off. This example illustrates an association that runs through almost all the cases between relative deprivation and perceived status incongruence.

Various points raised by the case studies may be summarised briefly. First, and obviously, each case supports the findings of Chapter 5 in respect of the significance of status in the daily lives of railwaymen. They also underline the extent to which it is status in the work context which structures both relationships and attitudes. The case material also illustrates some of the problems involved in restructuring networks of friends and associates after one of them has achieved rapid advancement. The particular data point to some further conclusions. Among certain groups of workers the objective rates of promotion are high, but it is clear that the expectancy that ambitions will be fulfilled by promotion is related to the frequency with which those who make up an individual's reference group in fact attain higher positions. The primary reference group in this context are 'contemporaries', usually those with whom the individual has been in close contact at the RTS. A less specific frame of reference is provided by standard of education, but this may also indicate another specific set of contemporaries, those who attended secondary school together. Even more diffuse frames of reference such as 'intelligence' and 'ability' are also employed. In so far as identification with a set of people defined in these terms is purely subjective, there is logically no limit to the number or kind of people with whom an individual can compare his lot. In fact Alan's ideas on this score were unusual in that for many ability and level of education are synonymous. The principal category of workers who would take exception to this equation are the skilled men.

Given the intensity of feeling surrounding the subject of promotion and the fact of competition for higher posts, the data from Nsambya present something of a paradox. In Chapter 5 we saw that close friends associate in cliques which are based on equality of status in terms of the industrial unit in which the members work, their occupation, grade, level of education and income. All these factors generate solidarity. At the same time the individuals making up a particular clique are likely to be involved in competition for posts further up their career ladder. The structure of the cliques is thus fundamentally unstable, first because of this competition, and secondly and more concretely because promotion inevitably separates clique members. In fact relationships generally remain amicable until such times as a promotion or other elevation of status occurs, at which point the group breaks up or at least sheds some of its members. Occasionally all or at least most members obtain promotion at roughly the same time, and the clique as a whole advances up the social ladder. In some ways the fact that the members of a clique are structurally in the same competitive situation enhances its solidarity. Jackson and Graham, the Station Master and the Goods Agent, for example, each felt that they were fellow sufferers 'overlooked' by the system.

This paradox of solidarity in the face of mutual competition is nowhere greater than in the case of relationships between the senior drivers, which are discussed in the next section. The example is also interesting for the choice of ideology through which the existence of intense competition is expressed.

RESPONSES TO SUCCESS AND FAILURE

Witchcraft and sorcery

It has long been established in the ethnography of Africa that accusations of the use of supernatural or magical powers to bring misfortune to others are usually uttered against those with whom the victim is in a particular relationship. Frequently such accusations are associated with competition between members of a close-knit community, a point that has been emphasised by a number of anthropologists (especially Marwick 1965). Although most studies of witchcraft deal with relations in rural communities, it has been argued, by Mitchell for example, that accusations of resort to supernatural attacks are likely to occur also in urban and industrial contexts, where 'townsfolk are linked in co-operative enterprises in which competition is nevertheless an essential element' (Mitchell, 1965: 210). The material from Nsambya largely supports this conclusion. A point much disputed in the literature is the need for a distinction between witchcraft and sorcery. Undoubtedly in many cultures such distinctions, among others, are frequently made. This includes both Luo and Luhya, though the terms 'witchcraft' and 'sorcery' do not necessarily provide an adequate framework for translating the many and varied categories which are in use. For the purposes of the present material, however, it is unnecessary to operate with any such distinction. Here the term 'witchcraft' is used to cover all forms of supernatural and magical attacks and it corresponds with how the English word is used locally, and with a Swahili equivalent – *uchawi*.

Belief in the efficacy of witchcraft is widespread in East Africa, and though detailed beliefs and practices vary from culture to culture the basic principles are similar. There is no anomaly, therefore, in the fact that accusations of witchcraft are made across ethnic boundaries. The similarity in beliefs extends from the methods thought to be effective to the contexts in which they are likely to be used. In Kampala, for example, people from many cultures would accept the idea that a jealous woman is likely to attack her lover, and it is widely recognised that accusations are likely to be made (or witchcraft practised) between those competing for power and status. Statements like the following are not uncommon. A young Soga fireman at Kampala said that his father, a peasant farmer, had been made very ill by a jealous person who had bewitched him. They had learnt this from the diviner. The young man claimed that in Buganda and Busoga many people became jealous and resorted to witchcraft, 'if a man tries to get on'. A young Gusii clerk on a tea estate near Kericho asserted that where he worked 'Many Luo are very active with witchcraft' which they use in order to get promotion.

During a stay in a Luo location in northern Tanzania I was able to study a number of accusations and confirmed that in the rural area they frequently occur between men in competition with one another for prestige in the local community. Both there and in the towns it is commonly held that struggles for status or power generate mystical attacks and cause misfortune, at least when other explanations may be discounted. Thus an MP whose car crashes may be said to have been destroyed by his rivals' witchcraft. As a corollary it is assumed that a successful man must *ipso facto* have access to very powerful magical resources both to have attained his eminence and to protect himself from the attacks of others. The particular examples dealt with below must be understood in terms of this general context (see also Kapferer 1969: 202–3, and Parkin 1969a: 67–9).

In Chapter 4 it was mentioned that the Loco Shed had a reputation as a 'terrible place' for witchcraft. Most of the cases of which I have record in fact emanate from there, in particular from among footplate staff.

The senior drivers at Kampala. For a number of months during 1964 I followed relations between a small clique of senior drivers among whom rumour had it that a war of magic was taking place. Matters came to a head when one of their number died in hospital from a septic ulcer. Some details about the three principal characters in the case are followed by the comments of various informants. The three were each over fifty years old, having joined the railways before 1935. All were illiterate, and all were Kenyans. One, Mfupi, was a Luhya, then on grade VI. The other two were Luo, Odhiambo being also grade VI, but Okello grade V, and the most senior driver at Kampala.

Comment: Luhya driver grade VIII. He said that Mfupi was blaming Okello for bewitching him and that the latter was 'very active' with medicines. The reason for this, he claimed, was that Mfupi was grade V and Okello grade VI. (Actually the reverse was true.) He later reported that Okello had been taken seriously ill and was accusing Mfupi of bringing this about. The latter had just left to go on leave in Kenya where he would 'fetch a really powerful medicine' with which to finish Okello off for good.

A Luo bar-owner. He said that he had heard that Mfupi had recently made a serious mistake at work. Driving the train out of Kasese he had allowed the boiler of his engine to burn out. For this he would be charged and his promotion stopped. The bar-owner thought that Mfupi would accuse someone of bewitching him. This practice was very common in the Loco Shed, he said, when a driver makes a mistake or has an accident. Very often a senior driver accuses a junior, for example, a man in grade VI accuses someone in grade VII. In a later episode of the same saga he told me that Odhiambo was suffering from swollen eyes and was claiming that he had been bewitched. Odhiambo was a suspicious man. If he were drinking in the bar with Okello and Mfupi and had to step outside for a 'short call' he would take elaborate precautions to ensure that his drink was not poisoned. He might, for example, put the top back on the bottle, or ask the bar-owner to watch it, or when he returned pour some into his companion's glass, waiting then until he had drunk from it, or even when the other was not looking, switch the bottles.

I actually observed antics of this kind. Mfupi had indeed made more than one serious mistake and had had his promotion held back.

Joseph, the RSF. Although he himself never believed in witchcraft 'since I was a young man', he admitted that many people in the Loco Shed did. Mfupi, Okello and Odhiambo in particular were 'always talking about medicines'. Mfupi would accuse Okello, and then Okello blame it all on Odhiambo, saying 'this Odhiambo is trying to poison us, we should not drink with him'. Joseph commented that it was common for a driver who had been charged as a result of an accident to go to a diviner and ask: 'Who has done this to me? Will I win the case?' When Okello became ill with his ulcer and finally died, Joseph reported the rumour that on his deathbed he had given his wife the names of two drivers, one from Kampala and another from Eldoret, who had accompanied him on his last drink. They had poisoned him and he would now die. In the hospital he had sent out for an African specialist saying his was an African sickness requiring African medicines.

At Okello's wake, held at his house at Nsambya, large numbers of men from the Loco Shed were present, and made a generous collection. His fellow senior drivers were, however, absent. Okello's senior wife in her keening repeated the phrase '*Alingalinga*' – 'I am keeping silent.' This was interpreted by those present as meaning that she would keep quiet for now, but would make her accusation when she got home. Although opinion generally fastened on either Mfupi or Odhiambo as the cause of Okello's misfortune, other explanations also circulated. For example, it was suggested that his death, Mfupi's accident and a number of other disasters had been caused by Ganda witchcraft, because the Ganda wished to drive all Kenyans out of the Railways. It was also rumoured that Okello had died because of a land dispute back home and that formerly he had been a notorious witch but that on his last visit he had called in the 'Legio Maria' – an anti-witchcraft movement – to exorcise his house, and hear his confession to a large number of killings.

Senior drivers at Eldoret. A similar situation was reported among the drivers at the Eldoret Depot. There the accusations centred on one Luo grade V driver – Orwa. Two cases came to my attention. In the first he was sharing a train with another high-grade driver, a Luhya. As Orwa was resting in the 'caboose', the Luhya who was driving the engine thought he saw 'devils dancing on the line ahead'. Back at the depot the Luhya reported to the Shedmaster that in future he would refuse to go out with Orwa as the man was using medicines against him. The second case likewise involved a Luhya driver, and also occurred while Orwa was sitting in the caboose. This time the driver suddenly put on the brakes for an emergency stop and got down from the engine. When Orwa came along to see what was wrong the Luhya shouted abuse and hit him. Later the Luhya claimed he could not understand what *kiserani* (evil spirit) had got into his mind to make him do what he did, and he blamed Orwa for bringing it on him.

Everyone agreed that these events reflected the competition between drivers. When Orwa was asked why he thought that he had been accused he replied at once that it was because people were jealous of his high grade and seniority. Although some people in the comments cited earlier, and in others not quoted, suggest that the principal direction of an accusation will be from a senior man to a junior with the implication that the junior is jealous of the senior's success, the cases indicate that accusations from both directions may occur. In fact both can be explained by reference to the underlying ideology, for an attack by a senior man on a junior is seen essentially as a defensive measure. The direction of the accusations is less significant here than their occurrence between a set of men closely bound together in a competitive situation.

Not all accusations of witchcraft necessarily reflect competition, as perhaps the case of Wellington, cited in the last chapter, indicates. Nor is the hostility between competitors always or even generally expressed through accusations of witchcraft. Why, then, in these cases were witchcraft accusations employed? The question poses a number of problems. First, is the extent to which such accusations are apparently confined to the drivers an accurate reflection of the true situation? It would indeed be very easy to miss any accusations that might be made, for there is no formal channel through which they can be aired. Everything is *sotto voce*, and information is passed on as gossip. Rarely was an accusation made to me directly, though one example is cited in the next chapter. Granted, however, that the incidence of accusations is higher in the Loco Shed, as seems to be believed by the people concerned, what is the explanation? It was often said, especially by clerks, that witchcraft accusations mostly came from 'illiterates'. It is impossible to show that witch *beliefs* are less among educated men, but it may be agreed that to express a belief in witchcraft would run counter to what an educated person is expected to believe. There is, then, perhaps an association between education and the culturally acceptable idiom for the expression of hostility. Let us also accept that opportunities for promotion among illiterates are greatest when they are skilled workers, and among skilled men the opportunities are greatest and competition stiffest among drivers. Since there is a high concentration of skilled men, and of course drivers, in the Loco Shed, it is not surprising that it has earned a reputation for witchcraft, or indeed that accusations most frequently occur there. That is not to say that accusations never occur between educated clerks, as an example will show later. The incidence, however, is apparently rare.

PROMOTION AND THE RESTRUCTURING OF RELATIONSHIPS

Social mobility among Nsambya residents derives almost entirely from promotion within the EARH, opportunities for which occur in some degree at all levels. The chances for advancement are, of course, much greater for some than for others in the normal course of events and this situation was intensified during the period covered by this study by the advent of Africanisation. Upward mobility forces the individual to readjust his relationships with fellow workers, making it necessary for him to reconcile former ties of equality with current differences of status. With former colleagues he must learn to operate a new mode of behaviour, taking care, as we saw in Chapter 5, that while the new distance between them is recognised it is not emphasised. He may also have to adjust to an equality with those to whom previously he was subordinate, and *vice versa*. In cases of the latter kind there appeared to be few difficulties except when an individual had risen exceptionally rapidly to a new post or when former subordinates were promoted to levels of equality with Europeans. Several newly-promoted African officers expressed the view that Europeans did not really accept them in their new roles.

In some respects the problems of adjustment are diminished by the extent to which promotion is accompanied by transfer. The individual is removed both socially and physically from the nexus of his old associates and can learn his new role in a fresh context and it may be some time before he is confronted with old friends. Nevertheless it may be argued that the problems of readjustment are much greater for railwaymen, and similar groups like the police or the army, than for the general run of office and factory workers in Kampala. Any urban African faces some restructuring of ties – especially with kinsmen particularly when he wishes to retain a rural foothold. It is perhaps the case that in this respect the problems of the upwardly mobile individual are greater among Luo and Luhya with their widely ramifying lineage systems and an ideology of brotherhood than for Ganda whose lineages are shallower. From this point of view railwaymen are no different from other Kampala residents. In other parts of the city, however, there is largely a separation of work and residence, and social mobility is often signified by a move from one housing estate to another. The interconnection of work and residence at Nsambya Railway and on the police housing estate mean that the successful worker, when not transferred or when re-transferred to his old depot, is likely to be forced into frequent encounters with his former associates, and that they, when not promoted, are continually confronted with the concrete evidence of their own failure.

Promotions in the EARH must always have posed such problems and Africanisation only made them more frequent and more visible. The implementation of this policy, however, has had consequences far more important in terms of the community than the exacerbation of interpersonal relationships. For it has been the mechanism through which there has occurred a restructuring of the community as a whole. By increasing or rather heightening the range of grades and occupations available to Africans, by widening the ranges of income in the population, it has created or at least intensified differences of status. By placing Africans in positions of power and authority over other Africans it has potentially divided the community into two classes who have differences of interest and allegiance which (also potentially) are in conflict. The immediate consequences of this have so far been small scale. In the long term the significance of this development could be profound.

CHAPTER 7

URBAN ASSOCIATIONS AND COMPETITION FOR STATUS

This chapter attempts to draw together a number of themes. It has been argued that relative status as measured by grade, income, education and occupation provides a framework for interpersonal and intergroup relations and that developments within the industry, which have given opportunities for the achievement of status, mean that interaction takes place in a highly competitive environment. Nowhere is this competition for prestige greater than in the various urban associations which operate both at Nsambya and in Kampala. Personal advancement in these associations, signalled by the achievement of office, brings both standing and power within the urban community. This chapter will illustrate this by way of an extended case study which outlines events surrounding competition for office in one urban association, the Railway African Union, during 1964/5. The material will document a range of themes which have already been noted in previous chapters including the significance of departments and sections as political arenas, and the extent to which ethnic alignments cut across those derived from the industrial framework. For it will be shown that during contests for control of the union claims are made that allegiances among groups of leaders, and between leaders and rank and file members, are determined by tribal identity and interest. This raises the question discussed briefly in Chapters 3 and 5 of the significance of 'tribalism' in a modern industrial context.

Some of the data contained in this chapter has been published previously (Grillo 1969a). The presentation here differs in a number of ways. First, the amount of ethnographic evidence discussed is considerably more extensive: in particular the history of events in the contest for power in the union is extended beyond the point at which it was left in the previous narrative. Second, the analysis has been expanded to include consideration of a wider range of problems, and in some respects the conclusions I now reach differ from those outlined in the earlier publication. Third, the wider theoretical implications which before could be mentioned only briefly are here given at least rather less superficial notice.

URBAN ASSOCIATIONS IN KAMPALA AND AT NSAMBYA

Railwaymen have the opportunity of joining a wide range of urban voluntary associations, some of which are directly related to employment in the

EARH and others independent of it. By association is meant any organisation or club or institution such as a church or political party. Associations unique to the railway community include: the two Railway Clubs and their committees and subcommittees, e.g. the management of the Railway football team; the welfare committee, a joint staff–management body concerned with all railway welfare activities including the clubs and to some extent the running of the housing estate – the nearest approach to a tenants' association that exists among railwaymen; and numerous bodies concerned with industrial relations – the local staff committees and, above all, the trades unions. Beyond these are the associations which railwaymen may join but which are not their exclusive province. Leaving aside sports clubs, political parties and churches, the most important of these are the ethnic unions. Membership in such bodies link railwaymen with the members of other urban communities in Kampala and with people much further afield, especially those in the rural areas.

Some idea of the extent of participation in the principal associations is conveyed by Table 37. Though further reference will be made to this table,

TABLE 37. *Association membership among railwaymen*

Association	Low status	High status	All
	% membership among:		
Railway African Union	69.0	37.1	54.3
Railway Workers Union	6.2	7.4	6.8
Ethnic association	47.0	37.1	42.5
Railway African Club	47.0	37.1	44.1
Association leader	12.5	33.3	22.1

two points may be made here. First, the trade union is the one association which stands out in terms of membership, followed by the Railway African Club and ethnic associations. Very few respondents were members of other clubs, apart from the churches, which are discussed separately. Second, when the sample is divided into high- and low-status workers it is found that proportionately many more of the former can be classified as association 'leaders', leadership being defined as membership of a committee or the holding of office.

Almost all associations are organised on a formal basis using the familiar 'Western' model. Each generally has a (written) constitution providing for the annual election of committee members and a hierarchy of officers which usually includes a president or chairman, a secretary and a treasurer. This form of organisation is favoured even in those ethnic associations whose members come from what are (or perhaps were) traditionally acephalous societies. Trade union constitutions are in some respects regulated by the law. The functions of urban voluntary associations have been extensively discussed in the literature, particular emphasis being placed on their 'adaptive' role, i.e. the way in which they help the incoming migrant to adjust to urban life by providing an institutional framework within which he can establish a network of friends and learn the rules of the new urban culture (e.g. Little 1965, Parkin 1966a). It is argued that the very structure of such associations may help him to understand the novel hierarchical system with which he is confronted. While historically these functions were, and perhaps still are, significant, in the present context more weight should be attached to their function as arenas in which competition for urban leadership at the local- or middle-status level may take place.

ETHNIC ASSOCIATIONS

At Nsambya membership of ethnic associations seems to be slightly greater among low-status workers, but the difference between their incidence of participation and that of high-status men is slight. More significant are differences between ethnic groups. In the sample membership was highest among Luhya (70%) and Luo (64%) while the figure for all other tribes combined was only 22%. The figures confirm an impression that it is among the Kenyans that associational activity of this kind is greatest, and support Parkin's findings for the estates in Kampala East. Outside the Luo and Luhya the highest incidence of membership appears to be among Soga where four out of five respondents claimed to be in an association. This is in contrast to Parkin's discovery that attempts to found a Soga Association in Kampala East failed (1966: 62). The Nsambya evidence is not necessarily inconsistent with this, however, and in fact illustrates a characteristic feature of many urban associations, their ephemeral nature. The existence of a Soga Association among railwaymen, suggested by the sample and confirmed by observation, may indicate little more than that a small group of townsmen, in one area of the city, have decided to have a formal organisation. Problems of legitimation come only when several groups independently claim to represent an urbanwide community.

The organisation of Luo and Luhya associations is more formal and to some degree centrally regulated. My own evidence largely confirms the work of Parkin in this respect. Each operates at three levels of organisation with, at the top, the Luo and Luhya unions formed on a pan-East African basis with headquarters in Kenya and branches in the various cities including Kampala. During the fifties and sixties they were political parties or pressure groups of a kind. Below these are the affiliated location unions based on the rural administrative units and having branches wherever sufficient numbers from the home area happen to live. Location union branches also have an ephemeral character, though perhaps less so among Luo than among Luhya where they are often dormant and are activated only for a particular purpose, often a crisis, or by particularly energetic or ambitious leaders. Location unions, too, are political pressure groups, raising funds and support for home interests. They sometimes, perhaps frequently, have close ties with their local members of Parliament. They also serve as social clubs, one of the principal occupations being the organisation of a location football team. At the lowest level are clan or lineage or sublocation associations which concern themselves almost exclusively with the moral and physical welfare of their members. There is wide variation in the extent to which there is continuity in and formal organisation of their activities. In some cases there appeared to be a thriving association, with committees meeting regularly and the full range of officers, while others meet sporadically, perhaps only at times of trouble – a death, a runaway wife, a case of incest. Comparing the Luo and Luhya at Nsambya with those in Kampala East there appears to be much less active involvement, as opposed to nominal membership, in ethnic associations. There are a number of possible explanations. The present study began after Parkin's work in Kampala East had been completed, and there seems to have been a general slackening of interest in ethnic unions during this period perhaps because leadership had largely been in the hands of those who after independence in Kenya were able to divert their interest and energies into other activities – politics or new careers – which the political changes made possible. Second, the structure of the railway community to some extent isolates railwaymen from ethnic associations in two ways. The welfare activities which on other housing estates are performed largely if not exclusively by ethnic groups are at Nsambya partly performed by other sets of people, e.g. the collections made in work sections at times of trouble. Moreover, the railway community has its own arenas within which leaders can operate, viz. the trades unions and the various clubs and committees mentioned earlier. Historically, however, railwaymen had previously played a prominent part in at least the Luo union, and according to informants a Luo association, not the union, had existed at Nsambya in the early thirties, when it was founded to help return the bodies of deceased men to their homes.[1]

A NOTE ON RELIGION

Some religious associations, especially the numerous sects, perform functions similar to those of ethnic associations by providing welfare for their members and arenas for leadership. A breakdown of religious affiliation among railwaymen is given in Table 38 which includes a comparison with

TABLE 38. *Religious affiliation at Nsambya and in Kampala East compared*

Denomination etc.	Percentage adherent at	
	Nsambya	Nakawa/Naguru
Catholic	45.8	45.9
Protestant (CMS)	37.3	39.1
Muslim	6.8	7.3
Seventh Day	6.8	2.4
Others	3.4	5.3
Total	100.1	100.0

SOURCE for Nakawa/Naguru figures: Parkin 1969a: Appendix III.

Parkin's findings at Kampala East. Among railwaymen, the most numerous sect is the Seventh Day Adventists. Their greater importance at Nsambya compared with other areas of the city probably derives from the fact that they have many adherents in South Nyanza, an area from which come large numbers of Luo railwaymen. Two other sects are 'Africa Israel' and 'the Saved Ones'. The former recruit mostly among Luhya unskilled workers. They hold their ecstatic meetings and marches most Sundays at the estate. The sect known in English as the Saved Ones and in Luganda as *Balokole* tends to recruit primarily among wives of high-status railwaymen. The tenant of the general store at Nsambya was a prominent member, and gatherings were held at his house. The sects take a strict line towards fleshly pleasures including smoking, drinking, popular music and women. Their adherents, though few in number, are devout, as are the followers of Islam. Other affiliations seem to be largely nominal. Church is a place to send the women and children. As one young man put it: 'One of the good things about Independence is that it means you don't have to go to Church on Sundays.' There is frequently a pragmatic and eclectic attitude to religion. For example, when a child in one Protestant family died he was buried in a Catholic cemetery and the service was read by a prominent relative from the lineage who was a devotee of Africa Israel. One elderly railwayman, baptised as Protestant, was planning to adopt the Greek Orthodox faith, which he had offered a considerable sum of money to establish a school in his home area. He also hoped that his marriage, now of some dozen years' duration, would be solemnised according to Orthodox ritual so that his wife could have some official standing to qualify for his pension after his death. Although religious affiliation appears to be unimportant for most railwaymen it must be said that the extent and significance of church organisation in Kampala itself remains a major gap in our ethnographic knowledge.

Participation in other associations – sports clubs, political parties and so on – is minimal. Railwaymen are in this respect primarily spectators rather than joiners. This is not the case with trades unions.

THE ORGANISATION AND FUNCTIONS OF THE RAILWAY UNIONS

Although the EARH is an interterritorial body there is no single union incorporating workers throughout the network. In the early sixties there were eight workers' associations with separate African, Asian and European unions in Kenya and Tanzania, and an African and an Asian union in Uganda. Most of the material discussed in this chapter is concerned with one of these only, the Railway African Union (Uganda) or RAU(U).

The RAU(U) recruits from among all full-time African railwaymen stationed in Uganda, and only from them. It is an industrial union whose members come from all grades and occupational groups, unlike in Britain where there are separate unions for clerical staff, footplate staff and for general workers. The union is organised on the traditional British model. At each depot where the numbers warrant there are branches which elect their own committee and officers. The branches send delegates to an annual conference which is the governing body of the union and which discusses policy resolutions. Conference also elects a national executive – president, vice-president, general secretary, assistant gen. sec., treasurer and assistant treasurer – who are responsible for carrying out conference decisions. The president is a full-time paid official in contrast to the British model where the permanent officer is usually the general secretary. This point has some bearing on what will follow, since the situation became an issue in the contest for power. Since its foundation the union had had only one president, the Hon. H. M. Luande, MP, who had formerly worked in the EARH as a telegraph clerk. When in late 1965 the union switched to the British pattern, Luande ceased to be president but became general secretary. The union has an office in Kampala near the railway station manned by a small permanent secretarial staff. The membership fee of 2s. per month is deducted from salaries at source – the 'check-off' system – and paid to the union. Membership is optional, though some unions leaders would have preferred a 'closed shop'. In early 1964 there were about 3,000 members, of whom a third were stationed at Kampala.

The Kampala branch committee consists of six officers – chairman, secretary, treasurer and an assistant for each office – who are chosen in annual depot-wide elections, and a number of representatives, sometimes referred to as 'shop stewards', elected by union members in each departmental section. There are usually ten representatives on the committee.

The functions of the union in industrial relations may be mentioned briefly. The formal position of the unions is recognised and regulated by the 'Industrial Relations Machinery Agreement, 1962' which established a hierarchy of consultative committees. At the level of the depot they are called 'local staff committees', of which at Kampala there are three, one for each major department. Their personnel consists of representatives of management together with workers' representatives elected by employees in each section. The union has one or more ex-officio places depending on the strength of its membership in the department. For each region there is a territorial council consisting solely of union and management nominees which may discuss matters referred to it by the local staff committees. Finally there is the central joint council which discusses major issues in industrial relations – pay claims, Africanisation policy and other matters affecting all workers. Apart from the central joint council the consultative committee has little relevance to industrial disputes and frequently negotiations between management and workers at the local level take place outside the framework of the machinery.

Within the depot the main activities of branch officials include helping members on disciplinary charges and negotiating with management in the event of a local dispute. They also mediate between the rank and file and the national executive, conveying information both ways. They have a particular role to play informing members of the progress of important negotiations and preparing them for any action that might be necessary. It is their task to mobilise the members should a strike be called. As was noted in the last chapter union officials have a quasi-career structure. Many of those now on the national executive worked their way up, first attaining prominence as a representative, then a branch officer. When they attain the level of the national executive their primary duty lies in conducting negotiations at the territorial and central joint councils, intervening in local disputes only when called in by either side. They are essentially politicians meeting with senior officials of management, with civil servants and with ministers of government. As representatives of their union they are also in contact with other trades unionists in the UTUC and with organisations abroad such as the ICFTU and the ILO. Since their decisions can bring rail transport to a halt in East Africa they are important men whose views are sought by the press. They may be fêted or abused, but they become nationally known figures. It is in the NEC that the real power, its trappings and its perquisites, actually resides. NEC members also have access to various forms of patronage of which the most important is the ability to nominate members for places on training courses either at the ICFTU College in Kampala or abroad on scholarships donated by one of the many international organisations. How important this is as a form of influence may be judged from discussion in the last chapter.

Who are the union members? To answer this question it is useful to distinguish between the ordinary rank and file and the leaders which in this case means officers and committee members at branch and national level.

TRADE UNION MEMBERSHIP

The rank and file

In early 1964 the union claimed a total membership of 3,000 out of approximately 4,000 workers eligible to join. About 500 members were in Group B, the rest in Group C. Since Group B staff in Uganda numbered about 1,000, the proportion of this Group in the union was roughly 50% while about 80% of Group C were members. The results of the Nsambya survey, which was conducted a year later and after the events to be described in this chapter, show rather lower proportions of union members even when the results for the RAU(U) and the Railway Workers Union are combined. This may be explained by the resignations that occurred during 1964, as we shall see. Nevertheless the difference in the incidence of participation between the two Groups remained, with 69% of Group C in the sample claiming membership and 40% of Group B. Evidence from the sample also shows an occupational difference with the following percentages of each occupational group in the union: unskilled 77%, semi-skilled 62%, skilled 71%, clerks 21%, supervisors 20%.

One aspect of membership composition which will have some bearing on subsequent discussion is ethnic affiliation. Table 39 compares the incidence of RAU(U) membership in each of the main ethnic groups. It will be seen that two groups, Luo and Acholi, form a higher proportion of union members than they do in the sample in contrast with Ganda/Soga and others.

TABLE 39. *RAU(U) membership and ethnic identity*

Ethnic group	% in sample	% among members	% of group in union
Luo	23.0	28.0	64.0
Luhya/Samia	23.0	22.0	54.0
Ganda/Soga	14.8	9.0	33.0
Acholi/Sudanese	9.8	19.0	100.0
Others (18 groups)	29.5	22.0	41.0
Total	100.1	100.0	54.3

When the sample is broken down by nationality a similar difference is revealed between Kenyans, 60% of whom are members, and Ugandans, 48%. Superficially, therefore, there appears to be some difference in ethnic propensity to join the union. However, the relationship between ethnic identity and union membership is obscured by the intervention of other variables. Thus all the Acholi in the sample happened to be unskilled workers, while the majority of Ganda and Soga were clerks in Group B. The sample numbers are too small for a full comparison, but the available evidence, including intensive data, suggests that Luo clerks, for example, are not notably more prone to join the union than their counterparts in other groups.

The leaders

Among leaders a different pattern is found. Including all those who sat on the Kampala branch committee and those who stood for office in the branch, but excluding members of the national executive, we may identify thirty-five individual 'leaders' in the period 1963/4. Out of the thirty-five, thirty-one were Group B, and of these no less than twenty-three were in grades VIII and IX.[2] Furthermore, about 80% were clerks. The leadership, therefore, may be contrasted with the rank and file on several points. The typical leader is a lower-middle echelon clerk, likely to have some secondary education, be about thirty years old, earning around 500s. per month. He is likely to have served for eight or nine years in the EARH, and to be the subject of frequent transfers between depots. This profile, which is derived largely from survey data, accords with the information that could be collected about specific leaders. On the other hand, the 'average' member is unskilled or semi-skilled, poorly educated, with a higher length of service and, of course, lower pay.

That union leadership is largely in the hands of the relatively well-paid and well-educated clerks – the NEC members consist entirely of this group – is not surprising considering the patterns of leadership that have been observed in other urban associations in Kampala. In Kampala East, for example, the essential characteristics of those who make up what Parkin calls the 'local elite' are: average age, thirty; mean years at school, 8.2; mean income, 485s.[3] Of the twenty-seven individuals he lists, twenty-one are in white-collar jobs. This 'local elite' tends to be involved in the running of most of the local associations, with individuals holding office on several committees at one and the same time. Similarly at Nsambya those in competition for office in the union are likely also to be found on the club committees associated with the Railway, and on non-Railway associations such as ethnic unions. As we can see from Table 37, one-third of high-status respondents claimed to be a leader in at least one association. Among clerks and supervisors alone the figure was 37%.

Interest in union leadership appears to be greatest among clerks in grades VIII and IX. Approximately half the clerks in the depot on those grades appear to have been involved. It is precisely in this occupational group that chances of promotion arising from Africanisation have been greatest. Thus competitors for office in the union are also in intense competition with each other within the industry. Interest decreases with higher grade, and indeed involvement in the union seems to be a stage in the individual's career, a phase which he leaves behind on achieving upward mobility. Once grade VII and above has been attained most drop their union interests.

Other features of the leadership group include a heavy concentration in the Commercial and Operating Department, 55% of leaders compared with 38.5% among the ordinary members. Only 10% of leaders are from Mechanical Engineering although that department reported the highest percentage of members – 61%. The ethnic origins of leaders are also of interest, the actual figures suggesting that Luhya/Samia and Ganda/Soga are over-represented taking into account their strength in the membership as a whole – 48.6% of the leadership group, 31% of union members.[4] There may, however, be intervening variables which invalidate a straight comparison, as we saw when comparing ethnic identity and union membership. The significance or otherwise of ethnic identity among union leaders will be discussed extensively later.

POWER CONTESTS IN THE RAU(U)

The heavy involvement of certain categories of staff in union leadership is consistent with the status system of the community as a whole. Control of an urban association brings power and prestige and it is considered not only a prerequisite for those who aspire to high social standing, but in some sense their perquisite. It is this as much as anything which explains why the unskilled and skilled union members who make up the majority allow the leadership to remain in the hands of another occupational group even when they feel that that group pursues policies which do not necessarily reflect the interests of the bulk of the members. It is precisely because, in the society as a whole, leadership is in the hands of people like clerks rather than unskilled workers that the former are able to control the union without opposition from the latter. That the union constitution contains a 'literacy' clause which leaders must pass is simply a product of this. Aware of the possibilities in this situation, I observed very closely to see whether unskilled or skilled workers, the bulk of union members, were becoming conscious of their position. With the exception of the abortive

' Enginemen's Association' and possibly the Parcels' Office Committee (see below) no such development appeared to be taking place. Such conflicts over union leadership as occurred ran along very different lines.

During 1963/5 the RAU(U) was rent by two serious disputes over the leadership, or 'splits' as they are called locally, the second of which culminated in the formation of a breakaway union, the Railway Workers Union (RWU). These were not the first of such crises to occur in the union, nor indeed the last. Nor was the RAU(U) the only union in Uganda or Kenya to experience such problems. In a chapter discussing earlier events in the RAU(U)'s history which forms part of a wider study of the Uganda trades union movement, one writer, a political scientist, has suggested that a major cause of the recurrent conflict has been ethnic rivalry principally between Luhya and Luo, who as we have seen form the two largest groups on the Railway (Scott 1966: Chapter 6). Here we will examine that contention among others. The events to be described here were significant in the life of the community since they forced many individual railwaymen to make a choice between one of two groups of leaders, a process which threatened at one time to divide the population of the housing estate into two warring factions. The analysis of how this choice was made and how the community divided illustrates many of the themes that have run through this monograph. The narrative follows the events of both splits which are then examined using a variety of methods. The last part of the chapter widens the discussion to include some comments on the significance of ethnic identity in urban Africa and the relevance of this material for the anthropological study of factions.

Phase one: the ' Shifta' Faction

In the middle of 1963 a new branch committee was elected at Kampala in accordance with the constitution. Following their election certain officers of the committee, led by the chairman, began to criticise the way in which the president handled union affairs. At the 1963 annual conference, which was held in December, the Kampala branch put forward a resolution urging that the office of president should be held by a working railwayman, and that of general secretary should become the permanent post. It was also urged that the general secretary should be an *executive* officer with authority only to carry out the decisions of conference and the national executive. The resolution was not accepted, apparently on the technical grounds that it had been sent in too late for inclusion on the agenda, though there is some dispute over this. Many of the members of the branch committee were dissatisfied with this result, and when shortly afterwards one of the members of the NEC (the Assistant General Secretary, Christopher, see Table 40) was awarded a scholarship to study industrial relations in the UK, and the branch's nominee passed over, the crisis came to a head. The branch committee called a succession of meetings and made certain serious allegations against the president. Relationships between the branch and the NEC deteriorated further when the committee was refused permission to hold a general meeting in the Railway African Club. They responded by closing the branch office, a corrugated iron hut on the estate, and called on all members to resign. Approximately 230 complied, about a quarter of the branch membership. The RAU(U) executive then reported the affair to the Registrar of Trades Unions and obtained permission to disband the committee and re-open the branch office by force. This was done amid scenes of some turbulence on the estate. Fresh elections were held and a new committee took office in March 1964. Resignations continued sporadically and the members of the disbanded committee threatened to form a new union, which did not materialise. Nevertheless, the repercussions of this crisis lasted through the year until early 1965 when a new group which contained some members of what had come to be called the 'Shifta' faction founded the Railway Workers Union. Of this, more later.

Briefly, then, this was the outline of events in the first phase. Most of the developments took place in and around Nsambya and the depot where public meetings and private caucuses were held in homes, at the club and in the open air. The affair was accompanied by considerable rhetorical and occasional physical violence. The word 'shifta' applied by the president's supporters to the rebels means 'bandit' and was the term currently used to describe Somali terrorists operating in Kenya's Northern Frontier District. It was taken to be highly abusive. They were also referred to as the 'Splinter Group' which is the term I used for them in a previous publication. The following analysis attempts to sort out three related aspects of the conflict: the issues at stake, the composition of the factions, and the processes the leaders used to mobilise support.

The issues. Although considerable confusion existed as to the issues, there was agreement on both sides on a number of themes. The first concerned the position of the president. Luande had long since given up his job in the EARH to devote himself full time to the union. This occasioned the criticism that he was now out of touch with the problems of the ordinary member. It was also felt that only a working railwayman should have the powers that Luande had as president. This was the reasoning behind the branch's resolution to conference. It was also argued that Luande, who besides being president of the RAU(U), was also president of the UTUC, a frequent delegate to international conventions, and a member of the Uganda Parliament, was attempting too much and consequently neglecting his duties towards railwaymen. Beyond these there were more serious criticisms, the tenor of which may be gauged from the strenuous denials issued by Luande in a handbill distributed to members at the height of the troubles.

RAU–Uganda still very strong

Quite recently there have been troubles and division in our Union which have been brought about by a few members who were in personal disagreement with me and have taken advantage of attacking me through the Union . . . They have gone to the extent of persuading you to resign from the Union now led by me and form a Splinter Union . . . Please do not be deceived. Your Union has for several years been run on constitution and this will continue. No Union money is wasted or used for personal convenience as has been alleged that I am using your money to build a six Story House. How can my sensible members believe such open deceipt or lies. Your money is looked after by a Treasurer who works in conjunction with the Secretary and Trustee. Without any of these three, not a single cent can be paid out. These office bearers are constitutionally elected. No Union money is being spent on individual scholarships.

Similar themes were stressed in an edition of the irregularly appearing union newsletter *Sauti ya RAU(U)* in an article entitled ' Away with blacklegs.' [5]

Time and again our leaders, Teachers and Inspirers have been warning us against subversion undermining intrigues, character assassination and rumour mongering. . . But it appears that the more these warnings are being sounded the more the perpetrators become heart hardened and continue to indulge in these social evils. . . For the past few years either by fate or Providence such blacklegs have been among our organisation. They have been cliquing, intriguing and undermining quite a lot the leadership of the Union. . . These self-styled unionists and know-alls had agents in the National Secretariat whose duty was to smuggle official documents and leak out official information to the subversionist camp. . . They have now resorted to new and subtle forms of undermining and subversion. These people have taken scholarships and Union funds as an Umbrella.

The allegations which the president refuted in the handbill were widely believed to be true, and a belief in their veracity would seem to present reasonable grounds for attempting his removal from office. The principal issue would therefore seem to be the welfare of the union. The same concern could be said to lie behind another theme. For it was alleged that the union was dominated by the president's own ethnic group, the Luhya-Samia, that his relatives were employed as officials at union headquarters, and that he gave preference to his tribe in the distribution of overseas scholarships. Against this the president's faction claimed that the Shiftas were dominated by Luo who were trying to control the union in the interests of their own ethnic group. Note that accusations of tribalism are always condemnatory when used as a theme in political debate. Neither side admitted that there might be any basis in the charge against them.

The ethnic theme re-appears under another guise in a third issue. The argument between the two factions frequently involved political jargon of the kind current in local politics, as the extract from *Sauti ya RAU(U)* shows. Terms such as ' neo-colonialist ', ' Imperialist ', ' opportunist ', ' subversive ' were employed with some abandon. Nevertheless, since the Shiftas seemed consistently to oppose the president's association with the Western-oriented ICFTU it is possible to conclude that the two factions at least represented themselves as supporters of two opposing ideological view-points. At that time there was a genuine difference of opinion within the East African trades union movements and elsewhere (cf. Ananaba 1969, Smock 1969) as to whether they should maintain links with international organisations such as ICFTU which are unambiguously aligned with one or other of the major power blocs or whether they should remain neutral. This issue re-appeared in the later split. In both conflicts, however, it seems that the ideological dispute was less a cause of the divergence than a device through which the opposition of the two sides was expressed. The dispute was not 'about' ideology, but ideological differences were employed as themes in the argument. Two other related political issues were raised. The principal events of the split occurred at the same time as the army mutinies and the Zanzibar revolution, a coincidence which led to the suggestion, made entirely without foundation, that all three events were linked in a plot by a prominent Luo politician with a reputation as a left winger to gain power throughout East Africa. Besides this, the president's faction was sometimes referred to as 'KADU', the Kenya African Democratic Union, the party then forming the opposition in Kenya. Since Luhya were supposed to be prominent in KADU this issue once more reflects the accusation of tribalism.

It is clear that the theme of ethnic interest and ethnic competition runs through the arguments in this and in other conflicts. Scott, referring to an earlier crisis in 1959, comments: 'Continuing resistance to Luande's leadership came from members of the Luo tribe . . . On three occasions the Luo tried to assert themselves without success. On each occasion, a basically tribal rivalry could be concealed beneath more legitimate complaints about the Union leadership' (Scott, 1966: 64). Superficial assessment of the data presented so far might justify this conclusion, but the picture is more complicated than this.

The personnel. Although I have referred to two factions it cannot be assumed that their composition remained constant. Therefore in considering the personnel on each side I will in the first instance take the factions at the moment that the break actually occurred, i.e. in the spring of 1964. The central figures on each side were relatively few in number. They are listed in Table 40 together with some details of their backgrounds. Those listed include all those generally considered on the estate to be linked in each faction. Each side, however, seemed to consist of a rather smaller inner core of leaders – the president, Christopher, Simon and Nathan on the one hand, and Arthur, Hamilton and Nicholas on the other. The rest represented an outer core of leaders less closely linked to the principal figure. Outside of those listed here were others more closely identified with each faction than the average rank and file supporter. The inner cores tend to become cliques of the kind described in Chapter 5, indeed that of the president's faction being the basis for clique (ix) in Table 34, the members of which assigned each other a series of comic nicknames – 'Mzee – old man', 'Highway (robber)', 'Okello' – after the unfortunate John Okello of Zanzi-

TABLE 40. *The personnel of the president's faction and the Shifta faction*

Name	Ethnic group	Grade	Occupation	Dept.	Section	Union post [a]
The president's faction						
Luande	Samia	-	Permanent union official			President
Omuntu	Soga	B VIII	Clerk	DTS	Station	Vice-president
Christopher	Luhya	B IX	Clerk	DME	Office	Vice-gen. sec.
Simon	Luhya	B VIII	Clerk	DTS	Office	Vice-treasurer
Nathan	Samia	B VIII	Clerk	DTS	Station	Branch chairman
Terence	Toro	B IX	Clerk	DE	PWI	Section rep.
Daniel	Toro	B X	Clerk	DE	Office	Section rep.
Michael	Samia	B IX	Artisan	DME	Loco	Staff committee
Alan	Luhya	C I	Storeman	DME	Loco	Branch secretary
The Shifta faction						
Arthur	Luo	B V	Clerk	DTS	Station	Branch chairman
Ibrahim	Nubi	B IX	Clerk	DE	Office	Branch vice-chairman
Hamilton	Lango	B IX	Clerk	DTS	Office	Branch secretary
Musoke	Ganda	B IX	Clerk	DTS	Station	Branch vice-treasurer
Alexander	Luo	B IX	Supervisor	DTS	Station	Section rep.
Omolo	Luo	B VIII	Clerk	DTS	Yard	Section rep.
Nicholas	Luo	B IX	Clerk	DTS	Station	Staff committee
Washington	Luo	B VIII	Clerk	DE	Office	Former gen. sec.
Non-aligned?						
Derek	Dhola	B VI	Clerk	DTS	Office	Gen. sec.
Mukwaya	Ganda	B V	Clerk	DTS	Office	Treasurer

[a] Posts held immediately before or after the split.

bar fame. The inner core of the president's faction was also known as the 'Cabinet'. In terms of grade, occupation and by extension educational level, age and pay, both factions consisted mainly of the same kind of people, thirteen out of eighteen (omitting the president) being in grades VIII and IX and no less than sixteen being white-collar workers. Neither faction could claim to represent a distinct grade [6] or occupational interest, both being formed largely from among the local elite of leaders who operate in all associations, and between whom in the EARH there is intense competition for promotion. A possible distinction between the two factions is that most of the Shiftas are from the DTS department while the president's supporters are drawn from a wider range of departments, especially Mechanical Engineering. Second, while the Shiftas include five out of eight Luo and no Luhya–Samia, the president's faction has six out of nine Luhya-Samia and no Luo. This seems to indicate some ethnic basis for the factions.

Now this was the position in March 1964. If we look back to the elections of 1963 the ethnic division does not appear so clear cut. At that time Arthur, Omolo and Christopher competed for the post of branch chairman, while Derek, Simon and Nathan were in the field for the secretaryship. In the first case a Luo competed against a Luo, in the second a Luhya against a Samia. This would seem to indicate that ethnic identity is not the only factor ranging opponents against each other, at least not all the time. In addition there were a number whose allegiance changed over time, as we shall see.

There is little systematic evidence available concerning the supporters of each faction. Besides information derived from personal contacts the principal source is a list of names of those who resigned in March 1964. Some evidence can be derived from the Nsambya sample since this was taken after the resignations. Those claiming RAU(U) membership in the sample can be taken to include the president's supporters since they did not in fact resign, or rather they did not apparently feel strongly enough about the issues to hand in their resignations. An examination of the list of those who opted out shows that the proportion of Group B and C is roughly the same as in the membership as a whole, but there is considerable variation in their departmental composition. In absolute numbers only twelve resigned from Mechanical Engineering but 120 from the DTS and eighty from the DE. Why were there so few resignations from Mechanical Engineering where union membership is quite high and where so many Luo work? Certainly large numbers of those who resigned were Luo, according to the list of names, but they were not in a majority, nor were the resignees largely Nilotic since many of the Shifta supporters appear to have come from Interlacustrine Bantu groups such as Ganda and Ankole. Note that even after the split a high proportion of Luo remained in the union (see Table 39). Given that few Luhya–Samia left the union it is clear that the dispute cannot be explained entirely in terms of rivalry between two ethnic groups. Some clarification of this problem may emerge if we consider how the split developed.

The process. We will first examine in some detail events that occurred in the DTS department. During 1963 it seems that some of those who later formed the core of the Shifta faction were steadily gaining prominence and power by winning places on this department's local staff committee. In January 1963, Martin, a Luo Group C man from Rusinga (see Figure 6), was selected by the then Station Master, an Asian, to represent the section on the committee. This appointment aroused criticism from staff in the section on the grounds that Martin was 'illiterate' and unable to oppose the management. The opposition to Martin was led by Alexander and Nicholas (see Table 40), both Luo. They advocated an election which Nicholas, who claimed to have successfully opposed the Station Master at another depot where they had been stationed, eventually won. Among his supporters were the Ankole from the Carriage Cleaning subsection of which Alexander was the Supervisor. A little later the representative from the Yard was also attacked as an 'illiterate' and in a subsequent contest Omolo was elected. When the resignations occurred many workers at the Station and the Yard, even non-Luo, came out for the Shiftas.

The situation in the Parcels Office where all but two of the twenty or so workers were Luo was also interesting. There some of the employees had formed an entirely unofficial and self-appointed committee which included nearly half the staff and which claimed to represent the interests of Group C men and sought to brief the section representative on the local staff committee regarding their problems. The chairman of this unofficial committee was John O., another Rusinga Luo Group C man (see Figure 6), who was or became what might be termed the local organiser for the Shiftas in his subsection. So successful were his efforts that only three workers in the subsection failed to resign. One of these, a Luo, thought he would be sacked if he involved himself. The second was a Luhya, Roy, who was in fact a relative of one of the leaders of the president's faction. Although he did not bring his allegiance out into the open by publicly resigning he supported the Shiftas in the subsection and held the post of secretary on the unofficial committee. The third was Francis, another Rusinga man, who did not resign because he thought Luande was doing a good job. Francis, whose problems we analysed in Chapter 5, was, of course, unusual in other ways, being a Group C clerk with a high standard of education and artistic pretensions. Francis came under pressure to resign from, among others, John O., who, as can be seen from Figure 6, was his father's brother's son. Francis was told, in private, that Luande had to be removed so that Luo could take over in the section. The case was put unambiguously in terms of ethnic interest, with no reference to the kin connection. Relevant here perhaps is that there was ill-feeling between John O.'s branch of the lineage and that of Francis and other Rusinga men – he had opposed Martin, for example. Francis did not agree, and shortly afterwards was approached by the union and asked to be their nominee on the local staff committee. Although reluctant to incur the excessive displeasure of his workmates, Francis thought that this might provide a good opportunity for his advancement and accepted. He mentioned this to Roy who promptly reported the matter to John O. When the unofficial committee learned that Francis was to sit on the local staff committee they went to the chief clerk of the department to complain. He told them that because Francis was a union nominee they should take the matter up with the branch. Since all but Roy had now left the union they felt that this tactic was closed to them. Francis's path thereafter was far from smooth. His first problem came when he went to collect the file belonging to the representative he was replacing. Most of those in the office where it was kept had resigned and passed remarks like: 'Who has chosen this young man to represent us on the committee? Oh, the union did because he is still a member.' His next test came when he was asked, presumably as a union official, to countersign a number of resignation slips and forward them to the management (so that the salary office could stop the deduction of the monthly subscription). When John O. learned that he had failed to do so, he remarked: 'If you want to remain KADU and keep separate from your people, it will be the worse for you sometime.' Francis was the subject of numerous insults. For example, Musoke, a Shifta leader, is alleged to have declared: 'Who is this man representing us? We don't want him!,' a remark which nearly led to an exchange of blows. Francis was told in no uncertain terms by Roy that he would receive no co-operation from the rest of the staff. In retaliation he threatened that anyone who opposed him would be transferred, but in the end the pressure of the remarks proved too much and he resigned from the committee, though not the union.

In a similar way the Shifta faction built up its support in various parts of the depot, employing techniques which, as we will see, were later used by the RWU leaders in their bid for power. That pressure could be applied by reference to an ethnic interest is obviously important in the present discussion. Occasionally such pressure created impossible situations, of the kind that the Welfare Officer, James, had to face. Among his duties was that of supervising the Railway African Club. When the president's faction heard that the Shiftas wanted to hold a meeting in the club hall, some members approached James and urged him as a Luhya to deny the club to their opponents. If he failed to do so, they said, he would be called 'pro-Luo'. He recognised that if he complied he would inevitably be seen as 'pro-Luhya'. In his job he had to be completely neutral. In fact the Shiftas presented him with no option, as he saw it, by failing to book the hall in advance and therefore, in strict accordance with the regulations, he had to deny them access. He immediately balanced this in his own eyes by performing a service for a Luo family on the estate who had lost a relative. The club incident had a number of repercussions. The Luo proprietor of the bar at Nsambya, who at the time also had the franchise in the club bar, was heard to sympathise with James' action on the grounds that he had acted in accordance with the regulations. He was promptly subjected to a boycott by the Shiftas. At the same time his bar was also being boycotted by some supporters of the president because, it was alleged, he had been told by Arthur, the Shifta leader, to poison their beer.

So then, both sides apparently used the theme that this was an ethnic dispute both in private manipulations and in public accusations of tribalism. At least one element in the situation, the management, was, it seems, convinced that this was a matter of tribal rivalry. The IRO (Isaac) who arrived in Kampala at the height of the troubles told me that he had been appointed because, as a Ugandan, it was felt that he would stand a better chance of being accepted as neutral in a dispute thought to be essentially between two Kenyan tribes. In fact he was immediately linked in the minds of the president's faction with the Shiftas through his connection with Hamilton. They were both members of the small closely-linked network of middle-status Lango who had ties with the highest offices of state. In this way the Shiftas were further seen as representing an element in the equation of Uganda politics.

Throughout the contest there were some leaders whose allegiance was either unclear or which changed. Derek and Mukwaya had been elected to their posts on the NEC at the December 1963 conference with the support, it was said, of the Shiftas in order to curb Luande's power – we may recall the 'agents' referred to in the article in *Sauti ya RAU(U)*. They were then alleged to have been 'bought' by the president, and indeed they supported him throughout the following year. By the end of 1964 the president's faction was convinced that they had been 'bought' by the faction which founded the RWU, and in the NEC elections of December 1964 Derek was opposed for the post of general secretary by Christopher and defeated, receiving demotion to assistant general secretary. Washington was another 'waverer', as they were called. In 1962 he had been secretary of the Kampala branch and subsequently became general secretary on the NEC. In both capacities he had been a strong supporter of the president, claiming that during this time 'Luande was my best friend'. However, during his tenure of office in 1963 he had gone abroad on an industrial relations course, and on his return was ousted from his position by Derek, i.e. at that time an alleged Shifta supporter. Shortly afterwards Washington himself joined the Shiftas. When they broke up he tried to come to terms with the president's faction, one of whom told me that Washington had been 'promised something' at the next annual conference. When that failed to materialise he returned to opposition and emerged on the committee of the RWU.

The extent to which one is able to assert that this contest represents primarily rivalry between two ethnic groups depends on which part of the conflicting evidence one wishes to emphasise. Clearly a different interpretation is possible, but before taking the analysis any further the developments which followed the Shifta split will be recounted.

Phase two: The Railway Workers Union (RWU)

In the months following the resignations several key members of the Shifta faction moved from Kampala. Hamilton left to join the army, Arthur, Nicholas and Omolo were transferred on promotion, though rumour had it that their transfer was due to pressure from the president. Arthur in fact had to return to Kampala some months later to face a court charge which alleged an assault on a Ganda ticket collector, an incident which apparently arose in connection with the events described above. Arthur pleaded guilty – the man had tried to bar his entry to the Station and had been brushed aside – but the magistrate expressed annoyance that such a trivial matter had come to court so long after the event and discharged Arthur with a caution. Many people supposed that the case had been raked up to cause Arthur embarrassment.

Towards the end of 1964 several informants reported that a new attempt would shortly be made to wrest power from Luande in a development connected with events taking place in the Uganda trades union movement as a whole. In mid-1964 a new national organisation, the FUTU, arose in opposition to Luande's UTUC. The origins of FUTU are obscure though it was apparently backed, if not founded, by the Minister of Labour in the Uganda government. FUTU opposed the UTUC's link with the 'imperialist' ICFTU from which they claimed it received money to carry out subversive activities. A consequence of the emergence of FUTU was that in a large number of the unions affiliated to the UTUC a struggle broke out between those wishing to remain in that body and those wanting to join FUTU. The struggles were hard-fought and at times violent and in the end almost every union in the country was affected. The newspapers carried frequent press statements from each side claiming victory in some union or branch, often simultaneously. In January 1965 the battle was taken to Luande's home ground when the Railway Workers Union was formed and its leaders said they would join FUTU.

The new union presented its case and its committee at a general meeting called in the Railway African Club, and at once began recruiting both at Kampala and in up-country depots. They claimed considerable success and their vice-president was quoted in the press in February as saying they had 2,700 members. Their strategy was to win sufficient support from the RAU(U) to be able to go to the Registrar of Trades Unions and claim that they now represented railwaymen in Uganda. This they failed to achieve, at least they were refused registration. Shortly afterwards in May their president resigned and the organisation collapsed. Although at the outset it had seemed a formidable threat to the RAU(U), in the end it was a complete failure. In the Nsambya sample conducted in April at the height of the campaign only 7% of respondents claimed membership in the RWU as against 54% in the RAU(U).

RWU aims and policy. The RWU case was as follows. Their union had been formed because of growing dissatisfaction with tribalism in the RAU(U). They claimed that at the annual conference in December 1964 seventeen out of eighteen delegates were Luhya–Samia (an exaggeration this) who had been 'handpicked by the president'. The RWU was to be non-tribal and non-racial, which was why its title did not include 'African'. At the inaugural general meeting speakers from the platform produced the familiar charges including (a new one this) abuse of the union's recently acquired motor car. This, they said, was being used as a taxi by members of the NEC and it had been seen very late at night outside one of Kampala's night clubs. 'Were they,' a speaker asked 'holding a committee meeting at the Satellite Club?' The RWU also criticised the union's handling of industrial matters, in particular alleging a dilatory attitude towards members on disciplinary charges and that management had not been pressed hard enough on pay claims and Africanisation policy. The president had also used his friendship with management to get trouble-makers transferred.

Joshua, the RWU vice-president, told me that since they had 'one hundred per cent Luo support', the president's faction were accusing him of being 'tribalistic'. On the contrary, in attacking the president he was not raising questions of tribalism. He simply objected to the union being dominated by what he called 'one clan', the president and his relatives.

The personnel. There is little evidence for the composition of the RWU's support. Among RWU members in the Nsambya sample were some Luhya and several Loco Shed workers, a point which has some bearing on subsequent discussion, but the numbers in the sample were too small to justify any serious analysis. The RWU had five officers, listed in Table 41, who

TABLE 41. *The officers of the Railway Workers Union*

Name	Ethnic group	Grade	Occupation	Dept.	Section	Union post
Alex	Dhola	B V	Clerk	DE	Office	President
Joshua	Gisu	B VII	Clerk	DME	Loco	Vice-president
Orema	Lugbara	B X	Clerk	DME	Loco	Secretary
Ibrahim	Nubi	B VIII	Clerk	DE	Office	Treasurer
Washington	Luo	B VIII	Clerk	DE	Office	Organising sec.

represented the core of the faction. There were several others on the periphery of the leadership, all clerks, but they took little part in events. As Table 41 shows, the basic characteristics of the RWU faction leaders are precisely the same as those of all other leadership groups discussed previously. Two of the committee, Ibrahim and Washington, were actually close to the core of the Shifta faction, though now, a year later, the latter has moved up a grade. Orema was another 'waverer', who at one time had been a Luande supporter. He had then been transferred to another depot and on his return had joined the Shiftas, though not as a member of the core. His reason, he told me, was that he had been promised a scholarship abroad, but when it had been given to someone else he had become disillusioned with the RAU(U) and 'crossed over' – another local term. Note that the committee contained representatives from the DE's Office and the Loco Shed, but no other section.

Process. To illustrate how the RWU set about recruiting support we will take the case of Joshua, the vice-president. The day the new union was announced he was very active in the bars at Nsambya buying drinks and talking with people. He was aiming specifically at Loco Shed workers, among whom he appeared to be receiving a lot of verbal support, particularly from footplate staff. He made much of his background, for his father had been an engine driver and knew many of the men involved, and of the fact that he himself had ties with them in his capacity as Shed Clerk. 'They all know me,' he said. He referred constantly to the complaints voiced by many Loco Shed staff which he claimed the RAU(U) had ignored. Among his most enthusiastic supporters at this point was Matthew O., a Luo driver, who until then had supported Luande, being the union's nominee on the departmental staff committee. Joshua was clearly trying to maximise support in his own section with some success, for Joseph the RSF told me that many at the Loco Shed supported him.

This change of attitude on the part of the Loco Shed which had stayed behind Luande at the time of the resignations is only partly to be explained by the personal influence of Joshua, for several specific events had undermined the president's support in that section, including the growing dissatisfaction with the union's handling of the interests of skilled workers, and the behaviour of union officials during an unofficial strike, details of which cannot be discussed here. Moreover, the principal supporters of the president in the section had either fallen into disrepute or lost their interest. In Mechanical Engineering these included Christopher, Michael and Alan (listed in Table 40), a Luo named Matthew, and Joseph, the RSF. The latter had at one time been very close to Luande, but drifted away from him, and the union, during 1964, a process which culminated, as we saw, in his opposing the strike of November of that year. Christopher, in the period following the resignations, had gone abroad for study and when he returned became, for a time at least, 'very proud'. The behaviour of Washington after his trip abroad had provoked from Joseph the comment that when a trade union man goes away he comes back very full of himself: 'Who are you? I've been to U.K. I have a passport. Then he tries to have his own Union.' Michael also suffered from a falling reputation on account of his propensity for drinking and fighting, while Alan, whose outlook on life we discussed in the last chapter, also lost support. He had been very popular with Group C men, including some outside the Loco Shed. One of the Ankole Compound Cleaners had described him admirably as '*Mtu hodari sana*' – a strong, brave man, a militant. Thus Joshua was simply exploiting a ripe situation.

He also struck out in another direction, using his position as Shed Clerk to secure the recruitment of a young Luo (Osbert) as a cleaner, despite an unofficial freeze on the employment of non-Ugandans. Joshua claimed that when he had done this, 'The Luo had been very pleased.' His action in this case had several angles. First, as he said, he specifically recruited a Luo to please other Luo and thus gain their support. He also pleased a number of other people for the boy he recruited was a friend of the brother of David who owned the bar at Nsambya. Joshua thus fulfilled an obligation to the bar-owner and demonstrated their mutual influence in the community. Finally Osbert himself had a number of unemployed friends whom Joshua was then able to recruit as his 'Youth Wing' – the local term for supporters, not necessarily young, who carry banners at meetings, lead the cheers and perform other necessary tasks, including strong-arm work.

Both sides employed some dubious methods in this contest. Joshua alleged that he had been offered 7,000s. to resign. Such allegations are naturally difficult to substantiate, but one important accusation was made publicly and never to my knowledge challenged. When Alex, the president of the RWU, finally resigned, he issued a press statement reported in the *Uganda Argus*, 6 May 1965, as follows:

> Mr. ––––– said yesterday that he had been deceived by some leaders of a political organisation that he would be granted a scholarship and money if he broke away from his former Union and formed another. . . 'I have received none of the big gifts I was promised and I have now decided to rejoin my former Union,' he said.

This statement, taken at its face value, would seem to dispel any suggestion that the breakaway union was conceived in terms of profound ideological commitment, despite its association with FUTU.

It was in connection with the contest between the RWU and the RAU(U) that there occurred one of the few instances of witchcraft accusation involving educated white-collar workers. My information here derives entirely from Joshua. One day, during March, I met him in the bar. He seemed very glum, and said 'I am now approaching my crisis.' He then related how members of the president's faction had summoned a witchdoctor from their home to destroy him, Joshua. He had not worried at first, had even greeted the man and asked him whether he knew that he had been stationed at Mombasa, and didn't he think he had some powerful magic? (The potency of medicine seems to be related to the distance from its source.) The witchdoctor's hands trembled. He had then returned home to get some really powerful magic. This is what worried Joshua, for he felt very tired and a bit ill, and wasn't there small-pox on the estate? He then said that some people were accusing him of having destroyed the union car which had recently crashed, injuring several of the president's faction. On the very day the crash occurred, Joshua had been arguing with Christopher in the latter's office and had told him, 'You'll see!' And they did. This was as close as any informant ever came to admitting responsibility for a supernatural attack.

So, then, the RWU offensive ground to a halt, ending in the defection of its president, though by that time it had clearly failed in its objective of winning support from Luande. The speed of its demise was surprising in view of the initial enthusiasm with which it had been received and in the light of the pessimism that some of the president's faction displayed in the face of its attack. Later, in 1965, the RAU(U) entered a new phase when the Uganda government enacted legislation compelling all trades union officials to be Uganda citizens. All its committees had to be reconstituted and the Kenyans replaced. This did not signify the end of rule by white-collar workers, however, for in this respect the new officials were no different from their predecessors. Nor did it bring an end to faction fights. In a later conflict fought primarily at the national level Luande eventually came to terms with his rivals and FUTU and the UTUC were amalgamated with Luande as president of the new body. This was after I left the field.

FACTION-FIGHTING IN THE RAILWAY UNIONS: AN ANALYSIS

Let us draw some preliminary conclusions from the material. In both episodes the issues involved were much the same as they appear to have been in all previous conflicts. Even the accusation of the abuse of union transport reflected an earlier dispute, that of 1960, though the vehicle then had been a scooter and not a car. Likewise, the competitors were similar in terms of status and background, almost all coming from the local elite, i.e. those who in the urban status system as a whole represent the emergent African middle stratum. It is they who are competing for prestige and positions of status, both in the industry and throughout the wider society, and one of the ways in which such status can be achieved is through the possession of office in urban associations. A position as a trade unionist brings both prestige and power and the stakes are high, as we saw earlier. A senior official can attain national prominence as a 'big man' and can also acquire access to patronage. Prominence in union affairs is used by some as a basis for an advance into other more influential and important social milieus, into the world of national and international trades unionism or into politics and Parliament or into management. While all these factors are sufficient to explain the intensity and frequency of power contests in the RAU(U) they do not necessarily explain the factional form those contests take, nor how and why individuals decide their allegiance to one faction or another. Nor can they explain why one side invariably seemed to win. We will consider each of these problems, taking first the question of allegiance.

To suggest, as Scott does, that competition for office in the RAU(U) is basically a form of ethnic rivalry[7] implies that among the competitors there is, consciously or unconsciously, a strong sense of ethnic interest which it is the goal of the contest to defend or advance. In the urban African literature the best account of a system where such an interest exists may be found in Cohen's study of the Hausa traders of Ibadan (1969). There the ethnic interest is clearly defined in economic terms and is organised and expressed within a legitimate institutional structure. Such does not appear to be the case among railwaymen. It may be agreed that domination of the union by one or other ethnic groups might be to the general benefit of members of the group, if it is accepted that control of the union also gives power, or is thought to give power over recruitment and promotion and thus provides control over channels of advancement and economic opportunity. Such a view, at any rate, seemed to be behind the arguments of John O., for example, in his attempt to persuade Francis to resign. On the other hand, it could be argued, the idea of group interest, rather than impelling individuals into political conflict, is used by them as a device for recruiting support for their own cause. It is far from proven that a desire to advance a particular section of the community is a fundamental force motivating competitors for office in the RAU(U). There are other difficulties surrounding the idea that the union power contests are basically ethnic, as we shall see.

The issue of allegiance raises two questions: how do rank and file members come to give their support to a competitor for office and why do individual competitors join together to form factions? Those aspiring to union office must have ways and means of acquiring support to vote them onto committees, to demonstrate for them, to overawe the opposition or, in the case of the RWU, to establish a claim to legitimacy with management and the Registrar of Trades Unions. The evidence from the case material shows that they are unlikely to rely on an appeal on ideological grounds since ideological differences are largely minimal, commitments to ideological positions loose, and an ideology of itself does not generate support. Nevertheless, ideological statements and themes are used, a point we shall return to later. Each individual, however, has a set of social statuses by reference to which he may be linked to other railwaymen and it is these that he first employs to win support. Some of these statuses are irrelevant to the competition in that they do not provide sufficient differentiation among the competitors. Since almost all contestants are clerks from a narrow range of grades in Group B an appeal to the interests of those occupational groups and grades is blocked. Note, however, that Joshua put himself forward as the advocate of another occupational group, the footplate staff and skilled men, by emphasising his father's link with them and his own status as Shed Clerk, a capacity in which he could claim he understood their problems. Similarly Alan's support came primarily from Group C. The example of Joshua illustrates how contestants exploit a primary line of differentiation within the community, the organisational division into sections and subsections. It is within these units that the aspiring leader makes his primary bid for support and prominence. We saw, for example, how Alexander was able to control the votes in his subsection while Nicholas gained prominence in the Station as a whole, partly with Alexander's support and partly with backing from the Parcels Office. At the same time Omolo established himself in the Yard. While these sections and subsections supported the Shiftas and resigned, the Loco Shed stayed behind Luande whose primary supporters were prominent in that section. When their influence waned, the Shed was ready to change sides. Interestingly, while Alexander's Ankole supported his alliance with the Shifta faction, the Ankole in another subsection – the Compound Cleaners – supported one of their own who was associated with the president's faction. Support within the section or subsection may be gained by appeals to an occupational interest or simply by reference to the important position held by the competitor in the hierarchy of the work unit. It is not unknown for such people to use or to be believed to be prepared to use, their disciplinary powers to generate a political allegiance.

Although an individual can attain prominence in a small work unit, the best office he can achieve in this way is that of section representative on the local staff committee of the union branch committee. If he wishes to become an officer in the union at branch or national level, he must appeal to a wider range of members. No section at Kampala contains more than a fifth of the African labour force, the largest sections (see Table 15) are the Goods Shed 20.6%, the PWI 19.2% and the IW 17.5%, Loco Shed 12.8% and the Station 7.2%, though this distribution does not directly enable us to understand the dynamics of union politics since some sections have higher rates of union membership than others. Unfortunately, the latter figures are not fully available. Nevertheless, the point remains that those who are in a subsection need to establish alliances with other subsection leaders to come to power in the section, and section leaders need alliances to gain prominence in the depot. Thus ambitious competitors are forced into coalition.

The other source of differentiation within the community to which an individual can make an appeal is the ethnic group or, where large numbers of the same group are present, the internal divisions within the group. In a discussion of ethnicity on the Copper Belt, Epstein notes ' Membership of a tribe . . . imposes an obligation, vaguely defined though it may be, to give mutual aid and support' (Epstein 1961 : 51). Parkin makes a similar point for the Luo and by implication the Luhya when he refers to what he terms the ideology of brotherhood which prevails in their cultures. It may be agreed that the assertion of common ethnic identity implies a claim to equality and solidarity and may be taken as a bid for support, but it is a bid that need not be answered in the affirmative. The fact of common ethnic identity does not entail an automatic obligation of unconditional support in the circumstances we are considering. One problem facing those appealing for ethnic support is the legitimacy of their claim. Even in the case of those groups for which there exists (or existed) a central authority (e.g. the Kabaka of Buganda) which can legitimately formulate a group interest and designate its representatives, that is, legitimate their claim to ethnic support, that authority is not irresistible. For those who come from societies which are traditionally non-centralised, such as the Luo and the Luhya, there may now exist centrally organised institutions, i.e. the ethnic unions, which may issue statements on the ethnic interest, but the authority of, say, the Luo union, or of those who hold office in it at any one time, need not automatically be respected. Indeed, one of the crucial problems for such a body is the establishment of authority and control over those it claims to represent. In the case of power contests in the RAU(U) never once did the possible sources of legitimate authority within any ethnic group show the slightest interest in the events at Nsambya, except in so far as the rumours about the involvement of a prominent Luo politician, but about by the president's faction, tended to suggest that there was a Luo bid for power backed by a source of authority within that ethnic group. Interestingly, no one in the Shifta faction claimed that this was true, perhaps for reasons discussed below.

Those making a bid for ethnic support do so by reference to a vaguely defined interest which they claim to be able to represent. They have to establish both that such an interest exists and that they have a right to expect support to represent it. Both are highly debatable points, as may be imagined. Nevertheless, competitors and others sometimes act on the assumption that ethnic loyalties exist. The Welfare Officer came under pressure to act as a Luhya, and then tried to amend his image by favouring a Luo family. Joshua placed a boy in employment to ' please ' the Luo. In the same way, perhaps, the appointment by the president's faction of a Luo driver as the union's nominee on the local staff committee of Mechanical Engineering helped that faction retain control in the Loco Shed. Such gestures assume a certain strength of ethnocentric feeling. Where such sentiments are weak there must be more than gestures or appeals – consider, for example, the pressures to which Francis was subjected in the Parcels Office.

Besides general appeals to the ethnic group as a whole there are specific appeals to people from the competitors' home area. Among both Luo and Luhya there are to be found at Nsambya large contingents from the major locations in Nyanza and western Kenya, among the members of which there may be numerous ties of friendship and kinship which cut across the boundaries of railway administrative units. Prominent among the Luhya supporters of the president's faction are those from Wanga and Samia Locations, in the latter case from the Samia areas on both sides of the Kenya–Uganda border, while among the Luo in the Shiftas those from Gem seem to have been particularly numerous. On the other hand, the Luo from Rusinga Island, with the exception of John O., tended to back Luande, a situation which may partly be a reflection of the fact that in Kenya Odinga Odinga's support mainly came from Central Nyanza, while Mboya's power base was in South Nyanza. It is to locational loyalties that Joshua was referring when he attacked what he called domination by ' one clan '. In order for an appeal to location or sublocation support to be effective the individual must have a good reputation at home. If he is ' proud ' or ' lonely ', known to be a bad kinsman, failing in his duties to parents and siblings, it will weigh heavily against him. In the elections for the branch committee in 1963 several candidates placed in this category, for example Jackson, failed abysmally.

Appeals for ethnic support of any kind must be used with caution for two reasons. No single group has sufficient numbers to dominate a depot-wide election or contest. Luo account for some 25% of the labour force, Luhya–Samia for about 22%, neither sufficient for absolute control. Once again contestants are forced into coalitions, this time of ethnic interests. There is evidence to suggest that Ganda and Luo made a somewhat unlikely alliance in the Shifta faction, while Luhya joined with Toro on the other side. Such alliances are by their nature highly unstable. It seems, for example, that on several occasions a 'grand coalition' of Luo and Luhya emerged for short periods. Appeal for the support of an ethnic group is, moreover, a double-edged weapon in that it makes the opposition's task of convincing their own ethnic group of the issues at stake that much easier. In addition, since the idea of tribal loyalty itself is under attack in East Africa as being against the values of modern nationalism, a public appeal for tribal support, even if it were not tactically undesirable, is politically impossible. Publicly each side comes out against tribalism, which is something they attribute to their opponents. One Luhya informant said that when Arthur emerged as an opponent of Luande he was told that he would be labelled as the leader of a Luo faction, and a similar threat was made to Joshua. If the opponents can be successfully associated with one ethnic group with which they are shown to have legitimate links, this can have the same indirect effect as an appeal to the loyalties of one's own ethnic group. It has the added advantage of attracting support from a wide range of ethnic groups, and also disrupting the opposition's ethnic alliance. This, for example, makes sense of the rumour regarding the prominent Luo politician. When ethnic appeals are made directly they occur in private, as we saw in the case of the Welfare Officer and Francis. One of Joshua's tactical errors may have been to bid openly for Luo support. Similarly, open appeal to a work section may be counter-effective, for a sectional interest is the concern of a permanent minority. An appeal made simultaneously, say, to Luo and Loco Shed workers, may end by generating support only among Luo in the Loco Shed.

Political contests in the union involve competitors in building up support using whatever relationships their social networks offer, appealing on various moral, emotional and pragmatic grounds. Those who succeed in establishing themselves in some sectional or ethnic constituency may then come to terms with each other to form coalitions. Sometimes these coalitions are brought together by one man, a leader, as is the case with the president's faction. Mutual support entails mutual benefits which may be as basic as a cash transaction, a post on a committee, or a scholarship abroad. To this extent the group which actually controls the union is in a permanently advantageous position in that it controls access to patronage. The opponents must rely largely on promises unless they have outside help.

Ethnic ties and ethnic themes are only two of the resources available to competitors, and sectional ties are of at least equal significance. Besides these a variety of methods may be employed to build teams and fight the contest, including bribery, threats, promises, rumour, gossip, abuse, witchcraft and direct violence. Each side may also stake its claim to an ideology and certainly offer a policy. In both episodes discussed here two themes emerged: the president's handling of union affairs, including both the internal affairs of the RAU(U) and relations with management, and his alignment with the ICFTU, an organisation which the RWU president was reported as calling an 'African bloodsucker' (*Uganda Argus*, 4 February 1965). A point made by one anthropologist in his discussion of factions is relevant here. Bailey argues that factions try on various kinds of normative clothing. Sometimes these are serious attempts to find a normative identity: sometimes they may be cynical manoeuvres parading one's own righteousness to discredit an opponent. But, sincere or not, one of these normative identities may be found appropriate and become the symbol of the group's new-found morality and a means of augmenting, and later replacing, the transactional basis of recruitment.

(Bailey 1969: 54)

A similar point is made by Kapferer, who suggests that: 'The general norms, values, attitudes and beliefs which are overt in a situation of conflict are more the banners under which people act: they do not necessarily betray the underlying reasons for their action' (Kapferer 1969: 20 (9)). A recent study of faction fights in the Nigerian Coal Miners' Union, where the issues were much the same as in the RAU(U), would seem to support this conclusion (Smock 1969: Chapter V).

The reasons why faction fighting seems to be endemic in the union follow from all that has been said. The rewards which are being contested are, by their nature, scarce. There are never enough to go round and competition is built into the system. Since support is built up largely by the operation of personal ties the individual can never command enough allegiance to dominate the depot. He, therefore, goes into an alliance, either with the ruling party or those who are left out. Factional coalitions are thus generated by the structure of the system. However, opposing coalitions are unstable since individual leaders may be transferred from the arena, change sides or simply lose their supporters. The party in power suffers less in this respect in that it is in a better position, having the patronage, to attract prominent individuals or seduce them from the other side. Above all, it has continuity in the person of the president and his aides who are *permanent* officials. An opposition faction may fall apart when its leaders are transferred, but when Luande loses personnel, as he does, he is in a position to replace them. In sum, to suggest that faction fighting is caused basically by ethnic rivalry overlooks the extent that the latter is the product of the former, and that both in turn are virtually inevitable in this system so long as the union itself remains a desirable prize.

A NOTE ON FACTIONAL STRUCTURE

Throughout this narrative the term 'faction' has been used without discussion, though the use here would seem to accord largely with that suggested by other anthropologists. Nicholas, for example, indicates five characteristics which define factions: they are conflict groups which are political and non-corporate, and which are recruited by a leader on the basis of 'diverse principles' (Nicholas 1965: 27–9). Each of these points apply more or less to the groupings in the RAU(U) provided that 'leader' is allowed to include a collectivity or clique of leading men. In fact Nicholas himself suggests that such cliques may exist 'composed of several leaders each of whom has a modest following, but none of whom is individually capable of mobilising an effective unit', precisely the conditions prevailing on Nsambya. Bailey specifies only two features, the absence of a common ideology and the transactional nature of relationships with the leader (Bailey 1969: 52). He does, however, draw a distinction between what he calls moral and contractual relations and suggests that as a faction achieves continuity it develops a set of people morally committed to each other and the leader. These he terms the ' core' and other supporters are described as the ' following'. Mayer's discussion of quasi-groups proposes a similar development (Mayer 1966). He starts with the notion of an 'action-set' which consists of a finite segment of an ego's social network activated for a specific purpose, e.g. an election. The quasi-group consists of those who repeatedly form part of the individual's action set. The quasi-group may develop a core 'when the more constant members are at the same time those directly linked to ego' (Mayer 1966: 116). This core may later ' crystallize into a formal group'. In the political field the quasi-group seems to be equivalent to the faction and therefore is a redundant term (cf. Harries-Jones 1969: 344).

Taking the president's supporters as an example, they may be said to constitute a faction consisting of a primary leader around whom is a central core of close adherents. Beyond these are three sets of individuals: a group of leaders not quite at the centre, a further set of prominent men, and finally the ordinary supporters. This pattern appears in the structure of both the Shifta and the RWU factions. The core of close adherents form a clique which meets regularly on unofficial occasions and may admit more peripheral leaders from time to time. In the president's faction one could draw the line between those who frequently went to his house for drinking parties and those who were occasionally invited as a reward. This device was used to signify both favour and disfavour. It was one of the president's strong points that he was able to develop and maintain a core despite the turnover of personnel.

Finally, it is possible to see over the history of the RAU(U) a cyclical pattern in the formation of factions, along the following lines. In the period from the foundation of the union in the early fifties up until 1959 there appears to have been in existence a ' grand coalition' of Luo and Luhya which controlled most of the positions in the union. From 1959–61 was a period of faction fighting, followed by two years in which the grand coalition returned. From late 1963 until 1965 was again a period of conflict. Numerous informants who had been prominent in the union in 1962–3 spoke of Luande as their ' best friend' with whom they had subsequently split. What appears to happen is that the big coalitions break up when it becomes apparent that not all the members can expect to receive a share of the available rewards. Individual competition gives way to coalition of opponents. As the factions recruit their supporters and the contest intensifies, ethnic differences, used to mobilise allegiance, become stronger. Finally, the president wins and the opposing faction breaks up. This is followed by a period in which the outsiders come to terms with the ruling party – a process in the interests of both – until the next round begins. The Shifta faction was forming throughout 1963, and did not make its main bid for power until the end of the year.

CONCLUSION

At the risk of some repetition I will summarise briefly the principal findings of this study. African railwaymen spend most of their adult working lives away from their rural areas of origin in employment in the cities of East Africa and at EARH depots where they happen to be stationed. As railway employees they belong to a distinct community which has local elements spread throughout the three territories. The social framework of the community, the categories of its culture, are provided in large measure by the industrial framework in that such organisational features as the departmental structure, the grading and salary systems, the industrial hierarchy, the distribution into occupations are taken up and used as a basis for relationships of solidarity and inequality. In this respect the industrial framework provides a specific form and content within the community for the general status system which now exists in East Africa. Status differentiation among railwaymen and an incipient division into classes have been created or at least intensified by recent political developments in which Africans have moved in increasing numbers into the middle and upper echelon positions in the industry and in the wider society.

At the same time most railwaymen are oriented towards social institutions and individuals outside the industry, notably those within their rural homes and hence their ethnic group. Almost all workers have a complex network of extra-town ties which links them socially and economically with their homes and continues to place them in special relationships with their home people. For most employees urban residence is temporary in that when they retire from their working life they plan to return to their homes in the rural areas. It is partly in preparation for this retirement that they maintain their networks of rural links, fulfilling important obligations, exchanging services, transferring wealth and so on. Perhaps less than 5% of the railwaymen at Nsambya do not retain such links, though the intensity with which they are fostered may vary with stages in the individual's personal and family domestic cycle. It may be added that the fact of birth in an urban area does not necessarily indicate an absence of 'rural' orientation. One of the largest and most successful farmers in the sample was Joshua, who had been born and brought up on Railway housing estates, and we saw in the case of David's search for a wife how those who may in most senses be said to be fully-fledged townsmen still utilise a network of rural connections. Although these links apparently fulfil the functions of providing long- and short-term social and economic security for workers at all status levels, they are significant also for those in high-status positions in that how they operate such relationships reflects on their reputations in both the urban and rural areas. Reputation is important not only in interpersonal relationships but also in competition for status and power in the urban political arenas such as ethnic associations and trades unions. Success in such institutions is both a reflection of and a boost for social standing both in town and at home.

The expansion of status differentiation has involved much restructuring of relationships in two ways. At the personal level it has frequently created problems for the upwardly mobile individual in that it forces him to re-organise his network of close associates and to re-order his relationships with a wide range of other people, especially those from his home area. At the community level there emerge new status boundaries within groups which were previously poorly differentiated in status terms or within which status differences took a different form. In fact for Luo, Luhya and other peoples for whom migration is, in the long run, still temporary, the status divisions are cross-cut by a series of complex ties. This does not mean to say that these status differences become irrelevant. Within each ethnic group the relationship between those in high and those in low status, between those in town and those in the countryside, is frequently operated by reference to an ideal model similar to that which elsewhere characterises links between patrons and clients. In fact we might propose the following equation of equivalents: urban : rural : : high status : low status : : father : son : : elder brother : younger brother : : patron : client. The operation of this model is at the present time apparently to the advantage of all parties.

MIGRANTS AND PROLETARIANS AND HOSTS AND MIGRANTS

This dual orientation, towards both the town and the country, which characterises the behaviour of railwaymen, appears to be widespread in East Africa and perhaps further afield. I term this the 'modern' pattern of migration in contrast with the 'classical' pattern which characterised the labour force in the fifties. These two patterns are, of course, intended to represent ideal types used to indicate large-scale developments or social tendencies and at the empirical level many exceptions may be found. The railway labour force as a whole appears to have consisted of 'modern' migrants for much longer than other industries in the Kampala area and it may be that 'classical' migrants can still be found in the city. In fact we have little hard information on this, though the studies of Parkin in Kampala East show that the modern pattern has many adherents at least on the organised housing estates. Further work by Parkin in Nairobi reveals a similar situation there (Parkin forthcoming papers). Throughout the text numerous references have been made both to the work of Parkin and that of Elkan which represent respectively a contemporary and an antecedent study in the city. Some general comparison of their findings with my own is appropriate.

Elkan's fieldwork was undertaken in the early fifties and while the conclusions he drew were valid for the situation as he found it they have, I believe, largely been superseded by events. In his major study published in 1960 Elkan drew a distinction between what he called 'Migrants', i.e.

those who for either shorter or longer periods work away from their homes but who eventually always return to farming, and 'Proletarians', a term which he uses in a highly idiosyncratic sense to refer to those workers in Kampala, principally Ganda, who live mainly on the peri-urban fringes where they maintain small-holdings and who commute daily into the town for work. It is these Proletarians, he says, who:

> provide the towns with their elite workers, their clerks, artisans, foremen and supervisors. Since they are able to enjoy the dual income from farm and employment without having to be away from home, the desire to maximise their incomes does *not* lead to short-term, temporary migration as in the case of people from a greater distance and their greater stability then leads naturally to their selection for the better jobs.
>
> (Elkan 1960: 6)

My own findings and those of Parkin suggest one immediate difference between the situation in the early fifties and early sixties. For it is quite clear that at the present time in a large number of industries, not least the EARH, the jobs of clerks, foremen, skilled men and so on are held at least as frequently by those in Elkan's Migrant category as by the Proletarians. It is also clear that many of the latter can now be found in unskilled employment. It will be noted that in the quotation cited Elkan sees the fact that it is the ability to have two incomes which leads to stability, commitment to urban residence and selection for higher paid work. This would not seem to be a relevant criterion for members of the Railway labour force or for the relatively stable elements on the housing estates of Kampala East.

The bulk of the industrial labour force in Kampala in the early sixties came from among those people who in the fifties Elkan would have categorised as Migrants and whose performance in work at that time could be classified as conforming to what I term the 'classical' pattern of migration. It is the behaviour of this element which has been the subject of the changes discussed in this monograph. A major weakness in Elkan's analysis would seem to be his failure to distinguish between the two types of migration which I have identified. Both short- and long-term migrants are included in Elkan's Migrant concept and the two types for him differ 'in degree and not in kind' (Elkan 1960: 6). On the contrary, I would argue that when the different patterns of migration are considered as a whole there emerge a number of crucial differences in the performance of the two types of worker that add up to a qualitative difference. These include: the length of stay in the urban and industrial milieu, the underlying change in cash needs which this represents, the extent to which employment becomes part of the individual's career rather than an interlude in his life, the consumption patterns which the change both reflects and allows, the lower costs in labour training for management, the increased level of skill and sheer industrial know-how which twenty years' work in an industry presumably generates, the fact that the situation allows many to follow a normal domestic life in the urban areas and the extent to which a worker

179

who spends most of his life in a single town and/or industry inevitably collects a network of urban associates to whom he has commitments and allegiances. Of all these factors, which taken together indicate a distinct type of situation, I would single out one as being of particular significance. The long-term modern migrant has an ongoing need for cash. He is not in any sense a target worker or a worker whose cash needs are intermittent. Because of this and because for most people the continuing income they desire can come only through employment, we may say they are dependent for their standard of living on the sale of their labour and that they are 'proletarians' in a more orthodox sense.

Elkan's distinction is drawn basically in terms of economic behaviour, though it obviously has some secondary social and cultural concomitants. In fact, since Proletarians tend to be identified with Ganda, this category overlaps with a term used by Parkin, viz. 'Hosts', which is one of a pair of terms that Parkin employs in his Kampala East study, the other being 'Migrant', a concept which overlaps but is not co-terminous with Elkan's usage (Parkin 1969a: Chapters 5, 7, 9). For Parkin, the Host/Migrant discrimination is largely cultural. The hosts are the Interlacustrine Bantu and include Ganda, Soga, Toro, Nyoro and Rwanda, but not the Ankole of Bairu caste. Migrants are the Kenyans and certain peoples from eastern and northern Uganda. I have found the distinction which is based partly at least on traditional and/or rural social and cultural practices (Parkin 1969a: 144) of only limited usefulness for the present study. For although it is undoubtedly significant for the interpretation of inter-ethnic relations in Kampala East and for indicating the persistence of certain cultural differences, particularly within the domestic sphere, within the urban areas, it seems less relevant for an understanding of relative involvement in the labour force or the extent to which industrial norms and values are assimilated. Superficially one might suppose that migrants from traditionally acephalous and egalitarian societies would be less willing or able to concur with the values of modern industry than those hosts from societies which were traditionally centralised and bureaucratic. In fact this does not seem to be the case. This may be partly because our notion of what constitutes the basis of the comparison is faulty. To say that Luo and Luhya were 'traditionally' acephalous and egalitarian does not mean to say that they are now or that the values prevalent in some previously existing system are relevant in a modern industrial context. I would argue that among both Luo and Ganda there is a general acceptance of the hierarchical order of modern society and that almost all of those alive at the present time have been socialised within such a system, at least outside the domestic arena.

This does not alter the usefulness of the distinction in other respects, for example, in the understanding of domestic relations. As far as can be seen Hosts appear to have a greater tolerance of marriage outside the immediate ethnic group, though still within defined ethnic limits, while Migrants tend to be ethnically endogamous. There are differences, too, in attitudes to women – at the Kiswa Housing Estate some 29% of household heads were found to be females independent of men and mostly from Host ethnic groups. Hosts also have much higher rates of divorce. They also give greater weight to matrilateral kin ties in preference to those of patri-kin. Because of the freer systems of land tenure prevailing in their home areas they may also more frequently move their rural residence, though this tendency did not appear particularly strongly in the Nsambya sample. Furthermore, because of their shallower lineage systems they tend to have fewer effective kin ties with relatives. These factors would seem relevant to the operation of the status system, since they apparently pose fewer problems for the upwardly mobile individual faced with the restructuring of relationships. In fact Parkin does not develop the argument in this direction as fully as might seem possible. The Host/Migrant distinction is primarily a device for understanding horizontal differences between ethnic groups rather than differences in their internal vertical structure. There is every indication, however, that the patron–client model of relationships between those of high and low status and between urban and rural areas operates within both host and migrant ethnic groups. Indeed, since this type of relationship may be said to be typical of the 'traditional' structure of Host societies it could be argued that the behaviour of Luo and Luhya in Kampala is converging towards a Host pattern.

In other respects my own data complement the findings of Parkin, in particular his views on the significance of occupation, income and educa-tion as status factors and the importance of urban associations in the status system of the local elites. Differences between Nakawa–Naguru and Nsambya in respect of the prominence of ethnic associations were discussed and I hope accounted for in Chapter 7. In terms of status composition the population at Nsambya Railway lacks one element who appear in Kampala East, namely, the self-employed businessmen and small traders. It includes another element of whom there are no representatives at Nakawa and few at Naguru, those who might be called the lower echelon upper elite – the officers. I have shown how at Nsambya, if data were fully available, it would be possible to map the population into fields of overlapping cliques roughly hierarchically ordered. In a similar way it could be shown how the local elites in each urban neighbourhood are integrated into an urban-wide network. To this extent I find that the model which Epstein envisages for a Copper Belt town is relevant to Kampala (Epstein 1961: 59). The demonstration of its usefulness is beyond the scope of this monograph.

THE RURAL–URBAN CONTINUUM: SOME CONCEPTUAL PROBLEMS

Some of the problems discussed in earlier paragraphs raise a number of conceptual and methodological difficulties. For example, I stated in the Introduction that an assumption is made that the rural and urban areas of East Africa constitute a single field of social relationships and that an under-standing of what happens in the town, and often in the countryside, can only be gained through the acceptance of that assumption. Many anthro-pologists – Mayer, Epstein, Parkin, among others – also accept that view. Nevertheless, we may still wish to make a heuristic distinction between the two for the purposes of studying, say, geographical mobility, the relative distribution of resources or the relevance of particular sets of values. This position may be set against an older view which tended to subsume the rural/urban distinction in Africa within the framework of a much broader set of distinctions identified by a variety of labels as follows:

A	B
Rural	Urban
Traditional	Modern
African	European
Tribal	Western
Subsistence	Cash
Agriculture	Employment
Farmer	Labourer
Kinship	Economic status
Status	Contract
Gemeinschaft	*Gesellschaft*
Simple	Complex

These two sets of categories form two ideal types representing two contrasted models of behaviour, sets of values and even moral fields. They form the basis for nearly all discussion of social change in contemporary Africa, with the direction of change being understood to be from some element in A to some element in B. That the categories of these models are used in this way may be seen by glancing at any text dealing with change in Africa, including the present monograph. Consider, for example, the two following extracts, the first of which is from a study by Guy Hunter published in 1963.

> The second serious problem [for industry in Africa] lies in the discrepancy between the traditional and industrial environment. This may start at the simplest level – the worker has never worn boots, used a shovel, seen stairs or an electric light switch. It may refer to hours of work; the eight-hour day, week by week is hard for many Africans to accept, since their own rhythm is broken by many pauses and unevenly divided through the year . . . attitudes to authority (traditionally directed towards the old or the well-born) and towards members of other tribes frequently conflict with the status and ranking systems of industrial organisation.
>
> (Hunter 1963: Para. 15)

The second comes from Gluckman and was published in 1961. He is discussing a parallel topic, that of 'detribalization', a concept which frequently confused movement from 'tribal areas' with loss of tribal identity. Gluckman says,

> It seems to me apparent that the moment an African crosses his tribal boundary to go to the town he is 'detribalized', out of the political control of the tribe. And in the town, the basic materials by which he lives are different: he walks on different ground, eats food at different

hours and maybe different food at that. He comes under different political authorities, and associates with different fellows. He works with different tools in a different system of organization.　　　(Gluckman 1961 : 69)

The basic model used by the two writers is very similar since each sees a strong discontinuity between the town and the country, etc., though the points they are making are different. Hunter emphasises the difficulties in the transition, while Gluckman stresses the rapidity. This leads him then to suggest that the starting point of any study of Africans in town must be the urban system of relationships ('An African townsman is a townsman, an African miner is a miner'). I would follow Gluckman in two respects. First, the problems of 'the African' in an urban and industrial environment are not as acute as Hunter seems to imply. This is certainly true of the present day, whatever may have been the case previously. Underlying Hunter's statement, which may be more widely accepted than many anthropologists suppose, are two assumptions, both of which are questionable: that Africans entering employment come into an environment in which the values and the ideas which they must employ are in strong contrast with all those in terms of which they have been socialised, and that as a general principle the individual's adjustment to a new situation is bound to be slow and painful. Neither of these suppositions seem to me, on the basis of my experience, acceptable. The first seems to imply a very strange view of the rural African, cut off from his fellows who may have made many trips to town, and isolated from all the changes of the last seventy years. It also ignores the extent to which changes have occurred in 'traditional' value systems, changes which I implied earlier make it virtually meaningless nowadays to talk about 'acephalous' societies, at least with reference to such peoples as the Luo and the Luhya. The second reflects an older tradition in anthropology in which change itself was considered something out of the ordinary and consequently difficult to handle, whereas nowadays perhaps we might almost accept the opposite point of view.

I also agree with Gluckman that operationally it is necessary to assume that townsmen are townsmen and that there is a distinct pattern of urban relationships, and indeed this was the method employed in the collection of data for this monograph. That such patterns may be perceived has been the experience of every urban anthropologist in Africa, *pace* Elkan and Fallers, who state: 'Relative stability of employment in town . . . involves no motivational commitment to a distinct urban social system. In these circumstances, indeed, the latter hardly exists' (Elkan and Fallers 1960: 254). This ignores a point made by Mayer who says: 'The ongoing nature of the urban social system has been successfully distinguished from the temporary or shifting nature of the migrant personnel' (Mayer 1962: 576). Nevertheless, the distinction between an urban system and presumably its rural counterpart(s) should always be recognised for the heuristic device which it is. For individuals in the kind of situation we have discussed are operating simultaneously in both rural and urban sets of relationships and the overall 'structure' must be understood in terms of the connectedness of the two systems and of the 'feedback' between them.

Interestingly the anthropological tendency to conceptualise the rural and urban as two distinct social fields is often followed by informants. Many people in Kampala and Nairobi seem to view the city as a place of evil and corruption in contrast with the rural areas. Among Luo, for example, the phrase *okethore town*, 'He/she has been destroyed (i.e. morally) by the town' is used frequently with reference, for example, to young men who are excessively fond of Ganda barmaids. It was a commonly-held view that townsmen are 'always' committing adultery, though all the information one could collect seemed to point to the conclusion that adultery was at least as frequent in rural as in urban areas. Luo also have a noun, *okora*, which means roughly a '(town) rascal'. On one occasion I heard it used to refer to Francis, the clerk in the Parcels Office, who was said to have gone home wearing 'shorts only fourteen inches long'. Another man admitted that others might classify him as *okora* because he had 'slept with women of every tribe'. It may be recalled that in the case of the search for a wife recorded in Chapter 3, as soon as it became clear that the unfortunate Matilda was familiar with the ways of the town she was excluded from the category of a woman eligible for matrimony and placed in a class of loose women, immediately acceptable as a bedmate. This conceptualisation of the urban and the rural in terms of two fields of morality is used frequently as a theme in Swahili popular music and, of course, appears in European literature from Hesiod onwards.

The ongoing continuity between the town and the country has a number of theoretical and practical consequences. The first concerns the definition of 'urbanised'. A wide range of criteria have been put forward in the attempt to locate the urbanised African, as the surveys of previous work contained in Mitchell (1956a) and in Mitchell and Shaul (1965) indicate. These include: length of residence in town and/or in one town either in total or as a proportion of the individual's life since turning some arbitrary age, severance from the political control of traditional rural institutions, presence of a wife in the urban area, lack of land or land rights, independence of rural kin ties, occupation, wage and education levels, and the expression of certain attitudes. According to some of these criteria railwaymen turn out to be highly urbanised, but by others they are manifestly not. For example, if we follow Mayer and define the 'process of urbanisation' as a 'shift in the balance between within-town ties and extra-town ties' (Mayer 1962: 580), it is clear that railwaymen exhibit a modest degree of urbanisation, though one would need to be able to devise an acceptable comparative measurement to justify the statement. On the other hand, it would also appear that in some respects the balance varies with the developmental cycle, and thus the individual is more or less urbanised according to the stage his domestic circumstances have reached. It should be noted that frequently attempts to measure urbanisation, stabilisation, detribalisation and so on are related to assumptions about the nature of change in Africa, for example: 'the growth of a body of wage labourers permanently settled in industrial towns has apparently had advantages for England, and all employers in Africa wish the same might happen there' (Elkan and Fallers 1960: 240). We have also seen how it is argued that the 'failure' to become urbanised in this sense apparently has severe consequences for the structure of urban life and for the productivity of labour (cf. ILO 1958: 145, Elkan 1960: 136–7, Elkan and Fallers 1960: 240, 254).

The search for the chimerical urbanised African often seems to confuse a number of logically distinct factors such as the length of residence in town, permanent commitment to residence in town, industrial stability, industrial efficiency, the existence of an urban system of relations, the operation of roles within that system, the acceptance of norms and values appropriate to modern industry, the abandonment of 'traditional' values and traditional identities. In fact 'urbanized' is often in practice a synonym for 'Europeanized'. Thus it becomes less interesting to ask how urbanised are railwaymen, than to consider the implications for each of the aforementioned factors of the pattern of life that they follow. For example, given that their dual orientation to town and country is unlikely in the foreseeable future to be superseded by a permanent commitment to urban residence accompanied by a severance of extra-town ties, what are the consequences for urban and industrial policy? It would seem, perhaps, that unless it can be shown that a labour force composed of such personnel is *inherently* less efficient than one whose members are totally divorced from the rural context (and further studies could look at this) then there need be no search for remedies on the part of employers or government. On the other hand, as I have argued elsewhere (Grillo 1969b: 82), there may be positive advantages in such a system which are at present overlooked. Thus the transfer of wealth from the town to the countryside may at least balance the disparity between the affluent worker and the poor peasant, a disparity which represents potentially an explosive cleavage throughout Africa.

ETHNICITY AND STATUS DIFFERENTIATION: SOME WIDER COMPARISONS

The Nsambya material bears out the findings of a multitude of urban studies throughout the African continent in two respects: the increasing significance of 'modern' status variables in structuring relations between Africans and the continuing significance of ethnic ties. There are two points that may be emphasised. First, most studies have reported the growth of *status* differences, and few have commented on those allegiances which following Dahrendorf and Marx have here been termed *class*. The differentiation of the urban community in terms of power and authority, usually in association with the unequal distribution of prestige resources such as wealth and income, may in the very long run be of greater significance as a factor determining social and political action than the existing differentiation into ethnic and status groups. As we have seen, there is already an emergent consciousness of class interest which appears at times of industrial crisis. It will be interesting to see how future industrial disputes in Africa intensify this consciousness and whether this in turn is translated into action of another kind. This, however, is speculation.

The second point relates to the kind of structure which is created by both the continuing significance of ethnicity and the growth of status differentiation. How are the two related? Some possible comparative models may be taken from the analysis of social relations in the United States, a society which, superficially at any rate, would appear to have little in common with urban Africa. Take, for example, the following model of contemporary American society which one sociologist, Milton Gordon, has proposed. Within America, he says, there are a large number of ethnic groups each of which 'may be thought of as being divided into sub-groups on the basis of social class, and that theoretically each ethnic group might conceivably have the whole spectrum of classes within it, although in practice some ethnic groups will be found to contain only a partial distribution of social class sub-groups' (Gordon 1964: 48). This contrasts with an earlier view of American society which suggested that the growth of differentiation on class and status lines would itself undermine ethnic identity: 'Our class system functions for a large proportion of ethnics to destroy the ethnic sub-system and to increase assimilation. The mobile ethnic is more likely to be assimilated than the non-mobile one' (Warner and Srole 1945: 284). An implication of this might be that ethnic identity remains strong in stable working-class communities while disappearing among the middle classes. This, however, is not consistent with Gordon's view. For him the intersection of ethnic and class boundaries has produced 'ethclasses' of the kind described above: e.g. working-class Italian, middle-class Irish, upper-class Jew, and that many communities across the United States contain representatives of each ethclass. He also suggests that a principle of 'transferability' exists, i.e. the ability of any individual to move from one area to another and take his place in his given ethclass (Gordon 1964: 162).

To some extent the ethclass model is not inappropriate if used in relation to the cities of East Africa, though there appears to be some variation in the strength of ethnic boundaries at different status levels, in different areas of a town and between towns. At Nsambya, for example, there appear to be more frequently ethnically mixed cliques among higher-status people than among lower, or, putting it another way, that higher-status individuals tend to have ethnically more heterogeneous networks of associates. The same appears to be the case in Kampala East (Parkin 1969b: 294), though there the intra-ethnic activities of higher-status people seem to be greater than at Nsambya. In Kampala, too, ethnic identity appears to be very important at the elite level, though for obvious reasons this is difficult to document. In Nairobi ethnic boundaries appear to be strong in all status groups, though the strength of the boundaries may vary in response to events in time (Parkin, forthcoming papers).

More important, for immediate purposes, than the boundaries between ethnic groups, is the structure of relations between those at different status levels within the group. I earlier argued that the extension of the status system has in many cases considerably changed the internal composition of the ethnic group. Each now has a set of high- and low-status members with leadership largely in the hands of the former. Between the two levels there are significant social, economic and political transactions which bind the two together. I have also argued that the continuance of this system, which has obvious implications for the continuing importance of ethnic boundaries as a whole, is ultimately related to dual urban–rural orientation, but that it also relates to the urban status system in that support within ethnic 'constituencies' is frequently essential for the ambitious individual competing for power in the political arena. This aspect could conceivably remain significant even if rural links were to be severed. This is the implication, for example, of Cohen's study of the Hausa trading community in Ibadan. It should be added, however, that because leadership in ethnic groups and in the urban areas is largely in the hands of men of high status who are competing with one another for power, any interpretation of the use of ethnic ideologies in political contexts as a manifestation of the interest of the ethnic group *per se* must be viewed with caution, as perhaps the material of Chapter 7 illustrates.

The literature on the significance of status differences for the internal structure of American ethnic groups is unfortunately sparse – with the exception of Black communities. Gans, who studied the working-class Italians of Boston's West End, however notes that among them, 'the peer group is limited to people of similar ethnic background and class' (Gans 1962: 76) and that they maintain 'friendly but infrequent' relationships with other ethnic groups. They also maintain social distance between themselves and middle-class elements and 'reject other West Enders who stray too far from the peer group society and adopt middle-class ways. . . Only those few who can achieve upward mobility in the occupational sphere without becoming " uppity " in their consumption patterns and choice of friends are likely to be spared scorn' (Gans 1962: 221). We are not, unfortunately, told what happens to those who break completely with the West End Community, though Gans subsequently implies that the theory, if not the practice of middle-class society, is to ignore ethnic boundaries. On the other hand, certainly among Italians and Irish, and possibly among other ethnic groups, there are in the political and business spheres ongoing relationships between those of high and low status which may be understood in general in terms of the patron–client relationships which I have said characterise links between similar people at Nsambya. The extreme examples of this are the 'mafias' of both the Sicilian and Irish variety. It may also be that the existence of such relationships in both ethnic groups derives ultimately from the processes used to effect migration from the home country to America and to establish themselves in the new land, and/or that there are similar patterns associated with polyethnic societies composed largely of immigrants in which status differentiation within the ethnic groups becomes of increasing significance.

To return to Nsambya. Given that ethnic ties continue to be used in the way described and that individuals at different status levels and with potentially divergent class interest are integrated within a single transactional system to the mutual benefit of all parties, then the incipient cleavage on class lines referred to earlier is likely to be delayed, if indeed it ever fully materialises.

G.A.R.—8

APPENDIXES

APPENDIX I: FIELD METHODS, THE NSAMBYA SURVEY

The bulk of the information discussed in this monograph was obtained by the traditional methods of anthropology, i.e. intensive fieldwork. I had hoped at the time to collect more systematic data using a variety of survey methods and tests (see, for example, the comments in Chapter 4). Although these proved to be beyond my resources I was able to conduct a general survey at the Nsambya Estate. Most of the material discussed in Chapter 3 was drawn from this. The survey at Nsambya formed part of a wider study entitled the 'Kampala Survey, 1965'. This was undertaken in April–June of that year in conjunction with the Department of Sociology at Makerere and the Government Town and Country Planning Department. Three areas of Kampala were taken, Nsambya, Kiswa and Kibuli, and in each a questionnaire was administered to a random sample of household heads. The questions were devised in seminars at Makerere under my direction and tested on college employees living on campus. The questionnaire varied slightly in each area in the light of what was known of local conditions. The full results of the survey have not yet been published, though some information is used in this volume.

For the survey at Nsambya, which was confined to African employees of EARH, the following sampling frame was devised. The EARH house classes (see Chapter 2) were used as strata,[1] classes 3 and 4 being amalgamated to form a single stratum. A list of all occupied housing was obtained from the EARH and arranged by class, the houses in each class being ordered by references to the numbers assigned by the EARH. Using random numbers, a 10% sample[2] was selected as shown in Table 42.

TABLE 42. *House classes in the sampling frame at Nsambya*

Class	Number in occupation	Number in sample	Sampling percentage
7 (i)	213	21	9.9
7 (ii)	168	17	10.2
6	81	8	9.9
5 (i)	73	8	11.0
5 (ii)	43	5	11.6
4/3	35	4	11.4
Total	613	63	10.3

Two respondents, both in class 6, were not contacted after repeated calls and two more in class 7 (i) failed to finish the questionnaire. In the tables giving the results of the survey, totals add to 59 or 61 depending on whether the aforementioned answered the relevant question. Out of 63, 59 complete responses – 94% – represented some measure of success, which may be attributed to the skill of those sociology students from Makerere who carried out the interviews. Four checks were available on replies: some information supplied by the EARH, questions in the survey designed to check consistency, spot checks with re-interviews, and my own knowledge of many of the respondents. I was satisfied that on all counts the answers received revealed a high degree of accuracy. It may be added that the survey was not undertaken until I had been in the field for a whole year. Without the background of intensive fieldwork, designing the questionnaire would have been a formidably difficult task.

APPENDIX II: DEPARTMENTAL AND SECTIONAL FUNCTIONS

THE GM'S DEPARTMENT

The main function of this department is co-ordination and planning. There are three sections devoted to Welfare, Industrial Relations and Public Relations which have been established in recent years and have not so far extended their activities to each district let alone each major depot. Each section has a Principal Officer at Nairobi. Among the functions of the Industrial Relations section, certainly at Kampala, is that of acting as secretary of the District Housing Committee.

THE COMMERCIAL AND OPERATING DEPARTMENT

The department is responsible for the working of all stations, goods sheds, marshalling yards, piers, jetties and inland ports, and for the operation and control of all trains, road vehicles and vessels. It also runs the EARH telephone, telegraph and wireless communications systems. Its heads are the Chief Commercial and Chief Operating Superintendents. In the district the department is headed by the DTS. The most important sections are stations (passenger traffic), goods sheds, marshalling yards and control offices, which are all to be found at Kampala.

THE ENGINEERING DEPARTMENT

This, the largest department in terms of numbers employed, is responsible for the maintenance of the permanent way, signalling installation, bridges, tunnels, wharves, jetties, and all buildings including housing. At the head is the Chief Engineer represented locally by the DE. The principal sections at Kampala are the PWI, which deals with track maintenance, the IW, in charge of construction and building maintenance, and the HI. At Nairobi the department maintains considerable workshops.

THE MECHANICAL ENGINEERING DEPARTMENT

This department, headed interterritorially by the Chief Mechanical Engineer and locally by the DME, is in charge of the maintenance of all locomotives, carriages, waggons, machinery, tools and plant, cranes and all other mechanical and electrical equipment. Its workshops at Nairobi are equipped to undertake the heaviest mechanical engineering work. At Kampala its principal sections are the Locomotive Shed and the CxRs. A small specialist electrical section was recently established.

THE PORTS DEPARTMENT

This department is represented only in coastal areas since inland waterway harbours are under the jurisdiction of the Commercial and Operating Department.

THE ACCOUNTS DEPARTMENT

Requires no comment except to say that until very recently the department maintained no staff outside Nairobi.

THE STORES DEPARTMENT

Existing in Nairobi and a few local districts, the department co-ordinates the purchasing, stocking and distribution of all supplies.

THE RTSS

The EARH runs two training schools, at Nairobi and Tabora. The activities at the school are discussed in Chapter 2 under 'Training and Recruitment'. In the figures given for the numbers employed in the EARH, students at the schools are included in the totals for the departments to which they are assigned.

THE RAILWAY POLICE

At the present time the Railway police force consists of officers and men from the various national forces on secondment to Railway duty. They guard Railway property and prosecute in the case of thefts, etc. They are not included in the EARH labour force figures which I give.

APPENDIX III: ADDITIONAL NOTES ON THE GRADING SYSTEM

SPECIAL SCALES

The titles and pay rates for those in the special scales mentioned in Chapter 2 are as follows:

TABLE 43. *EARH grading system, special scales*

Title and grade	Equivalent grade	£ per annum Minimum	Maximum
Secretarial grades			
Personal secretary I	B III	786	903
Personal secretary II	B IV	618	726
Stenographer I, Telephonist I	B V	510	582
Stenographer II, Telephonist II	B VI/VII	402	474
Stenographer III	B VIII	294	366
Stenographer IV, Telephonist III	B IX	222	270
Footplate staff on consolidated salaries			
Loco driver V	B V	606	678
Loco driver VI/VII	B VI/VII	498	580
Loco driver VIII	B VIII	354	426
Loco driver IX/X	B IX/X	225	321
Running staff on consolidated salaries			
TTE VII, Guard VII	B VII	447	519
TTE IX/X, Guard IX/X	B IX/X	225	297

THE HARRES COMMISSION CHANGES

The grading system and salary structure have been subject to a number of commissions of enquiry and subsequent changes, most recently the Harres Commission set up in 1962 to report on the system and on the process of Africanisation. The findings of the commission were implemented in 1963 (see EARH Special Notice No. 4, 1963). Harres advised the reduction of the number of grades in Groups B and C, and the establishment of a new pay scale which raised the basic pay of those in Group C and in Group B grade XI. At the same time the basic rates in the higher grades were *reduced*, as may be seen in the accompanying table.

In Table 11 I have used the titles applying in the old grading system, but the pay scales of the Harres system. This is because in 1964/5 many workers were still on the old grades and, in fact, in the everyday speech the old titles were used to describe the new points in the Harres system. Although Harres reduced the pay scales, no individual experienced a direct cut in salary, since staff were retained on their old grades at the old rate, provided this were to their advantage, until they received promotion when they were appointed to a grade in the new system. Although no individual

TABLE 44. *EARH grading system, pre- and post-Harres scales compared*

Former grade	£ per annum		'Harres' grade	£ per annum	
	Minimum	Maximum		Minimum	Maximum
Executive A	1,494	1,551	Senior executive A	1,500	1,500
Executive B	1,380	1,437	Senior executive B	1,350	1,350
Executive C	1,275	1,326	Senior executive C	1,200	1,200
I	876	966	Executive I A	1,065	1,110
II	1,026	1,104	Executive I B	975	1,020
III	876	966	Executive II	786	903
IV	726	816	I	618	726
V	609	681	II	510	582
VI	501	573 ⎫	III A, III B	402	474
VII	396	480 ⎭			
VIII	309	369	IV	294	366
IX	252	297 ⎫	V A, V B	222	270
X	198	246 ⎭			
XI	127	186	VI	150	186

suffered, it was clear to everyone that the long-term effect of the change was to cut the wages paid to Group B staff. The issue assumed some importance in industrial relations in 1964/5, as I will describe in a subsequent publication.

NOTES

1: THE SOCIAL AND ECONOMIC FRAMEWORK

[1] Sources for population figures used in this monograph are, unless otherwise stated, the various volumes of the 1948, 1959, 1962 and 1969 censuses conducted in Kenya and Uganda. Employment figures are generally taken from Uganda's annual *Enumeration of employees* and Kenya's *Reported employment and wages*. Full details are given in the list of references.

[2] Males between 15 and 60 form roughly 25% of the population. See Uganda Census 1969.

[3] Uganda data derived from *Enumeration of employees* 1963 and 1969. The Kenya figure from Labour Department Annual Report, 1962.

[4] The comparison of employment figures between the two countries and at different periods must be treated with caution. The Kenya figures include domestic servants which are omitted in Uganda. The Uganda figures also omit those employed as wage labourers on peasant farms. These who are mostly Rwanda and mostly in Mengo were in the early fifties estimated at 100,000, a figure seemingly plucked out of thin air which has been retained in successive enumerations. In both countries successive enumerations have become more sensitive and the scope broadened. Thus the earlier the figures the more conservative they are. These provisos do not undermine the fact that the employed proportion of the population is small and has not increased significantly in the last fifteen years. Indeed the latter point is strengthened.

[5] The figures for income from non-employment sources for 1954 and 1963 are derived from Ghai 1964: 12–15. A similar method has been employed to arrive at 1969 figures. The mean income is found by dividing the gross sum by the estimated total of non-employed males.

[6] Uganda, Govt. of, 1964: Tables UF.6 and UP.10, 1970: Tables UF.6 and UP.9 (b).

[7] Derived from Uganda, Govt. of, 1964: Tables UF.2, UF.6. Cf. also Elkan 1960: 14, Parkin 1969a: 9, and World Bank 1962: Table S.5, p. 442.

[8] Derived from Kenya, Govt. of, 1964b: 35, Table 6, and census figures.

[9] Baryaruha 1967, and United Nations Economic Commission for Africa, *Social factors affecting labour stability in Uganda* Document No. E/CN 14/SDP/20 (Addis Ababa, 1963).

[10] For purposes of comparison Greater Kampala in 1948 and 1959 has been defined as the census areas of Kampala Municipality and the Ggombololas of Mumyuka and Omukul w'eKibuga of Kyaddondo County. The present area of Kampala is greater than this.

[11] Southall and Gutkind 1957, Parkin 1966a, 1966b, 1969a, 1969b.

[12] That unemployment is one of the crucial problems of the present period has become increasingly recognised by social scientists in Africa. The proceedings of a conference held on this subject at the Institute of Development Studies, University of Sussex, September 1971, will, when published, add considerably to our understanding of the issues, as will the work of C. Hutton, especially for Uganda.

2: THE RAILWAY COMMUNITY IN EAST AFRICA AND AT KAMPALA

1 Throughout this chapter, unless otherwise stated, statistical and other information relating to the Railways has been obtained from EARH sources. The responsibility for interpreting the data rests with me.
2 For a detailed history of the Railways, see Hill 1961.
3 Uganda, Govt. of, 1966: Table UA.10.
4 EARH Annual Report 1964: 3.
5 *Spear* Vol. VIII (1): 2.
6 Class 7 (i) units numbered 213, class 7 (ii) 212.
7 For other descriptions of zoning in Kampala, see Parkin 1969a: ch. I, Southall 1966: 352–3.

3: TOWARDS AN AFRICAN PROLETARIAT?

1 Cf. Menzies 1961.
2 Uganda Census 1959a: Appendix X, p. 70.
3 Because the middle value of the groups employed is usually higher than most of the individual ages collected in the group.
4 Census returns show that in Kenya and Uganda as a whole males and females, adults and children, are in roughly equal proportions.
5 It is hoped to undertake a further analysis, using the combined results of the surveys at Nsambya, Kiswa and Kibuli.
6 The figure was calculated from the total amounts stated as remitted during the five month period January–May 1965. A second method, using the average time elapsed since the last remittance, and the average amount sent, produced a figure of 33.2s. per person per month. This confirms the figure derived by the first method.
7 Kenya, Govt. of, 1964a: Appendix Table 2 (a).
8 'Location' is the administrative and popular term for local districts in western Kenya and Nyanza. They correspond largely with what have been called 'tribes' in the ethnographic literature on the Luo and the Luhya.
9 W. Sytek, personal communication.
10 Hutchinson 1956: 302, Mitchell 1961: 207ff. Both references explain how the index is constructed.

4: SOCIAL RELATIONSHIPS AND THE INDUSTRIAL FRAMEWORK

1 *Sikio* No. 149, 1 April 1966, p. 3.
2 In the UK there are three railway unions of which one is the Associated Society of Locomotive Engineers and Firemen (ASLEF).
3 Mitchell 1956b, Mitchell and Epstein 1959, Hicks 1966, Xydias 1956, Parkin 1969a: Ch. III, and Lloyd (ed.) 1966 passim.

5: STATUS, REPUTATION AND CLASS

1 See references cited, Note 3 to Chapter 4.
2 The four status variables–grade, income, education and occupation–were each divided into five ranked categories to which the following weights were assigned: 10, 30, 50, 70, 90. These weights are somewhat arbitrary, and better values might be obtained, perhaps through a process of iteration.
3 Epstein 1961, Mitchell (ed.) 1969, Parkin 1969a 119, 132, Pons 1961, Southall (ed.) 1961: 25.
4 See the relevant articles in Mitchell (ed.) 1969.
5 Status congruence or crystallisation is calculated by taking the square root of the sum of the squared deviations from the mean of the individual's status score on

each of the four variables. The result is subtracted from 100 to give an index figure for degree of congruence. (See Lenski 1954: 412, and Lenski 1956. See also Goffman 1957, Malewska 1963.)

6: SOCIAL MOBILITY

[1] In the EARH Uganda District in 1965 there were 109 station masters, assistant station masters and station foremen, forty-eight yardmasters and yard foremen, and two goods agents.
[2] See EARH Annual Report for 1954. Separate figures for clerical staff are not available.
[3] James and other actors in this narrative appear in a different context and with different names in Grillo, forthcoming. There James is referred to as 'G', Jackson who appears later as 'C' and Graham as 'B'.

7: URBAN ASSOCIATIONS AND COMPETITION FOR STATUS

[1] For other versions of the myth-history of the Luo union, see Parkin 1969a: 155.
[2] Actual distribution: Group C–4, Group B XI–I, B X–3, B IX–II, B VIII–12, B VII–3, B V–1.
[3] My own calculations derived from Parkin 1969a: Table V, pp. 75–6.
[4] Actual ethnic distribution: Luhya–Samia 9, Ganda 5, Luo 4, Soga 3, Toro 3 and one each of Nubi, Teso, Dama, Lango, Ankole, Gisu, Chagga, Taita, Nyoro, Tanzanian and one half-caste.
[5] *Sauti ya RAU(U)* Vol. 33, 23 April 1964.
[6] This is perhaps in contrast with the RAU(K) situation. A recent D.Phil. thesis, as yet unpublished (Sandbrook 1971: 353–74), seems to indicate that differences between Groups B and C formed the basis of RAU(K) factions in the early sixties. Although the evidence for this is largely in the form of statements by faction leaders, which must always be treated with great caution, it seems likely that social differences between the two Groups are more intense at Nairobi where they live on different housing estates (cf. the statement by James in Chapter 5, p. 94).
[7] The assumption that ethnicity is a causal factor in intra-union conflicts is made also by Amsden (1967: 152ff.). For example, she suggests that the downfall of Dennis Akumu, the well-known Mombasa dock leader, in 1966 was due to his being a Luo in an industry dominated by workers from coastal tribes. This would seem to ignore the fact that Akumu held his position in the same industry for the previous decade.

APPENDIX I: FIELD METHODS, THE NSAMBYA SURVEY

[1] The Town and Country Planning Department, who paid the Makerere students for helping with the survey, was primarily interested in household size. Since house classes varied in numbers of rooms available it was necessary to ensure that the several classes were 'correctly represented in the sample' (Moser 1958: 79) thus controlling variation between strata and reducing the standard error of the variable of most concern to the planners, viz. mean household size.
[2] I first decided to use a uniform sampling fraction of 1/10th, but since the numbers in classes 5 (i), (ii) and 4/3 were so small increased this to 1/9th in those strata. I must confess that subsequently I realised that the gain in precision was tiny and that unless a larger fraction were used the operation was pointless. I also concluded that for most purposes the extra labour involved in adjusting the results in the tables to take into account the use of a variable sampling fraction greatly outweighed the returns to be gained. Thus the results show a very small error due to the processing of the data as if a uniform sampling fraction had been employed.

REFERENCES

OFFICIAL PUBLICATIONS

General economic statistics

Kenya, Government of, 1964a. *The pattern of income, expenditure and consumption of African middle income workers in Nairobi: July 1963.* Nairobi: Ministry of Finance and Economic Planning.

1964b. *Development Plan, 1964–70.* Nairobi.

Republic of, 1965a. *Economic survey, 1965.* Nairobi: Statistics Division, Ministry of Economic Planning and Development.

1965b. *Statistical Abstract, 1965.* Nairobi: Statistics Division, Ministry of Economic Planning and Development.

Uganda, Government of, 1964, etc. *Statistical Abstract.* Entebbe: Statistics Division, Ministry of Planning and Community Development.

Employment figures

Labour statistics for Kenya for 1954 and 1958 are contained in the annual *Reported employment and wages in Kenya.* Nairobi: East African Statistical Department, Kenya Unit.

Labour statistics for Uganda may be found in the annual *Enumeration of employees.* Entebbe: Statistics Division, Ministry of Planning and Community Development.

Census figures

Kenya Census 1948. *Geographical and tribal studies, African population of Kenya Colony and Protectorate.* Nairobi: East African Statistical Department. (Published September 1950.)

1962a. *Kenya Population Census, 1962: advance report of Volumes I and II.* Nairobi: Economics and Statistics Division, Ministry of Finance and Economic Planning. (Published January 1964.)

1962b. *Kenya Population Census, 1962: Volume I.* Nairobi Directorate of Economic Planning, Ministry of Finance and Economic Planning. (Published July 1964.)

1969. *Kenya Population Census 1969, Volume I.* Nairobi: Statistics Division, Ministry of Finance and Economic Planning. (Published November 1970.)

Uganda Census 1948. *Geographical and tribal studies: African population of Uganda Protectorate.* Nairobi: East African Statistical Department. (Published 1950.)

1959a. *Uganda Protectorate, Uganda Census 1959: African population.* Entebbe: Statistics Branch, Ministry of Economic Affairs. (Published April 1961.)

1959b. *General African Census 1959, Volume I: population by sex and age group.* Nairobi: East African Statistical Department.

SECONDARY SOURCES

Amsden, A. H. 1967. 'Trade unions and politics in Kenya', pp. 122–53 of *Institute of Commonwealth Studies collected seminar papers on labour unions and political organisations,* ed. W. H. Morris-Jones. London: Athlone Press.

1971. *International firms and labour in Kenya: 1945–70.* London: Cass.

Ananaba, Wogu. 1969. *The trade union movement in Nigeria*. London: Hurst & Co.

Bailey, F. G. 1969. *Stratagems and spoils*. Oxford: Blackwell.

Banton, M. (ed.) 1966. *The social anthropology of complex societies*, ASA Monographs No. 4. London: Tavistock Publications.

Baryaruha, A. 1967. *Factors affecting industrial employment: a study of Uganda experience*. Nairobi: Oxford University Press.

Berg, E. J. 1961. 'Backward-sloping labor supply functions in dual economies: the Africa case.' *Quarterly Journal of Economics* 75: 468–92.

— 1965. 'The economics of the migrant labour system', pp. 160–81 of *Urbanization and migration in West Africa*, ed. H. Kuper. Berkeley: University of California Press.

Cohen, A. 1969. *Custom and politics in urban Africa*. London: Routledge and Kegan Paul.

— (ed.) forthcoming. *Urban ethnicity*, ASA Monographs No. 12. London: Tavistock Publications.

Dahrendorf, R. 1959. *Class and class conflict in industrial society*. London: Routledge and Kegan Paul.

Dubb, A. A. (ed.) 1961. *The multitribal society*. 16th Conference Proceedings of the Rhodes–Livingstone Institute, Lusaka.

Elkan, W. 1956. *An African labour force*. East African Studies, No. 7. EAISR, Kampala.

— 1960. *Migrants and proletarians*. London: Oxford University Press.

Elkan, W. and Fallers, L. A. 1960. 'The mobility of labor', pp. 238–57 of Moore and Feldman 1960, q.v.

Epstein, A. L. 1958. *Politics in an urban African community*. Manchester: Manchester University Press.

— 1961. 'The network and urban social organization.' *Rhodes–Livingstone Journal* 29: 29–62.

— 1969. 'Gossip, norms and social network', pp. 117–27 of Mitchell (ed.) 1969, q.v.

Gans, H. J. 1962. *The urban villages: group and class in the life of Italian-Americans*. Glencoe: Free Press.

Ghai, Dharam. 1964. 'Some aspects of income distribution in East Africa', EAISR Economic Development Research Project, Working Paper No. 24. Kampala: cyclostyled.

Gluckman, M. 1961. 'Anthropological problems arising from the African industrial revolution', pp. 67–82 of Southall (ed.) 1961, q.v.

Goffman, I. 1957. 'Status consistency and preferences for change in power distribution.' *American Sociological Review* 22 (3): 275–81.

Goodenough, W. 1961. 'Comment on cultural evolution.' *Daedalus* 90: 521–8.

Gordon, M. 1964. *Assimilation in American life*. New York: Oxford University Press.

Grillo, R. D. 1969a. 'The tribal factor in an East African trade union', pp. 297–321 of Gulliver (ed.) 1969, q.v.

— 1969b. 'Anthropology, industrial development and labor migration in Uganda', pp. 77–84 of *The anthropology of development in Sub-Saharan Africa*, ed. D. Brokensha and M. Pearsall, Society for Applied Anthropology Monograph 10. Lexington, Kentucky: University Press of Kentucky.

— (forthcoming 1974). *In dispute: race and class in the development of worker-management relations on the East African Railways, 1939–1965*.

— (forthcoming). 'Ethnic identity and social stratification on a Kampala housing estate', in Cohen (ed.), q.v.

Grillo, R. D. and Parkin, D. J. (eds.) (Manuscript). *Kampala: profiles of a modern African city*.

Gugler, J. 1965. 'Life in a dual system', EAISR Conference Proceedings. Kampala: cyclostyled.

— 1968. 'The impact of labour migration on society and economy in Sub-Saharan Africa: empirical findings and theoretical considerations.' *African Social Research* 6: 463–86.

References

1969. 'On the theory of rural–urban migration: the case of Sub-Saharan Africa', pp. 134–55 of Jackson (ed.), q.v.

Gulliver, P. H. 1955. *Labour migration in a rural economy.* East African Studies, No. 6. EAISR, Kampala.

1960. 'Incentives in labor migration.' *Human organisation* 19 (3): 159–63.

(ed.) 1969. *Tradition and transition in East Africa.* London: Routledge and Kegan Paul.

Harries-Jones, P. 1969. 'Home-boy ties and political organization in a Copperbelt township', pp. 297–347 of Mitchell (ed.) 1969, q.v.

1970. 'Tribe, politics and industry on the Zambian Copperbelt.' D.Phil. Thesis, University of Oxford.

Hicks, R. E. 1966. 'Occupational prestige and its factors.' *African Social Research* 1: 41–58.

Hill, M. F. 1961. *Permanent way: volume one, the story of the Kenya and Uganda Railway,* 2nd edition. Nairobi: EARH.

Hillery, G. A. 1955. 'Definitions of community; areas of agreement.' *Rural Sociology* 20.

Hunter, Guy. 1963. *Tropical Africa Project: supplement on manpower and training.* London: Oxford University Press.

Hutchinson, E. P. 1956. *Immigrants and their children 1850–1950,* Census Monograph Series. New York: Wiley.

Hutton, C. 1970. 'Rates of labour migration', in *Urban growth in Sub-Saharan Africa,* ed. J. Gugler, Nkanga Editions 6. Kampala: Makerere Institute of Social Research.

ILO 1958. *African labour survey.* Geneva: International Labour Office.

Jackson, J. A. (ed.) 1969. *Migration,* Sociological Studies 2. Cambridge: Cambridge University Press.

Kapferer, B. 1969. 'Norms and the manipulation of relationships in a work context', pp. 181–244 of Mitchell (ed.) 1969, q.v.

Lasswell, T. E. 1965. *Class and stratum.* Boston: Houghton Mifflin.

Lenski, G. 1954. 'Status crystallization: a non-vertical dimension of social status.' *American Sociological Review* 19: 405–13.

1956. 'Status participation and status crystallization.' *American Sociological Review* 21: 458–64.

Little, K. 1965. *West African urbanization.* Cambridge: Cambridge University Press.

Lloyd, P. C. (ed.) 1966. *The new elites of tropical Africa.* Oxford: Oxford University Press.

MacDonald, J. S. and L. D. 1964. 'Chain migration, ethnic neighbourhood formation and social networks'. *Millbank Memorial Fund Quarterly* XLII (1): 82–97.

Malewska, A. 1963. 'The degree of status incongruence and its effects'. *The Polish Sociological Bulletin* VII (1): 9–19. (Reprinted in M. M. Tumin (ed.), 1970. *Readings on social stratification.* New Jersey: Prentice-Hall.)

Marwick, M. 1965. *Sorcery in its social setting.* Manchester: Manchester University Press.

Mayer, A. 1966. 'The significance of quasi-groups in the study of complex societies', pp. 97–122 of Banton (ed.) 1966, q.v.

Mayer, P. 1962. 'Migrancy and the study of Africans in town'. *American Anthropologist* 64: 576–92.

Menzies, I. R. 1961. 'Tribalism in an industrial community', in Dubb (ed.) 1961, q.v.

Merton, R. K. 1957. *Social theory and social structure.* Glencoe: Free Press.

Mitchell, J. C. 1956a. 'Urbanization, detribalization, and stabilization in Southern Africa', pp. 693–711 of UNESCO 1956, q.v.

1956b. *The Kalela dance,* Rhodes-Livingstone Papers No. 27. Manchester: Manchester University Press.

1959. 'Labour migration in Africa south of the Sahara: the causes of labour migration.' *Bulletin of the Inter–African Labour Institute* 6: 12–46.

1961. 'Wage labour and population movements in Central Africa', Ch. 12 of *Essays in African population,* ed. K. M. Barbart and R. M. Prothero. London: Routledge and Kegan Paul.

1965. 'The meaning in misfortune for urban Africans', pp. 192–203 of *African Systems of thought*, ed. M. Fortes and G. Dieterlen. London: Oxford University Press.

1966. 'Theoretical orientations in African urban studies', pp. 37–68 of Banton (ed.) 1966, q.v.

1969. 'Structural plurality, urbanization and labour circulation in Southern Rhodesia', pp. 156–80 of Jackson (ed.) 1966, q.v.

(ed.) 1969. *Social networks in urban situations*. Manchester: Manchester University Press.

Mitchell, J. C. and Epstein, A. L. 1959. 'Occupational prestige and social status among Africans in Northern Rhodesia'. *Africa* 29: 22–40.

Mitchell, J. C. and Shaul, J. H. R. 1965. 'An approach to the measurement of commitment to urban residence', pp. 625–33 of *Science and medicine in Central Africa*, ed. J. Snowball, Oxford: Pergamon Press.

Moore, W. E. and Feldman, A. S. 1960. *Labor commitment and social change in developing areas*. New York: Social Science Research Council.

Moser, C. A. 1958. *Survey methods in social investigation*. London: Heinemann.

Munger, E. S. 1951. *Relational patterns of Kampala, Uganda*, University of Chicago Dept. of Geography Research Paper No. 21. Chicago: University of Chicago Press.

Nicholas, R. W. 1965. 'Factions: a comparative analysis', pp. 21–61 of *Political systems and the distribution of power*, ed. M. Beaton, ASA Monographs No. 3. London: Tavistock Publications.

Northcott, C. H. (ed.) 1949. *African labour efficiency survey*, Colonial Research Publications, No. 3. London: HMSO.

Nosow, S. 1962. 'Labor distribution and the normative system', in Nosow and Form (eds.), q.v.

Nosow, S. and Form, W. H. (eds.). 1962. *Man, work and society*. New York: Basic Books.

Parkin, D. J. 1966a. 'urban voluntary associations as institutions of adaptation'. *Man* (N.S.) 1: 90–5.

1966b. 'Types of urban African marriage in Kampala'. *Africa* 36(3).

1969a. *Neighbours and nationals in an African city ward*. London: Routledge and Kegan Paul.

1969b. 'Tribe as fact and fiction in an East African city', pp. 273–96 of Gulliver (ed.) 1969, q.v.

(forthcoming). 'Congregational and interpersonal ideologies in political ethnicity', in Cohen (ed.), q.v.

(forthcoming paper). 'Migration, settlement and the politics of unemployment'.

Peil, M. 1972. *The Ghanaian factory worker: industrial man in Africa*, African Studies Series 5. Cambridge: Cambridge University Press.

Pons, V. 1961. 'Two small groups in Avenue 21', pp. 205–16 of Southall (ed.) 1961, q.v.

Powesland, P. G. 1957. *Economic policy and labour*, East African Studies No. 10. EAISR, Kampala.

Price, C. 1969. 'The study of assimilation', pp. 181–237 of Jackson (ed.) 1969, q.v.

Richards, A. I. (ed.). 1954. *Economic development and tribal change*. Cambridge: Heffer.

Runciman, G. 1966. *Relative deprivation and social justice*. London: Routledge and Kegan Paul.

Sandbrook, K. R. J. 1971. 'Politics in emergent trade unions: Kenya 1952–1970'. Unpublished D.Phil. Thesis, University of Sussex.

Scott, R. 1966. *The development of trade unions in Uganda*. Nairobi: East Africa Publishing House.

Silverman, S. F. 1966. 'An ethnographic approach to social stratification: prestige in a central Italian community'. *American Anthropologist* 68.

Smock, D. R. 1969. *Conflict and control in an African trade union*. Stanford: Hoover Institution Press.

References

Southall, A. W. 1954. ' Alur migrants ', Ch. VI of Richards (ed.) 1954, q.v.

1966. 'The concept of elites and their formation in Uganda', Ch. XVII of Lloyd (ed.) 1966, q.v.

(ed.). 1961. *Social change in modern Africa*. London: Oxford University Press.

Southall A. W. and Gutkind, P. C. W. 1957. *Townsmen in the making*, East African Studies, No. 9. EAISR, Kampala.

Stouffer, S. A. *et al.* 1949. *The American Soldier, Volume I: adjustment during army life*. Princeton: Princeton University Press.

UNESCO. 1956. *The social implications of industrialization and urbanization in Africa South of the Sahara*. Switzerland: UNESCO.

Warner, W. L. and Low, J. O. 1962. ' Wages and worker solidarity ' in Nosow and Form (eds.) 1962, q.v.

Warner, W. L. and Srole, L. 1945. *The social system of American ethnic groups*, Yankee City Series Vol. III. New Haven: Yale University Press.

Weber, M. 1947. *The theory of social and economic organisation*, ed. T. Parsons. New York: Free Press.

1948. *From Max Weber*, ed. H. H. Geerth and C. W. Mills. London: Routledge and Kegan Paul.

Weeks, J. F. 1971. ' Wage policy and the colonial legacy: a comparative study '. *Journal of Modern African Studies* 9(3): 361–87.

Whyte, W. Foote. 1943. *Street Corner Society*. Chicago: University Press.

Williams, R. M. jnr. 1964. *Strangers next door: ethnic relations in American communities*. New Jersey: Prentice Hall.

Willis, R. 1968. ' Kamcape: an anti-sorcery movement in South-West Tanzania '. *Africa* 38(1): 1–15.

World Bank. 1962. *The economic development of Uganda* (International Bank for Reconstruction and Development, report.) Baltimore: John Hopkins.

Xydias, N. 1956. ' Prestige of occupations ', pp. 458–69 of UNESCO 1956, q.v.

INDEX

Index

Labour, casual, and day wage, 22, 39
Labour force, in Kenya and Uganda, 8–
   10; *see also* EARH, Employment,
   Kampala EARH Depot, Migration
Labour stability
   Copper Belt, 16, 36
   Elkan on, 13–14, 48
   increasing, 14, 16; reasons for, 16–18,
    62, 179
   in EARH, 14, 38–40, 44, 62
   problem of, 13, 19, 65, 184–5
   see also Commitment, Labour turnover,
    Land, Migration, Rural-urban links,
    Urbanisation
Labour turnover
   EARH, 14, 38–9
   other industries, 14
Land
   continued significance of, 13; for rail-
    waymen, 47–9, 61, 63
   theories of labour stability, 13–14, 18,
    48
   see also Agriculture, Farming, Rural-
    urban links
Landies, 33
Leadership, 64, 111, 149–50, 155–6, 178;
   see also Local elites, Patrons, RAU(U)
   leadership, Urban associations
Leading artisans, 30, 123
Leave, 23, 45
Lenski, G., 92, 108, 110
Life-styles, and status, 96–102, 137–8
Light-ups, *see* Footplate staff
Local elites, 155–6, 162, 170, 181; *see also*
   Leadership, RAU(U) leadership, Urban
   associations
Local staff committees, 70, 73, 131, 153,
   163, 173
Loco Shed
   at Kampala: staff employed, 28 (by
    area of origin, 59) (Kenyans, 58–9)
    (Luo, 162, 168, 173–4)
   farewell party for Shedmaster, 72, 103
   organisation and functions, 29–30, 68,
    190
   relations in, 70–4, 78–84, 104, 123, 144
   reputation for militancy, 73; for witch-
    craft, 73, 111–12, 143, 145–6
   solidarity, 70–3 *passim*
   supervisors, *see* RSF, Shedmaster
   support for Luande, 162, 167, 171; for
    RWU, 167, 171, 174
   union representative, 93
   see also Footplate staff, Mechanical
    Engineering Department, RSF, Sec-
    tions, Shed Clerk, Shedmaster, Skilled
    workers

Luande, Hon. H. M., M.P.
   career, 153
   position nationally, 153, 166, 170
   position in RAU(U), 153–4, 166, 170,
    175–6; critics of, 157–9, 166–7
   seen as big man, 93
   see also RAU(U) president, and fac-
    tions, *especially* president's faction
Luhya
   at Nsambya and Kampala East, 151
   cliques, 101, 107, 160
   compared with Ganda, 146, 180–1
   ethnic associations, 150–1
   identified with Samia-Gwe
   in EARH, 3, 37, 173
   in RAU(U), 155–7, 159–64, 166, 172–4;
    identified with KADU, 160, 164; with
    president's fraction, 157, 159–60, 162,
    164, 166, 172–3
   relations with Luo, 143–5, 157, 160–4
    passim, 168, 170, 173; grand coalition,
    174, 176
   see also Samia-Gwe
Luo
   at Nsambya and Kampala East, 151
   attitudes to occupations, 75
   cliques, 105, 107
   compared with Ganda, 146, 180–1
   ethnic associations, 114, 150–1; Luo
    Union, 57, 150–1, 172
   in EARH, 3, 37, 52–5, 113, 162, 173;
    Loco Shed, 162, 168, 173–4; Parcels
    Office, 61, 163 fl.; recruitment, 56,
    103, 168–9, 174
   in Kampala, 60
   migrations of, 55–6, 58, 63
   RAU(U), 154–7 *passim*, 160–4, 172–4;
    identified with opposition, 157, 160,
    162, 163, 167, 172–3
   relations with Luhya, 143–5, 157, 160–
    4, 168, 170, 173; grand coalition, 174,
    176
   RWU, 168, 173
   witchcraft, 54, 142–3

Makerere University College, Fig. 1, 4,
   188
   as social category, 67
   extra-mural classes, 130, 137
   scholarships, 135, 137
Management, *see* EARH management
Marcus, 52–5, 56
Marriage
   courtship, 51–5
   divorce, 43
   education, 53
   ethnic endogamy, 51–2, 113, 180

United States, ethnicity and status in, 186–7
Unskilled workers, 86–7, 89, 118
as illiterates, 89, 119
length of service, 38
status, 89; score, 97
union membership, 154
see also Carriage Cleaners, Compound Cleaners, Group C
Urban associations
in Kampala, 148–50
leadership in, and status, 64, 111, 150, 155–6
railwaymen, 149
see also Ethnic associations, Religion, Trade unions
Urbanisation
concept of, 65, 184–5
trend towards, 15–16, 19, 44, 61
urban growth in Kenya and Uganda, 14–16
see also Labour stability, Migration, Rural-urban links
UTUC, 154, 166, 170; *see also* H. M. Luande, RAU(U)

Visits
from rural areas, 42, 46–7, 55, 61
to rural areas, 4, 44–6, 51–5, 61

Wages, *see* EARH wages and salaries, Grading system, Incomes
Wanyama, 139–40
Waragi, 94, 101
Warner, W. L. and Low, J. O., 57
Washington, 161, 165, 167
Watchmen in Goods Sheds, 125
Waverers, 161–2, 165, 167
Weber, Max, 91

Welfare committee, 149
Welfare officer
at Kampala, 29, 76; organises sports, 103–4; post Africanised, 32; seen as big man, 93, 95; union factions, 164, 173; *see also* James
section, 28–9, 189
services, 23–4
Wellington
career, 111, 124
reputation, 112, 115
suspicious death, 111–12; witchcraft, 112, 145
White-collar workers, *see* Clerks
Whyte, W. F., 4
Witchcraft and sorcery
competition, 142–6
education, 145, 169
Ganda, 60, 144
Loco Sheds, 82, 111–12, 143–6
Luo, 54, 142–3; *juok*, 54
status, 93, 145
union politics, 168
Wives, of railwaymen, at Nsambya, 41–6, 152; *see also* Children, Families, Marriage, Rural-urban links
Work units, 74
Work process, 6, 65–6, 68, 71, 74
Workers, as social category, 68, 118
Working life, 39, 120

Yard, 68, 126, 189
at Kampala, Fig. 2, 28–9, 31, 70, 129; labour force in, 28, 59; politics in, 163, 171
Yardmaster, Kampala, 29, 31–2, 137

Zoning, at Nsambya, Fig. 2, 32–4, 87, 97–8